POLICIES AND PERCEPTIONS
OF INSURANCE

An Introduction to
Insurance Law

MALCOLM CLARKE

CLARENDON PRESS · OXFORD
1997

Oxford University Press, Great Clarendon Street, Oxford OX2 6DP

Oxford New York
Athens Auckland Bangkok Bombay
Buenos Aires Calcutta Cape Town Dar es Salaam
Delhi Florence Hong Kong Istanbul Karachi
Kuala Lumpur Madras Madrid Melbourne
Mexico City Nairobi Paris Singapore
Taipei Tokyo Toronto
and associated companies in
Berlin Ibadan

Oxford is a trade mark of Oxford University Press

Published in the United States
by Oxford University Press Inc., New York

British Library Cataloguing in Publication Data
Data available

Library of Congress Cataloging in Publication Data
Clarke, Malcolm A. (Malcolm Alistair)
Policies and perception of insurance: an introduction to
insurance law/Malcolm Clarke.
p. cm.—(Clarendon law series)
Includes bibliographical references.
1. Insurance law—Great Britain. I. Title. II. Series.
KD1859.3.C58   1997   97–24355
346.41'086—dc21   CIP
ISBN 0–19–876340–9 (hb)   99020031
ISBN 0–19–876341–7 (pb)   29.9.99

1 3 5 7 9 10 8 6 4 2

Typeset by Cambrian Typesetters, Frimley, Surrey
Printed in Great Britain on acid-free paper by
Bookcraft Ltd., Midsomer Norton, Somerset

CLARENDON LAW SERIES

Edited by

PETER CANE, TONY HONORÉ AND JANE STAPLETON

CLARENDON LAW SERIES

Preface

The book is an introduction to insurance contract law in the United Kingdom today. As such, however, it contains not only summaries of settled and satisfactory legal rules but also discussion of more controversial matters, with an attempt to flag which is which. On these matters, it is less an insider's invitation to come in and look round than a view from the outside, the view of an academic of an industry which in the past has not exhibited a conspicuous regard for academe. It is said, and not only by insurers, that academics sit in silicone towers and suffer ivory illusions. Be that as it may, from some towers on a good day one can see a long way. Whether this book was written from the right tower on a good day is for the reader to decide.

I have been helped in various ways and various degrees by many people, among them Derek Cole, Gordon Cornish, Martin Davies, Valerie Fogleman, Lis Frost, Charles Goldie, Marit Halvorsen, Brian Haynes, Bob Hepple, Martin Hoskins, Gareth Jones, Ben Jupp, Martin Kemp, Keith Loney, Robert McCorquodale, Tony Paish, Laurie Slade, John Spencer, Peter Stein, Lloyd Watkins, and Gunther Wiese. I am most grateful to all of them. Above all, however, I have had the scholarly support of Peter Cane and Jane Stapleton. It has been a great good fortune to work with them, not only because of their devotion as editors but also by reason of their expertise in some of the areas touched on in the book.

Finally, I hope that readers from other parts of the United Kingdom will forgive the author, who was born in Wales, for referring to what is their law too as English law.

MALCOLM CLARKE
October 1996

Contents

THE PLAYERS

THE PLAY

THE WIDER SCENE

**Chapter 9. The Sequel: Perceptions of the Past
and of the Future 298**

Table of Cases

Australia

Belgium

Canada

Table of Legislation

UK

Australia

Belgium

Canada

Denmark

The Insured

Risk

To the actuary, risk is the 'probability that a particular adverse event occurs during a stated period of time or results from a particular challenge' where 'an adverse event is an occurrence producing harm'. This was the conclusion of a report of the Royal Society,[1] which was not confined to insured activity but at a broad spectrum of activity.

To insurers, probability matters in order to rate the risk and calculate premium: see 38 below. To insurers, the risk is the chance of loss of the kind insured. Loss means both loss in the literal sense of deprivation (e.g. robbery) and financial loss—the impact of events (e.g storm damage) on the economic well-being of the insured. Insurers are concerned not only with whether the loss will occur (e.g. fire) but also, in cases in which loss is more or less bound to occur, with when it will occur (e.g. death) or the extent of loss (e.g. the damage to a London taxi in the course of the period insured).

To the insured, as conceived by the insurance economist, the 'concept of risk comprises two components—a detriment aspect and an uncertainty aspect'.[2] As regards the detriment, by taking insurance, the financial element in the detriment, although no longer a risk but a certainty, is reduced to the level of the premium; and the inconvenience element is curtailed to the time it takes to find insurance and, if the risk strikes, to obtain indemnity. As for the uncertainty and whether the risk will strike, that is not reduced objectively. Subjectively, however, just as some people

[1] Royal Society, *Risk Assessment* (London, 1983).
[2] P. M. Wiedermann, 'Taboo, Sin, Risk: Changes in the Social Perception of Hazard', *BayerischerR* 44.

say that as long as they take an umbrella it never rains, some people feel that insurance serves as a 'charm' which wards off the danger. Uncertainty is reduced objectively, however, as to the extent of the detriment, notably the cost. Moreover, if the insurer offers advice on or incentives to risk avoidance, the likelihood of the occurrence and thus, if the insured responds appropriately, the amount of uncertainty are reduced further: see 42 below.

To the ordinary actual insured, who is not a model of behaviour or rationality, something is risky if loss is relatively likely to happen or, although it is not likely to happen, if the effect will be disastrous if it does. An instance of the first is an injury playing rugby; an instance of the second is an accident at a nuclear reactor. The insured is less concerned with the precise probability than with whether the risk seems probable or bad enough to justify paying (premium) to soften its effects; that depends on his view of things—his risk aversion.

Risk Aversion

In the words of *The Economist*, risk aversion is the feature of human nature that explains why 'when given a choice between, say, losing 1 dollar and a 10 per cent chance of losing 10 dollars, most people would prefer a certain outcome (losing 1 dollar) to a risky one (losing 10 dollars or nothing)'. 'Prospect theory' tells us that people making decisions in uncertain conditions weigh prospective losses twice as heavily as prospective gains. If a person knows that there is a one per cent chance of total loss of his £100,000 house, he may be willing to pay more than £1,000 for insurance, and one of the main reasons is that he is willing to pay to offload anxiety. He is 'risk averse'. The Association of British Insurers (ABI), the organization that speaks for the insurance industry, projects insurance as something that enables people who are insured to organize their household budgets, or plan their business activities, with greater certainty. Indeed, one insurer, taking the idea from the United States, recently offered businesses a fixed premium for three years, because research indicated that stable insurance-planning could be used as a selling point. This raises the question what is it that makes a risk so unacceptable that the person decides to do something about it and, in particular, to buy insurance cover?

Anxiety and Stress

Risk aversion grows from stress aversion. Psychologists tell us that stress levels are directly related to whether we feel that we can predict or control our situation. An everyday illustration of this, that has been confirmed by research, is that in a given risk situation on the roads the anxiety levels among passengers are higher than among drivers.

One of the ways in which people seek to regain control of their lives, to reduce stress, and to move towards some kind of peace of mind is by taking out insurance. Insurers know this, and some send their sales staff on courses to learn about the 'emotional needs' of the customer. Most of all, it is seen in their advertising. For example, one company recommends its life insurance for 'life-long peace of mind'. A leading retailer of travel cover offers 'a service to give you peace of mind when travelling'; and one of the main banks offers 'a free home insurance review to ensure peace of mind'. When we sign a certain 'Health Care Contract', we 'give up one very important thing. Worrying'. Best known is the promise of the Commercial Union 'not to make a drama out of a crisis'.

Advertising of this kind has an enduring appeal. Associated with the wish for peace and certainty is a desire for security. Sociologists tell us that just after people's basic needs for food, clothing, and shelter comes the need for security.[3] Security is a prominent feature of the image that the insurer projects of himself and his product to the insured: see 36 ff. below.

Associated with the desire for peace and security is an aversion to 'aggravation', and thus to litigation. Genn claims that society values the coercive and menacing character of the court process because it is the anvil against which the hammer of negotiation strikes. It is the menace of the court process that gets people to settle rather than to pursue their suit to judgment.[4] If people thought they could go to court for quick and sure compensation, perhaps they would; perhaps they will in future, but for the moment they do not.

---

[3] B. Strümpel and P. Michael, 'The Security Requirements of Private Households', *BayerischerR* 113–33.

[4] H. Genn, *Hard Bargaining* (Oxford, 1987), 11.

A racing cyclist whose road injuries kept him off his bicycle for a year said that the pain and anguish of a prolonged court case was as bad as, if not worse than, the pain and anguish of his injuries. Moreover, at the end of a case over bullying at school, it was the judge who observed that six years of recourse to complaints procedure and litigation had caused more lasting damage to the pupil than the acts alleged. According to a survey of 'ordinary people' in 1995 by the National Consumer Council, three out of four people involved in 'serious legal disputes' were dissatisfied with the system of civil justice in this country. The reaction of the Law Society was not to dispute the conclusion but to agree that it was natural enough that people wanted to avoid having to go court—just as they would avoid going to the dentist.

Businessmen, too, according to a senior judge, want to keep out of court, although for different reasons. If a lawyer tells businessmen that the result is uncertain or even that they will lose, he said, they take no notice; or at most dispense with his services and engage another lawyer. If he tells him that the costs will be enormous, they reply that that was what they expected. 'But tell them that days or weeks of executive time will be involved, in attending court, and they sit up and take notice'. What they want is 'to be allowed to go on running a business instead of sitting for days in court, while the competition make hay in their absence'.[5]

Whether in business or not, most people are afraid not only of the formality of the court process but also of the uncertainty of the outcome. A tort action, for example, has been described as a:

'compulsory long-distance obstacle race' in which the amount of the prize 'must remain uncertain until the last moment because the umpire has discretion to fix it individually for each finisher. None of the runners is told the distance he must cover to complete the course; nor the time it is likely to take. Some of the obstacles are fixed hurdles (rules of law), while other can, without warning, be thrown into the path of a runner. . . . In view of all the uncertainties, and particularly the difficulties which could be presented by the unknown, future obstacles, many runners drop out of the race at each obstacle'.[6]

---

[5] Staughton LJ, 'Good Faith and Fairness in Commercial Contract Law' (1994) 7 JCL, 193–6, 194.

[6] D. Harris *et al.*, *Compensation and Support for Illness and Injury* (Oxford, 1984), 132–3.

In a situation such as this it was no surprise that a Law Society survey found that most people felt that 'accidents happen' and took no steps to seek compensation. This, said the Society, is an 'alarming ethos' and it started a campaign against public 'ignorance' and 'the great British reserve'. In consequence, perhaps, there has been some increase in negligence actions, but mostly against the medical profession and actions arising out of sports injuries. Until recently, people have tended to litigate less in England than, for example, in the United States and in Germany. They have not bought legal expenses insurance, which sells well elsewhere and which would enable them to go to court for 'a good fight'. They prefer insurance which gives them the clear prospect of indemnity without altercation with neighbours and without having to spend time and money going to court to get it. The effect of contingency fees, whereby the plaintiff's lawyer gets paid only if he wins the case, may be more litigation. Certainly, some professional negligence insurers are alarmed at the prospect. Recently, a company in Tyne and Wear set itself up to sell the names of the 40,000 accident victims it has on its books to solicitors. Enterprise like this may change the picture and with it the culture in which we live. This remains to be seen.

Spreading of Risk

In *The Merchant of Venice*, Shakespeare's Antonio had few of the anxieties we have been considering because, he says,

> My ventures are not in one bottom trusted,
> Nor to one place; nor is my whole estate
> Upon the fortune of this present year.

Although we are often told to act like Antonio, if the modern Antonio is an exporter of eggs he may have to put them all in one ship. He may not be able to spread the eggs between different ships, but he can nonetheless spread and share the risk of breakage with others. The risk that the ship will sink is spread via insurance among all those who insure risks of that kind with the same insurer, who may well pass on some of that risk to other insurers. The availability of insurance encourages new ventures and new adventurers. One of the main purposes of insurance is to achieve a rational and reasonable spread of risk, and to help people to do things which, otherwise, they would hesitate to do. If Antonio turns out to be a bad businessman who chooses badly-maintained ships, his premium will rise. If risk is spread efficiently, he will be charged according to his expected loss (from neglect) but still the risk of random loss (from swordfish) is spread among all in the insured group. So is the random element provided by inaccuracies in the underwriting such as the classification of the risk group: lines between good and less good risk groups are not always perfectly drawn, but, on the whole, these errors are sufficiently evenly spread for the insurance to be sold at what is perceived to be a reasonable price and for a reasonable return.

The efficiency of the spread depends also on the data available to those who spread it. The insurer must rely on information from other experts—who may strive for objectivity but not always achieve it. Studies speak of 'affiliation bias'; for example, toxicologists working for industry see chemicals as more benign than do their counterparts in academia and government. Still, relatively speaking, and with one reservation concerning his fear of fraud (169 below) and another about 'instinct' underwriting at Lloyd's in the 1980s, the insurer's approach to risk endeavours to be objective and rational.

The Insured's View of Risk

The model insured is a close relative of *homo oeconomicus*, who is concerned mainly with utility i.e. the maximization of personal material self-interest. Such persons make wise decisions in the light of personal goals. At worst, they can be tricked into collectively irrational behaviour by systematic errors in the social rules of the game. *Homo oeconomicus* is an invention of economists and no more a figure of 'real life' than the model insured.[7] Nor is a more sophisticated descendant of the species, the person of qualified economic 'rationality', who is characterized by self-interest in a broad sense that includes non-material factors, such as a desire for more leisure, and consistency. Having decided what he wants, this person then works out correctly how to get as

---

[7] H.-W. Sinn and A. J. Weichenrieder, 'Biological Selection of Risk Preferences', *BayerischerR* 67–83, 68 ff.; see also Tyler and Dawes in Mellers and Baron (eds.), *Psychological Perspectives on Justice* (Cambridge, 1993), ch. 5.

much of it as he can. This model, too, is accepted even by many economists as unrealistic. In December 1994 *The Economist* observed ruefully that a deeper understanding of what makes people tick could transform economics. The wisdom of mankind is limited by 'bounded rationality': people still pursue self-interest but are constrained by lack of information and the cost of getting it. But the figure of 'bounded rationality' is still a model which ignores other factors that influence actual decisions, including both fashion and fear. So, a further development of recent times is 'quasi-rational economics', which looks to experimental psychology and cognitive sciences; and this has led, for example, to the setting up of 'risk appraisal initiatives' on an inter-disciplinary basis. Even so, some economists still assume in people a consistency and predictability in their perception of risk, and thus in their behaviour, which is scarcely credible.

Sir Phillip Brocklehurst was a scarcely credible figure too; he was the insurers' and the economists' nightmare, but, evidently, Lord Denning found him rather endearing. Although Sir Phillip had 'had a conventional upbringing at Eton and Trinity Hall', he was, said Lord Denning,[8] 'the most unconventional of men' because he took the 'line that the insurance company never paid him anything, so why should he go on paying them?' Many people who have had a less conventional upbringing than Sir Phillip share his unconventional view of insurance, because they sometimes take a less than objective perception of risk. Even so, their perception of risk is not for that reason alone inferior to that of the expert. It is simply different. For those people whose concerns do lead to insurance, one of the goals is peace of mind and, whether their fears are rational or not, they are real to them and cannot be ignored.

Knowledge of Risk

The fears of the layman depend on his perception of risk, what is sometimes called his 'risk cognition'. This depends, first, on his knowledge of risk. He may be unaware of the very existence of risk. In the seventeenth century, for example, people smoked (pipes) in the belief that smoking was good for their health.

[8] *Re Brocklehurst* [1978] 1 All ER 767, 769–70 (CA).

Today, people are better informed, but not much. They may be aware of the risk but not of its extent. Sports injuries are many, but competitors with cover are few. Again, in spite of recent ministerial statements, many people believe that the State provides a sufficient safety net for long-term illness and disablement, and insurance against loss of income (PHI) is taken by only a few. And again, many more people take life insurance than any form of disability insurance, even though, for all but the oldest or terminally ill, the likelihood of illness or injury is appreciably greater than the likelihood of death. The average businessperson has a one in three chance of contracting a critical illness before reaching his retirement age, but only one person in four is even aware that insurance against critical illness is available.

Experience of Risk

Perception of risk depends, secondly, on a person's experience of the risk, directly or indirectly. One factor that 'plays a part in risk assessment is the gearing of judgments towards the cognitive "prominence" or "availability" of events. The lay person regards an event as being more probable, the easier it is to recall or imagine similar events'.[9] Psychologists speak of the 'availability heuristic', which is the human tendency to assess the frequency of an event by how quickly instances of the event come to mind; and of the 'simulation heuristic', which is the tendency to assess frequency by how quickly an image of it comes to mind.[10] The quicker it comes the more likely it is thought to be to occur. The person who has experienced an event of loss knows, of course, that it does not happen only to other people, and is more likely to register the event when it happens to others, thus reinforcing the process.

Fire insurance spread after the Great Fire of London in 1666—partly on the initiative of a housebuilder, who required insured claimants to rebuild with his bricks. Personal accident insurance

[9] H. Jungermann and P. Slovic, 'Characteristics of Individual Risk Perception'. *BayerischerR* 85–102, 87; R. Kemp, 'Risk Perception: The Assessment of Risks by Experts and by Lay People—A Rational Comparison?', *BayerischerR* 103–18, 107.
[10] S. T. Fiske and S. E. Taylor, *Social Cognition* (2nd edn., New York, 1991), 384 ff.

surged on a sense of the destructive power of railway trains. With industrialization came special cover, such as boiler insurance. Burglary insurance was born of the fears of houseowners in London, fuelled by the newspapers, of a Yorkshire burglar called Charles Peace. Although an attempt in the seventeenth century to market ransom insurance for travellers was unsuccessful, today there is a niche for cover against kidnapping and a much bigger platform for covering property against terrorists.

Today, for example, most people move on or near the roads; they both underestimate and exaggerate the dangers. Although, on the one hand, drivers tend to underestimate the dangers they create, on the other hand, all road users are conscious of the threat posed by others. So, the promoters of road safety can say things like 'even a million to one risk of death is unacceptable'. People nod their heads and support the promoters; but risk analysts from Harvard have pointed out that a list of 'million to one' death risks includes eating forty tablespoonfuls of peanut butter, drinking the water of Miami for a year, and living for two months with a smoker. To little avail. People are more risk averse in some situations, such as the roads, than in others.

Experience may be acquired second-hand. Emotions aroused by media reports 'act as controls on cognition, alerting people to important goals'.[11] In other words, emotions are the 'springs of action', which spur people to avoid risk, *inter alia* by seeking insurance, and on which the media play. The effect of the media on the popular perception of risk has been the subject of considerable study.[12] This shows, for example, that the public perception of the risk of death, although not in line with the statistics, is roughly in line with the amount of media coverage; and that, within any one area of risk, the media tend to select alarmist reports or opinions, which distort people's perception of those risks. An example of the latter is the 'salmonella scare' about eggs in the early 1990s. Ironically, perhaps, the cry that fear of crime is out of all proportion to reality and that broadcasters and

---

[11] Fiske and Taylor, n. 10 above, 433.
[12] See S. Dunwoody and H. P. Peters, 'The Mass Media and Risk Perception', *BayerischerR* 293–317 and references cited. Also G. Loewenstein and J. Mather, 'Dynamic Processes in Risk Perception', 3 *J Risk & Uncertainty* 155–75, 158 and 172 (1990).

the press must shoulder much of the blame has been taken up by the newspapers in order to attack television.

National media tend to focus on large-scale accidents, such as air crashes, rather than more frequent but small-scale accidents, such as befall motorists, whereas in the local media the latter feature more frequently. For different reasons, all the reports have this in common that they have a relatively large impact on the insured because they are less distant in the imagination. People are hoist by the petard of morbid curiosity. Our perception of risk depends significantly on media perception of what we want to read, see, or hear. If insurers could manipulate the media they could manipulate the market for insurance. Of course, they cannot do so, but it should be no surprise that a popular television 'soap', which is centred on a medical practice and (ill) health, is sponsored by a health insurer. Although sponsorship is hardly manipulation, it has been seen as a step in that direction. Insurance companies, said journalist Polly Toynbee, together with burglar alarm manufacturers and private security firms all have a financial stake in fear.

Journalists individually are not immune to manipulation. Some are specialized, but, in many cases, it has been shown that journalists are less educated in scientific subjects than their average readers, and that they are often unable to judge the soundness of their scientific sources. Moreover, for reasons of speed and economy, there is now less investigative and searching reporting than before and more reliance on 'sources' such as company press releases.[13] So they consider that they have complied with a standard of 'truthful' reporting if they present a range of views without any real assessment of their relative merits; equal space is given to the ideas, whether established or eccentric, with some extra space perhaps for the sensational or alarmist.

Any suggestion of manipulation of journalists by insurers would be simplistic and untrue. Studies suggest that the relation between media presentation and public response is complex and that for a force behind the media to produce a specific response in the public would be difficult. Response there is, but it is somewhat random and diffuse. People tend to use the mass media to find out about the nature of the risk and personal contacts to find out how much

---

[13] Dunwoody and Peters, n. 12 above, 301 ff.

they themselves should be concerned about that particular risk and what, if anything, they should do about it. There are several variables between the newspaper or television report and the contract of insurance. Insurers wishing to inform the public should therefore use the mass media as no more than one of several sources of information. Indeed, if, as other studies suggest, the best predictor of risk perception is cultural bias (12 below), we may find in future that, as marketing becomes more precise, insurers will divert their energy and expenditure from the media and the public in general to the direct mailing of individuals.

Context

Perception of risk depends, thirdly, on the context in which the risk is perceived.

Presentation

The manner of presentation is important to people's perception of risk. For example, the advocate of nuclear power might state that new measures will reduce the risk of meltdown by 70 per cent, whereas the opponent of nuclear power will point to the 30 per cent of the risk that still exists. In the insurance market, however, advertising that stresses the unpleasantness of risks has been censured by the advertising authority. Moreover, if the presentation is too disturbing people respond negatively by pushing the issue aside rather than positively by seeking insurance. So insurance against illness is described as health insurance, insurance against death as life insurance, and fire insurance is described as house insurance; it is the positive features of the product that are stressed. Insurers have brought the need for insurance home to the public indirectly by sponsoring television drama. A striking example is a fire insurer's sponsorship of a peak-time drama about fire-fighting. Episodes ended with a telephone number for fire-prevention information. Callers were sent an information pack which also included information about the policies offered by the sponsoring insurer. One episode alone produced 10,000 calls.

Distraction

People's perception of risk may be affected by the pull of other worries, some real, others not. On the one hand, the person who knows that he has terminal cancer may neglect to renew his house insurance—but not his life insurance. On the other hand, people who walk the streets in fear of muggers should be more concerned about the chance of being struck by a car. Those who walk the jungle looking down in fear of snakes should be looking up for falling coconuts. In many areas of England, those who worry about radioactive waste are more likely to be damaged by natural radiation in the soil; and a study in New Zealand has shown that those who had the highest aversion to the dangers of technology were more ready than most to assume the risk of skiing or smoking. In these examples, the dominant anxiety is that which subjectively arouses the most fear. In other instances, the dominant anxiety may simply be that which is associated with what happens next. The smoker may promise himself that he will give up smoking if he gets the job he so desperately needs. Not surprisingly, people worry most about the risks that seem to them most directly to threaten their wellbeing at the time.

The Context of Society: Time and Place

As a general predictor of risk aversion, the personality of the insured is not helpful, because individuals who take high risks of certain kinds also avoid other risks at all costs. Cultural and social factors are thought to be more significant.[14] In England, the cult of the self-reliant consumer, encouraged by governments of recent years, has led *inter alia* to more purchasing of insurance, such as health insurance. But people in the United States are willing to spend more than twice as much as people in the United Kingdom to mitigate the risk of loss due to road accidents. Again, over half the global premium for life insurance comes from Japan and the United States; *per capita* spending is highest in Japan, followed by Switzerland. In some eastern countries, however, life insurance has been slow to develop, because people saw contracting life insurance not as a wise investment but as a foolish temptation to fate. The sense of risk and the focus of fears often differ from country to country. One reason lies in differences in affluence and the way affluence affects the purchase of insurance.

In the United Kingdom between 1984 and 1994 the amount

---

[14] A. Wildavsky, 'The Comparative Study of Risk Perception: A Beginning', *BayerischerR* 179–220, 188–90.

spent on general (non-life) insurance went up, well ahead of inflation, from £8.76 billion to £30 billion. Within the United Kingdom today, the number of households without contents insurance in Northern Ireland is about three times higher than in East Anglia. Part of the explanation for such differences lies in differences in affluence. The more people have got, the more they are afraid of losing it, and the more they are willing to pay to protect it.

The famous journalistic rule of thumb—two dead in Putney is worth as much space as 200 dead in the Phillipines . . . recognises the difference between societies dominated by wants and those dominated by worry, between societies who cannot pay enough for safety and those who can. The biggest worry of all, for those in the second category, is that they are slipping back into the first.[15]

Moreover, people in the second category have more leisure to worry and more 'information' to feed their anxiety; their perception of insecurity has increased.

A particular anxiety for people in the more 'advanced' countries, who have become more aware of their world, lies in the potential hazards over which they, as individuals, have no control. Examples are pollution, global warming, and the spread of nuclear or chemical weapons. That kind of anxiety is not eased by the knowledge that they cannot live in society without trusting the skill, knowledge, and care of others, whether the scientists who advise the government about food safety or other people with whom they must share the roads. All this fosters a general sense of insecurity, not least because sections of the public now feel that in times past trust in experts and in public institutions has been misplaced. Once again we see a sense of helplessness (lack of control) that feeds stress.

On the other side of what is almost, but not quite, the same coin, studies suggest that people are more ready to accept risks which they have voluntarily assumed, such as smoking, or risks which they feel they can control, such as motoring. This is one reason for the special importance of motor insurance, and why it is compulsory.

---

[15] Martin Woollacott, *Guardian*, 24 Feb. 1996. See also R. B. Bovbjerg, 'Liability and Liability Insurance: Chicken and Egg', 72 *Tex. LRev.* 1655–79, 1669 (1994).

Compulsory Insurance

In certain situations Parliament has been convinced that the experts are right, that the rest of us underestimate and under-provide for risk, and that the cumulative actual loss or damage to the community is unacceptably great; so in these situations Parliament has made insurance compulsory. One instance is insurance of the liability of employers to their employees, which was first required in England in 1969. Another instance is motor insurance. Insurance against liability incurred on the roads was first required in England by the Road Traffic Act 1930 but had been foreshadowed by legislation in other countries, such as Sweden (1906), although it was not found until 1939 in Germany and 1958 in France. Such is its importance today that it has been the subject of three EC Directives designed to ensure and to harmonize compulsory motor insurance in Europe.

Whereas most people worry too much about travel by air, they worry too little about travel by road which, on any statistical basis, is more hazardous. 'Shortfalls in the cognition of danger and playing down of the probability and consequences of accidents go hand in hand with the conviction of being in complete control.'[16] It is one of the attractive features of motoring that the driver believes, encouraged by advertisements selling cars, that he is in control of a marvel of technology and that he is master of his situation. Moreover, because:

driving is an activity which everyone, or almost everyone, practises successfully, it is generally felt to be an easy task, an everyday activity at which everyone is almost perfect and whose risks are therefore under-estimated. Accordingly, a failure in this apparently easy task is particularly wounding to self-esteem. Consequently, defence mechanisms are more frequently encountered here than in other areas of life.[17]

A survey conducted by Mori for the British School of Motoring in 1995 showed that 25 per cent of drivers thought they had no bad

---

[16] H. D. Somen, 'Experience of Risk in Road Traffic Situations', *BayerischerR* 119–54, 136. See also Jungermann and Slovic, n. 9 above, 92 ff.; Kemp, n. 9 above, 107; B. Corby, 'On Risk and Uncertainty in Modern Society', *Geneva Papers on Risk and Insurance* 19 (1994), 241.

[17] Somen, n. 16 above, 137.

driving habits and that 90 per cent rated their driving as fairly good to excellent. The reality is different. In any one year in the United Kingdom, one in five of drivers comprehensively insured and 65 per cent of all fleet cars will have an accident. In any one year among children under 15 years of age one child in fifteen will be killed or injured by road vehicles and their drivers. The cost of road accidents in the United Kingdom is estimated to be in the region of £12 billion a year. Not many insurers make a profit on their motoring account and one reason is that it is hard to persuade the insured that the risk is high and that premiums have to rise accordingly.

The Demand for Insurance

The lines of insurance available depend on demand and, thus, largely on perceptions of risk and need. In the eighteenth century, there was an 'assurance of female chastity', a very personal line, for which, it seems, there is insufficient demand today. A line that prospered mightily until it faltered in 1994, but which has now begun to prosper again, is life insurance. Life insurance has origins both commercial and non-commercial. Life insurance in England may have begun not as a matter of family provision but because creditors realized that their chance of repayment depended largely on the labour, and thus the longevity, of the debtor. Today life insurance is seen not only as a means of family provision but also, a related matter, as an investment. In England, life insurance, together with fire and marine insurance, was the first on offer. Most of the other established classes of cover offered by insurance companies were introduced between 1840 and 1900.

More recent developments include contractors' all-risks insurance. As building and engineering projects have got larger, so has awareness of the need to cover work under construction, work in which much time and money has been invested. Customized insurance cover of great complexity is arranged for new airports, tunnels under the sea, and so on. Another recent development of a more personal kind concerns people whose continued prosperity depends on all or part of the anatomy—their own or that of those they employ. To a football club, a star player is an asset to be insured not only against the slings and arrows of outrageous spectators but also the attentions of opposing players—usually for the amount of the player's potential value in the transfer market. The idea, said the *Financial Times* 'that Pat van den Hauwe, Spurs' redoubtable left back, is an intangible asset may be news to some opposing forwards'. But for many businesses the most valuable resource is people. Almost anything and anyone can be insured, if the insurer can assess and quantify the risk. However, although a famous actress associated in the public eye with her bosom insured her bosom, and a popular comedian with prominent front teeth insured his teeth, a high priest of *haute cuisine* was unable to insure his sense of taste: the insurer did not dispute its importance or value but could not see how he would be able to assess a claim. A further and 'final' instance of the new products of our time is this: those who do not die quickly on the roads but die slowly in their beds can buy 'dread disease' cover to ease the financial burden and thus the discomfort of their decline. The range of insurance products on sale is considerable.

The Insurance Marketplace

The Produce on Sale

If a person demands insurance, the next question is whether he can get it—which is really not one question but two. Is it available at all, and, if so, is it available to that person. The answer to the second question depends on whether that person has what the law regards as an insurable interest in the matter: see 20 ff. below. As regards the first question, cover may not be available because the risk is one that insurers cannot rate or, being too expensive, the cover may be one that insurers cannot sell.

For cover to be offered at all, the risk must be one which can be assessed and perhaps controlled (other than by prayer or taboos) by human action. Partly this is a question of technological advance, such as the invention of the lightning conductor in about 1750. Partly it is a question of information, such as the development of probability theory and data to which it can be applied; see 38 below.

From the earliest days, demand for cover that is not offered by insurers on the market has led to mutual self-protection in 'clubs' of those who want it. Traces of such 'mutuality' are found from Roman times and, later, in the protection offered by guilds. In 1782, sugar refiners, who were regarded as a bad risk by the market, formed the Phoenix Fire Office to cover their own fire risks. Today, at one end of the financial spectrum shipowners still 'club' together to take risks which the insurance companies will not touch. At the other end, we find mutual benefit societies, such as local burial clubs, which arose out of the custom of passing around the 'hat' on the death of a fellow workman to collect something for his funeral and his family. Indeed, the earliest English life insurer was a mutual and in the life sphere mutuals are still found. Mutuality is not necessarily a solution of last resort: in some instances, it is cheaper or more effective anyway—or so it is believed, for example, by solicitors whose professional liability is insured mutually. Generally, however, the appearance of insurance companies marked the point in time when the need was sufficiently widespread for cover to be offered to people who were risk-averse by others, who then formed companies for profit. Today, the potential buyer finds that most insurance is offered by companies; and that these companies market standard insurance 'products' by reference to the peril against which cover is offered, or to the subject-matter of the insurance, the person, or property at risk.

Personal lines, he will find, include not only life and accident insurance but also, for instance, health and long-term care insurance. Accident insurance began with the railways as personal-accident insurance, but has since acquired a broader meaning. Although people think first of personal-accident insurance for what befalls the human body, the insurer thinks first of loss to property. For him the primary meaning of accident insurance embraces all commercial insurance, including motor and liability insurance, except marine, aviation, fire, and life. From accident insurance in this sense, the premium income (in the United Kingdom) is greater than all the rest together except life insurance, which, in the 1990s, outstripped all the rest.

Property insurance, he will find, is separated into insurance on tangible property, including specific items of money, and insurance on intangible wealth, known as pecuniary-loss insurance. Insurance of tangible property is divided according to the kind of property (livestock, cargo, house, etc.) and also according to the peril (fire, theft, etc.). Pecuniary-loss insurance includes cover against the insolvency of debtors, loss sustained by guarantors under their contracts of guarantee, and consequential loss, which is also called business interruption cover.

For the convenience of the customer, a cocktail of different kinds of cover may be offered in one package. Just as he will find audio equipment sold both as units and as integrated 'systems' of units, he will also find that, for example, fire cover can be bought on its own or as part of a package, such as 'householder's comprehensive' cover. This may be divided into sections covering not only fire and theft but also the liability of the householder for things that go wrong (e.g. falling slates), with an 'all-risks' extension (e.g. for protection against theft) on his valuables when taken out of the house and, perhaps, some cover for legal expenses (e.g. for proceeding against noisy neighbours).

If none of the standard products meets the perceived needs of the purchaser, he may get his broker to seek customized cover in the market or, perhaps, at Lloyd's. At Lloyd's, some insurers are celebrated for covering non-standard risks, whether the movement of satellites in space or of paintings by Cezanne from Paris for exhibition in London, or, on one occasion, the voyage of the insured from Dover to Cap Gris Nez in a bathtub—on condition that he did not remove the plug. Customized cover can be obtained—at a cost. In some instances cover might be available in theory but, in practice, the high chance of loss and associated cost rule it out on a regular or commercial basis.

The Choice of Insurer

At the point of choice, like the purchaser of any other product, the purchaser of insurance may be torn between price and reliability, i.e. security. Some will go for the lowest premium; others for the insurer with the reputation for support and prompt payment.

The choice may depend on whether the insured has to live with consequences of his decision. A longer view may be taken by the householder buying fire insurance than, perhaps, the exporter of goods who sells an occasional buyer a package including insurance on the goods; he is obliged only to provide commercially acceptable insurance, and, if there is a claim and if the insurer drags his feet over a claim, it is the buyer rather than the seller who suffers. In between, perhaps, is the purchaser of motor insurance who wears risk lightly and buys insurance only because he must. Convinced that 'it won't happen to him', he seeks the cheapest insurance he can find.

The choice may also depend on the experience of the purchaser. Although price is still a factor, some recent surveys suggest that, among buyers of commercial lines, security, integrity, and continuity are now more important. The speed with which Lloyd's paid on the Californian earthquake of 1906, when other insurers were dragging their feet through the dust and the small print, did much for the prosperity of Lloyd's in subsequent years. Much more recently, it has been plausibly argued that the ruling of the courts[18] that, under a compensation scheme, the insurance industry at large must pay claims against a failed insurer not only to policyholders in the United Kingdom but also to policyholders abroad, although painful in the short term, will benefit the image and thus the prosperity of the English insurance industry in the future.

If the insurance buyer is confused about the array of products available, he may seek advice; but from whom? Traditionally, he turns to a broker: brokers see their role as specialist retailers of insurance, as providers of independent 'best advice' about the insurance available: see 48 below. But many potential purchasers are confused about brokers too. A short walk down the High Street will reveal not only insurance brokers but insurance consultants, as well as banks and building societies offering advice about insurance. A survey jointly sponsored by brokers and insurers in 1990 showed that the public had an almost total lack of understanding of the role of the broker. Little has changed since. Moreover, having heard that something called ABTA is responsible for travel agents, the buyer of insurance may want to know who or what is responsible for controlling the sale of insurance. In 1995 he would have found not only the DTI but also an array of acronyms, ranging from FIMBRA and LAUTRO to SIB, IBRC, and PIA. Even the industry recognizes that this is confusing, and so it is. Buying sound insurance is not an easy matter.

[18] In *Scher* v. *Policyholders Protection Board (No 1 and No 2)* [1994] 2 AC 57. But cf. the Policyholders Protection Act 1997.

Insurable Interest: Why?

If a person has decided that he wants a particular kind of insurance, the next question is whether the law allows him to have it at all. The law states that he must have an insurable interest: he must stand in the 'right kind of relationship' to the person or property that he wants to insure. The insured must be acceptable as a risk—not only to the insurer but also to society, which must be satisfied that he is a person whose purpose in seeking insurance is a proper purpose. The law takes the matter seriously: an insurance contract made in the absence of insurable interest is void.

One reason given for the requirement of insurable interest is that it stops people using insurance for wagering. If I insure my cargo worth £100,000 against total loss on a voyage to New York for a premium of £100, that is valid insurance. If, however, the cargo is not mine but that of someone else, that is a 1,000 to one wager on whether the cargo will get there. The insurance is void. Why such a severe and censorious response to wagers?

Originally, wagers were seen less as a social or moral evil than as a nuisance. In a case in which P had paid D 100 guineas for D's promise to pay P a guinea a day for as long as Napoleon Bonaparte should live—a dinner-table wager on whether Napoleon would be assassinated, the court refused to enforce D's promise simply on account of the 'inconvenience of countenancing wagers in Courts of Justice'. Wagers occupy the time of the court and divert 'their attention from causes of real interest and concern'.[19] Indeed, elements of the argument are still found today in the argument of 'diminishing marginal utility': time and money, whether that of the insured or the insurer, should not be diverted to a matter that serves no useful social or economic purpose. But, be that as it may, the use of insurance for wagering is surely a thing of the past. Whatever the merits of legislation against wagering, the Supreme Court of Canada was surely right to say that, today, there 'seem to be many more convenient devices available to the serious wagerer'.[20]

Another reason for the requirement is that the existence of an

---

[19] *Gilbert* v. *Sykes* (1812) 13 East 150, 162.
[20] *Constitution Ins. Co.* v. *Kosmopoulos* [1987] 1 SCR 2, 22.

insurable interest reduces any temptation to bring about the loss insured against. A person with a large overdraft but little love for his neighbour might well be tempted to insure his neighbour's warehouse against fire and then burn it; and, if he really dislikes him, to insure his life and lock him in the warehouse at the same time. The assumption is that, when it comes to his own life or his own warehouse, there is not the same temptation.

Another related reason is that people take better care of their own things than those of other people. Economists, Rea for example,[21] speak of 'the externality' that is created when one party insures another's property. The 'externality' is the 'cost' imposed on the property owner who is not a party, and who is thus external to the transaction in question:

> Most insurance reduces the insured's incentive to take care because it is not efficient for insurers to monitor perfectly the care taken by the insured. When there is an insurable interest, the added expected loss caused by the moral hazard is borne by the two parties to the insurance contract. When a third party owns the property, that party bears the increased risk of loss without compensation. Therefore, an insurance contract without insurable interest is not 'Pareto efficient'.

The contract makes the insured better off and the owner of the property worse off—and, the argument assumes, the benefit to the insured does not outweigh the 'cost' to the owner. The argument concludes that the 'insurable interest doctrine exists to prevent such inefficient contracts'. Pareto efficiency occurs if the winner (the insured) compensates the loser (the owner) and retains a net benefit from the insurance contract. This clearly does not happen here. If we take a looser (Kaldor-Hicks) definition of efficiency whereby, although the winning insured *could* compensate the losing owner but does not, the two are lumped together and there is a net benefit to the lump and thus, in a sense, to society. As a justification of the rule of insurable interest, it is not convincing unless it at least takes account of the cost to the market of enforcing the rule. Rea also comments that the 'doctrine seems to be designed to avoid a costly investigation of the amount of care [taken of property insured] by focussing on the insured's

---

[21] S. A. Rea Jnr., 'The Economics of Insurance Law', 13 *Int. Rev. of Law & Economics* 145–62, 147 (1993).

interest'.[22] Criticism of this kind of the requirement of insurable interest, which is found in particular in the United States, carries some conviction.

Is all this really a sound and sensible basis for such a strict rule of law? On the one hand, people have sometimes taken their own life to pay debts and salvage honour, and, especially in times of recession, people have sometimes tried to reduce a large overdraft at the bank with a large fire at the warehouse: this has been described in the insurance industry as 'ash for cash'. On the other hand, most insurers, although they do not agree about its extent, insist that the temptation is real. They also agree with the economists about Pareto efficiency, although they are more likely to do so in the language of moral hazard and risk: 216 ff. below.

If the need for an insurable interest of some kind is real, it cannot be said with the same confidence that the strict rules of English law are the rules to meet that need. In many, if not most, cases of temptation, the insurer can also resist payment on other grounds. Although the law does not require a person to prove his interest, either when he contracts insurance or when he makes a claim, in practice he will find it difficult to insure property of any value in which he has no interest at all without falling foul of the rules about misrepresentation or non-disclosure. If he does insure it and then burns it, he will find it impossible to obtain the insurance money without fraud. Of course, fraud is sometimes successful. However, although the insurer may be reluctant to defend a claim on the ground of fraud (174 below), the insured may well find the insurer is slow to pay and, if the insurer does pay, that even then his enjoyment of the money is spoiled by the unwelcome attention of the police. The strict rule of English law, to which we now turn, is neither sensible or necessary.

Indemnity Insurance

In its detail the rule about insurable interest depends on the kind of insurance; it depends on a distinction, which is basic to insurance law, between indemnity insurance and non-indemnity insurance.

---

[22] S. A. Rea Jnr., 'The Economics of Insurance Law', 146.

Indemnity insurance pays compensation up to the amount of actual measurable loss. An obvious example is the amount recoverable under property insurance against fire. Non-indemnity insurance (also called contingency insurance) does not have this purpose, but pays a predetermined sum on the occurrence of a specified event, and the *amount* payable does not necessarily turn on the nature or importance of the event. An obvious example is life insurance payable on death: the amount does not usually depend on how the insured dies or how much the insured was 'worth' to family and friends but on how much premium was paid for the cover. Some kinds of insurance contract have both features. One is personal-accident insurance; the skier may get more for breaking a leg than an arm, but the insurance payment for medical expenses is the actual cost (indemnity) as well as a specified sum for the general pain and inconvenience (non-indemnity), regardless of which limb is broken and of whether it is broken in one place or two.

The distinction between indemnity insurance and non-indemnity insurance leads to the following difference. The insurable interest for indemnity insurance is tested at the time of the actual loss, which is the time at which the amount of the indemnity is measurable. For non-indemnity insurance, however, measurement is neither necessary nor, usually, possible. The interest is tested at the time of contract, which is when it can best be seen whether the insurance is really a wager or whether, in the example of life insurance, society might want to ask whether it is likely that the insured will be tempted to take the life insured. Moreover, when life insurance is a vehicle for investment, calculations have to be made at the time of contract based on as few variables as possible; so that is when the life insured must be identified and, incidentally, when the insurable interest must exist.

Life Insurance

Ties of Affection

The classic case of non-indemnity insurance is life insurance.[23]

---

[23] See M. A. Clarke, *The Law of Insurance Contracts* (3rd edn., London, 1997) 3–1 ff. and 4–4A.

From the reasons for requiring an insurable interest (21 ff. above), it follows that a person is allowed to insure only the lives of those whom, it can be presumed, he will not be tempted to kill. The law's view of human nature is dismal and the list of insurable lives is short: spouses. The law's view of human nature also seems uninformed and unconvincing. It is uninformed because many, if not most, murders are committed inside the family. It is unconvincing because it can scarcely be said that a mother is more likely to kill her child than her husband. At 3 am in a state of post-natal depression perhaps, but will she telephone for life insurance on the child first?

A more positive view of human nature has been taken in the United States. In many, if not most, states, life insurance is allowed not only by spouse on spouse but also by one sibling on another and by children (legitimate or not) on parents. Moreover, some courts have allowed insurance between engaged persons, 'partners', and 'significant others'. In Texas, however, the court disallowed insurance between unmarried couples because, said the court, it 'is a matter of common knowledge that the practice of such relations often results in a fertile field for the breeding of violence which too frequently ends in the wanton destruction of human life'.[24] Perhaps the only real lesson to be drawn from these differences is that general conclusions about likely human behaviour are unsafe.

Dependence

The restriction relating to natural affection is neither natural nor normative. So, an alternative basis for the requirement of interest in England was found in financial dependence. Outside the family circle, this was the explanation for the decision over a century ago that a creditor could insure the life of his debtor: if his best chance of repayment lay in the continued life and labour of the debtor, society had no reason to worry about the safety of the debtor, if the creditor had insured his life. Inside the family circle, however, financial dependence as a criterion of interest emerged more slowly. As early as 1830 it was argued that a father had an interest in the life of his son because, if the son died, the chance of

---

[24] *Biggs* v. *Washington National Life Ins. Co.*, 275 SW 2d 566, 569 (Tex, 1955).

the father being maintained in old age was diminished. The court rejected the argument, saying that, as the parish was bound to maintain him, it was a matter of indifference to the father whether he were maintained by the parish or by the son.[25] This was probably no more true then than it is now. Children are still seen by the poor as a source of security in old age. Some people would rather starve than take 'handouts' from the state—the same state that is now telling its citizens that state pensions will not suffice, and that, in future, most of them must provide for old age themselves. For some especially, the argument that the parents have a financial interest in the life of their child has lost little of its force.

The argument fared no better when it came from the child to establish the child's interest in the life of the parent. Was it because judges feared the thin end of a wedge, whereby a range of poor relations might insure the life of a prosperous relative on whose generosity they depended? The reason given was that the child had no right to maintenance—with the corollary, however, that, when a child does have a right to maintenance under a maintenance order of the court, the child can insure the life of the parent. A similar reason was given for rejecting the argument that the potential burden of funeral expenses gave the child an insurable interest in the parent: the child was not obliged in law to pay for the funeral. Eventually, however, the law relented on this and allowed limited cover for this kind of expense under the Industrial Assurance and Friendly Societies Act 1948 (section 2). Inside the family, financial dependence was finally recognized in 1909—not to extend the range of insurable interests but as an alternative basis to natural affection for allowing insurance between spouses.[26] Although one alone was earning, there might be mutual financial dependence because, as one judge put it, the cock bird can feather the nest only because he does not have to sit on it all day. Nonetheless, this leaves English common law looking clear but censorious; yet, if the insurance law is clear, the insurance practice is not.

In practice, although in contrast to married couples there is no insurable interest in the life of a cohabiting 'partner', some

---

[25] *Halford* v. *Kymer* (1830) 10 B & C 724, 728.
[26] *Griffiths* v. *Fleming* [1909] 1 KB 805 (CA).

insurers do offer cover and the Insurance Ombudsman will enforce it. The Scottish Law Commission has recommended that this practice should be confirmed by statute and, moreover, that no qualifying period of cohabitation should be required.[27] Further, although by analogy with debtors firms can insure the lives of key employees, sparse precedent says that the amount must be limited to the pecuniary value of the employee's unexpired period of employment. That is adequate for those who have contracted golden handshakes, but not for those who have not, and the legal limit is widely ignored. This is the kind of muddle that occurs when a rule does not have a rationale that meets the needs of commerce or commands respect. Can a rationale be found?

The Problem of Finding a Rational Basis

Clearly, affection is some kind of guarantee against murder; but what is not clear at all is when affection can be presumed. Marriage is not always a bond of affection; like charity, murder begins at home. But murder at home is mostly hot-blooded murder, whereas the requirement of interest only makes any sense at all if people think before they kill. Nor, of course, is marriage the only bond of affection. Indeed, it is strange that, on the one hand, tort law states that a third party owes a duty of care to a partner because, if one partner is killed by the third party in front of the other, the other will be so upset that nervous illness is a reasonably foreseeable result. Yet, on the other hand, the same partners are not allowed to insure each other's lives, because they might be tempted to kill each other. So much depends on the particular relationship that categories of relationships are a poor guide.

A second possibility, as we have seen, is to base the interest rule on financial dependence. However, readers of Agatha Christie may recall *Murder on the Nile* and its theme of dependence that bred abuse of power, resentment, and murder. Still, the idea of dependence does reflect a common purpose of life insurance: to indemnify the survivor against the financial consequences of death—consequences which are difficult to measure or predict and, perhaps the nub of the matter, distasteful as the subject of

[27] Report 135 on Family Law, para. 16.41.

proof by a survivor in mourning. There is perhaps an underlying sentiment that the widow should not have to prove to an insurer that her widow's weeds were paid for by a dress allowance from her husband which, as a result of his death, she has lost.

In cases like that of spouses dependence can be presumed and, it is argued, in other cases it can be proved. However, as the basis of a rule requiring insurable interest, does it prove too much? Might it not result in a rule that is too wide to be useful? If a bomb blasts a tourist to death in Oxford, that is bad not only for the tourist's spouse but also for hotels and shops in Oxford. If the monarch dies today, that is bad for business throughout the realm tomorrow. But, just as the hotel cannot insure the life of its guest, the subject cannot insure the life of the Queen.

In the realm of reality, however, what business needs and what it gets is not insurance on the life of the tourist or the life of the Queen, but insurance of the business. So, to take this kind of example a stage further, although a supermarket cannot insure the life or health of a TV star, it can insure profits against the star's non-appearance to open the new store. Moreover, bearing in mind the cost, a wedding can be insured against non-appearance of the bridegroom—as long as the cause is not cold feet. Again, the death of the driver, Ayrton Senna, in 1994 was a blow not only to motor racing but also to the insurers who had to pay on the 'death or disgrace' policies taken out by some of Senna's sponsors to cover loss of advertising revenue resulting from his death or injury. In his case, insurers paid his employer US$17.5 million. Indeed, one can even insure against the death of an image: a firm that employs a star to advertise low-alcohol lager can insure against the fall of the star when the star is driving over the limit. And, indeed, why not? In all these cases, the insured has a legitimate interest in insurance against damage to his 'pocket'. Insurance practice has outflanked the law of life insurance, by calling it consequential loss (or business interruption) insurance; and, of course, it is not contingency cover but indemnity cover, and the insured recovers no more than his actual loss.

As for life insurance, an alternative criterion to affection or dependence is consent. In certain other jurisdictions,[28] for

---

[28] France (c. ass., Art. 132–2, Germany (VVG, Art. 159), Ontario (RSO, 1980, s. 155(2)(b)), Switzerland (Loi fédérale sur le Contrat d'Assurances (LCA) Art. 74) and the State of New York (Ins. Law, sect. 146(3)).

example, there is the same social concern but a different rule, one which requires the written consent of the life insured. However, that is no guarantee against murder unless the consent is independent and informed. Consent may be obtained by the influence of charm over innocence.

Finally, in the extreme case of insurance contracted with murder in mind, perhaps there is another partial, albeit extreme, answer. As the law of insurance now stands, the insurer has little incentive to concern himself with the motives of a person applying for insurance on the life of someone else. In England, however, it has been suggested[29] and in the United States it has been decided in some states that, if the seller of a gun is aware that the buyer will use it to shoot his wife, the seller may be liable to the victim in tort. In the United States the basis for the rule is that a person has a duty 'to use reasonable care not to create a situation which may prove a stimulus for murder'; and this was stated not in a case about the sale of guns but in a case about the sale of insurance.[30] If the seller of insurance to the spouse of the life insured is aware that the buyer has already got the gun, the insurer may be liable to the victim in tort.[31] In England the law has not gone this far, and perhaps it never will. However, the possibility does raise the difficult and important question, to which we return (96 ff. below), of the extent to which the insurer can be expected to investigate a risk proposed.

In conclusion, if A, for reasons which A knows best, values B's life enough to pay premiums, why not let A do so? Why not trust people? Why not trust society and its policemen, who will be the first to look at A if B dies suddenly, to create a framework in which B is safe from A? Why not trust A to appreciate that there are better ways of making money than insuring B one day and killing B the next?

Property Insurance

The paradigm of indemnity insurance is insurance of property.

---

[29] *Paterson Zochonis Ltd* v. *Merfarken Packaging Ltd* [1986] 3 All ER 522, 540, *per* Goff LJ (CA).

[30] *Ramey* v. *Carolina Life Ins. Co.,* 135 SE 2d 362, 367 (SC, 1964).

[31] See B. Kingree and L. Tanner, 'Life Insurance as Motive for Murder', 29 *Tort & Ins LJ* 761–72 (1994).

The insured has an insurable interest in property, if he has an 'economic interest' in the property. That should have been enough for the law of England, as it is in other countries, to allay any anxiety about wagering or arson, but it was not. In England, the insured is also required to stand in 'a legal or equitable relation' to the property insured.

The economic interest is simply a 'factual expectation' of loss, i.e. that there is a sufficient chance that damage to (or loss of) the property will cause damage or loss to the insured—financially; and that therefore, if damage or loss occurs, he will need indemnity.

The extra requirement of 'legal or equitable relation' arose out of a controversial case, *Macaura*.[32] The claimant insured the timber on his estate, and then sold it to a company of which he was the main shareholder and the main creditor. Soon after that, the timber was destroyed by fire. Although, for all practical purposes, he was the company and the person who stood to lose most by the fire, his insurance claim failed. The reasons were that the insurance was in his name and not that of the company; and that his role neither as shareholder nor as creditor gave him a legal relationship of any kind, such as ownership or possession, with the timber. After the sale that relationship was that of the company and the company alone.

The effect of the decision is that, on the one hand, an insurable interest in property is enjoyed by persons such as owners, trustees, personal representatives, mortgagors, mortgagees, lessors, lessees, and bailees. On the other hand, an insurable interest is not enjoyed, for example, by the beneficiary named in a will in the inheritance; nor with two exceptions (30 ff. below), until possession or ownership passes, by the buyer of goods in transit—even though the very future of the buyer's business may depend on their safe arrival. Moreover, a person who puts money, time, and effort into a business, whether as investor, employee, or subcontractor, cannot insure the factory or equipment on which the work or the venture depends.

These are hard cases. They help to explain why the requirement of 'legal relation' was dropped in Australia, Canada, and the United States; and why in these countries, as well as others such as

---

[32] *Macaura* v. *Northern Assurance* [1925] AC 619. See further, Clarke, n. 23 above, 4–3.

Switzerland, the law is satisfied with expectation of loss, the economic interest, alone. Indeed, the logic of the rule in these countries suggests a further step from a rule that requires expectation of loss at the time of contract to one which drops that too and, like the law of France (Code d'assurances (c.ass.), art. 121–1) and Germany (Gesetz über den Versicherungsvertrag (VVG), art. 55), is content simply with proof of actual loss at the time of claim. In other words, in the case of property, the law must have some kind of rule against voluntary destruction by the insured (218 ff. below) but it does not need a rule of insurable interest; all it needs is what it has already got (186 below), a principle of indemnity.

As often happens when English law is too tight, it has been stretched to accommodate the pressure of commerce. The law states a rule, which the insured did not expect in the first place, and then confuses him further with special cases. Among the special cases are buyers and bailees.

Buyers of Goods

Although generally the buyer of goods, who has yet to acquire possession or ownership of the goods, cannot insure them in transit, an exception is made when they are at his risk—which is usually from the time of shipment. Until shipment, he stands in no legal or equitable relation to the goods. After shipment his position is no different except that, as a matter of contract with the seller, the goods are at his risk because he must pay for the goods if they are lost or damaged. To say that this puts him in a legal relation with the goods is to extend the second leg of the rule (legal relation) from its characteristic base to the terrain of the first (factual expectation of loss). The explanation of this extension lies not in logic but in the law's concern about speculative loss and speculative connection. Once risk has passed, it is clear beyond doubt that damage to the goods will damage the buyer; that is what really matters. The line has been clearly drawn; however, it is not clear at all how to explain it to the buyer. The buyer is unlikely to understand why the line is drawn at the point of shipment rather than earlier, for example, in the seller's factory when the goods are being packed.

A second exception has been made for the buyer if he has paid all or part of the price. This, said the courts, gave him an 'equitable lien' and thus an equitable relationship to the goods.[33] But the lien is window-dressing. Again, the real explanation is that the payment is evidence enough that damage to the goods will damage the buyer; that is what matters.

Bailees

A person has a legal relation to any goods in his possession—not only his own goods but also goods which are not his and for which, therefore, he may be liable to the owner, if they are lost or damaged, as bailee. So, a man may insure not only his wife's jewellery but also his son's bicycle, even though the jewellery is in his wife's handbag and even though his son is a student and neither son nor bicycle spends much time at home; once a year is enough. The explanation is that the father's interest lies in liability to his family, if its property is stolen because, for example, the father did not mend the lock on the back door. This explanation does not bear close examination, but it is not meant to: everyone agrees that it is sensible to allow the insurance.

The same possibility of liability is also the reason given why another bailee, the warehouse, is allowed to insure all the goods in the warehouse, its own as well as those of its customers. In the warehouse, the rule has been stretched further by what is called—confusingly as it is not a trust at all—the commercial trust. Not only is the warehouse allowed to insure the goods of its customer but, in the event of (loss or) damage, it may recover the full value of the goods from the insurer, even though the loss has been suffered not by the warehouse but by the customer. If, however, the warehouse does claim and recover the insurance money it cannot keep it: the customer can compel the warehouse to account for the money over and above the loss, if any, suffered by the warehouse itself.

In recent years, the warehouse rule has been extended to other bailees in commerce. On a construction site, especially a large one such as that for the Millennium Exhibition, there can be no doubt about the convenience for all concerned of allowing one person, usually the head contractor, to take out a single policy covering the

---

[33] *Ebsworth* v. *Alliance Marine Ins. Co.* (1873) LR 8 CP 596.

whole of the risk and for the benefit of all those working on site. Otherwise each sub-contractor, for example, would have to take out a separate policy. This would mean, at the very least, extra paperwork; at worst, in the event of an accident, there would be multiple overlapping claims and cross-claims. One solution to the problem might be for the head contractor to contract insurance as agent for the sub-contractors, but there are difficulties here about that well-worn device. One is that the law does not allow agents to contract for unknown principals: when the head contractor insures, the sub-contractor may not have been appointed. Another is that the cost of liability insurance might be too much for the small sub-contractor, and tempt him to do without insurance. So, in situations like this, the court has held that the position of a contractor in relation to contract works is sufficiently similar to that of a bailee in relation to goods bailed that he is entitled to insure the entire contract works, and in the event of a loss to recover the full value of those works in his own name.[34]

Extended like this, the rule has implications for any collaborative activity on a large scale, where there is a potential for damage to property and liability between collaborators. Factories, hospitals, and colleges come to mind. As Lord Diplock has explained the original rule as one based on commercial practice,[35] however, we cannot predict a similar extension for these places unless it can be said that, on account of manifest convenience, the basis lies more in the element of convenience than in the element of commerce. The law has been stretched to achieve a sensible result, but its extent is uncertain.

[34] See *Petrofina (UK) Ltd* v. *Magnaload Ltd* [1983] 2 Lloyd's Rep. 91, 96-7.
[35] *The Albazero* [1977] AC 774, 846.

2

The Insurer

The Emergence of Insurers

In Chapter 1 we saw that the insured seeks insurance, in part at least, to find some degree of peace of mind concerning the risk insured. Insurers are aware of this and, to sell their insurance, have projected a certain image of themselves and of their products. This image is the main subject of Chapter 2.

The earliest insurers were mutuals: persons in need of what we now call insurance got together in 'clubs' of such people for mutual protection and indemnity: see 17 above. Later, insurance was offered on a commercial basis by companies set up to provide the service of insurance and to make a profit for those who invested in the company. In parallel, certain kinds of insurance, originally marine but later other lines too, were arranged at Lloyd's.

As the market grew, intermediaries came into the market to bring people together. Indeed, insurers have done much of their personal lines of business through intermediaries, usually brokers (44 below), and chose to have little direct contact with the client insured—until the mould was broken by the arrival of 'direct' insurers who market their products directly to the client by mail or by telephone. The older way of doing business left it to the broker to identify need and design products; the new pattern found some insurers ill-equipped to take the initiative which the new market-place required.

First, some insurers did not know how to deal with the customer in the flesh. Some simply did not listen to the customer; they were unable to appreciate the particular concerns of the customer and to tailor cover accordingly. For example, in 1995 the head of risk management at London Transport was reported as saying that it did not see why it should be told by insurers what it could and could not have by way of cover; it was for the insurer to come up with the cover required.

Further, the older pattern left the industry with a remote and monolithic image which has failed to attract the best graduates of the best business schools or, indeed, graduates of any kind at all. Those who entered the industry were more likely to be promoted for loyalty than for talent. The 'successes' of this system reinforced the process by showing little enthusiasm for education, within the firm or in the world outside; and in turn they tended naturally to promote those they could trust and understand, cloning their own kind: the graduates of the university of life—company life.

Of the three underwriters found to have been negligent in a celebrated case in 1993, two had left school at 14 and 15 respectively, and had gone straight to Lloyd's. Notwithstanding what they had learned at Lloyd's, the judge found that one of them 'never had a proper appreciation of the excess of loss business that he was writing' and was still unable to appreciate his own lack of understanding.[1] The case established, said an industry journal,[2] 'what we always knew—that some underwriters at Lloyd's during that period', the late 1980s and early 1990s, 'were simply not up to the job'. After Hurricane Andrew in 1992, reinsurers swore that they would introduce discipline to the insurance industry which, said *The Economist* in 1994, remains 'notorious for relying on gut instinct rather than actuarial tables'. In the heat of competition in the common European market, it has been forecast by leading management consultants, McKinsey, that about half of the (2,000) European insurance companies will disappear. In particular, it was predicted that general multi-line insurers will suffer in competition with specialist insurers who have identified and focussed on a particular part of the insurance market.

Meeting or Making the Need

Insurers appeared on the scene in response to a perception in the public that people needed insurance. It is the role of the insurer to meet that need, to spread risk, with the aid of the law of large numbers and within the framework of the law of the land.

The response of some parts of the industry, to some of the

---

[1] *Henderson* v. *Merrett Syndicates Ltd, sub nom. The Lloyd's Litigation* [1994] 2 Lloyd's Rep. 193.
[2] *Post Magazine*, 13 Oct. 1994, 19.

newer needs of society has been impressive. Engineering and construction projects have increased in size and complexity, and insurance has been found for them. In 1969, for example, some people doubted whether the insurance industry had the capacity to cover the loss that might arise out of the crash of a Boeing 747 aircraft. By the 1990s, passenger miles had increased by a factor of four, the number of western passenger jets in service was over 10,000, and it is estimated that a serious crash of a 747 would cost insurers of the hull alone fifteen million dollars—and be paid. Each death in such a crash might cost a further three million dollars. Even so, the cost of an airline's insurance for a passenger aircraft is only about 0.8 per cent of the operating costs of the aircraft, and for one of the 747s it is less. The 747 and other large aircraft offer a good illustration of the function of insurance to spread risk and loss. In 1984 five crashes caused three fatalities but in 1985 thirteen crashes caused 1,489 deaths. Fluctuations and losses of this magnitude can be covered only by spreading loss— over the years and over the market through many insurers and many layers of reinsurance.

In contrast, it is still not possible to get flood insurance for buildings in certain parts of Holland: the likely cost of a breach in the dikes protecting the densely populated areas of South Holland would exceed the total capacity of the entire Dutch insurance industry. Nor is it possible to get market cover above a certain ceiling for accidents at nuclear energy installations in England and, in certain other countries east of the Oder, it is not possible at all.

The insurance industry has done more than simply react to the needs perceived by the potential insured. Insurance is a product, which is marketed like any other product. A need may be seen more in the eye of the insurer than the insured and, if so, the insurer may foster its growth. Between 1992 and 1994, the amount spent by insurers on advertising in all the UK media doubled from £70 million to £163 million. At the end of 1995, one company alone was paying nearly half a million a month for time on TV, and another was paying £75 million over a five-year period. Studies have confirmed what the companies apparently assume—the power of the media to influence the public perception of risk: see 9–10 above.

A brilliant and innovative underwriter at Lloyd's was Cuthbert

Heath. In the smallpox epidemic that hit London in 1901, Heath was quick to realize that, at a time of great anxiety, people needed some kind of talisman; and the talisman might be insurance. So he offered them insurance against their catching the disease, provided that the insured was vaccinated. He thus promoted risk-management and prevention, and made a lot of money. Today, a life insurer has taken the service a step further by selling term life insurance with counselling for the bereaved survivor; and a health insurer is offering medical advice by e-mail. As we have seen (at 3 ff. above), insurance contracts differ from most other commercial contracts, in that a significant part of what the insured buys is peace of mind. Insurers know this and are developing their services beyond the payment of money to a wider range of services to meet the needs of the insured.

Inspiring Confidence

To satisfy the insured's desire for peace of mind, the insurer must offer cover in which the insured has confidence. He must convince the buyer that, if loss occurs, money will be paid and paid reasonably quickly. To overcome the lingering frisson caused by the public perception of City scandals in recent years, one of the main objectives of advertising by insurers has been to create an image of financial security, enduring trustworthiness, and fair dealing.

As for trust, 'when it comes to life', ran an advertisement in the United States, 'there are two things you can always count on. A mother's love and your State Farm agent.' In England the prose is more restrained but the message the same. General Accident, for example, claims simply to be 'a name you can trust'. This is an important aspect of the persona of the insurer and his relationship with the insured, and one to which we return: 307 ff. below.

As for security, that is associated with endurance—with a known and, by implication, established, name. To achieve this, some insurers advertise simply to increase name awareness. As with washing-powder and whisky, people are more likely to choose an insurer they have heard of. One of the big insurers ran the same advertisement for over fifteen years not only because it was successful in attracting attention and, therefore, premium, but also because repetition, while risking boredom, suggests consistency and stability. For similar reasons, life insurers are loath to change their names because research indicates that people want an 'old' name, a company with pedigree, which they can rely upon to be there in the future as in the past. Ecclesiastical, for example, with 'over 100 years of experience in property insurance' offers 'insurance you can believe in'.

The image of security is also built on associations with solidity—sometimes quite literally. One company advertises with television pictures of the Great Wall of China and the claim that 'no-one protects more' than it. Another ends its television advertisement with the unmistakable voice of an actor associated with classical theatre and the words 'At every stage of your life Friends Provide'. Again, a Swiss insurer chose the image of a St Bernard dog, not only on account of the association with Switzerland but also because it was a breed associated with rescue and reliability.

Sponsorship, which is often cheaper than advertising, is chosen with equal care. Some insurers have associated themselves with classical arts, and thus with enduring values, and others with community involvement, especially organizations concerned with caring for those in need—or organizations caring incidentally for insurers. One insurer sponsors crime prevention; and an insurer based in East Anglia sponsors coastline protection. A number of insurers have chosen to sponsor sport. One company, seeking perhaps a fresher image with a younger market, sponsored football with a 'Safe Hands Award' for the best goalkeeper. However, most insurers seem to have some reservations about the image of association football. Cricket is another matter. The industry's image of fairness took a battering in the 1990s: newspapers attacked insurers as tight-fisted (claims resistance) and profiteering (the pension transfer 'scandal'). That is partly why one insurer sponsors cricket, as for many people cricket still has connotations of fair play and honesty.

Much remains to be done, and such was the damage to the image of the industry that there have been calls for collective action. Yet, when in 1994 the Association of British Insurers (ABI) organized a conference to discuss the image of the industry, it had to be cancelled for lack of support among insurers: some perhaps consider that it is for the ABI itself to repair the image and others do not trust anyone else to project the company image and prefer to do it themselves through a public-relations (PR) department. However, there is surely something to be said for the view of a PR consultant that, although there is a PR problem, the solution is not to be found through PR, for PR should be used as a means of communication, not as a sticking plaster; and that images or reputations are built mainly on good products, service and handling of complaints. The image of the industry will improve only when the volume of complaints goes down and the daily newspapers lose interest.

If the desired image is to be created, the implied promise kept, reassurance and peace of mind provided, insurance and the law that underpins it must meet the expectations induced by the image: certainty of cover and reasonable speed of settlement. This book seeks to assess the law of England against these standards.

Risk Prediction

The insurer is concerned to know 'what he is letting himself in for'; in other words, he needs to know the extent of the risk proposed, in order to decide whether to take the risk at all and, if so, what premium to charge and what conditions to impose. The risk contains two major elements.

First, much of what the insurer promises is money and, for the insurer, the risky feature of money is inflation. For the liability insurer, for example, the premiums collected this year must be enough to pay claims, claims which may arise this year but which may not be quantified for some years to come, and in the light of prices and wages then. Secondly, the chance that he will have to pay money at all, the extent of the risk insured, depends not only on physical factors associated with the perils insured against and the 'state of the art' of ways to mitigate loss, but also, especially in the case of liability insurance, on the state of the law.

Risk on the Ground

Above all, the insurer needs to know about the peril to be insured. He must try to predict events. This means, first, a judgement about the person insured, the 'moral hazard': 216 ff. below. Secondly, the insurer must consider whether the risk will be affected by people in general—by governments which may intervene to affect the risk, for example, by changing the law of liability or regulating insurance. Last but not least every risk has an actuarial aspect. 'I have but one lamp by which my feet are guided, and that is the lamp of experience. I know no way of judging of the future, but by the past.' This lesson, thus expressed by an American lawyer, Patrick Henry, in 1775, was well understood by insurers then and now. The insurer must have enough data from the past to predict the future and, in particular, to have some idea about the largest possible single loss, the average size of the loss in question, and how frequently losses are likely to occur. Insurers prefer risks with a high frequency on a low scale.[3] They prefer, for example, to cover damage to taxis than damage to space vehicles.

The importance of data is illustrated by the underwriting of life insurance. Lives were insurable only after Edmund Halley, the Astronomer Royal, had drawn up mortality tables and these had been published by the Royal Society in 1693. Insurance covering the consequences of disease was possible as regards many diseases (and then on a limited scale) only with the information resulting from the Infectious Diseases (Notification) Act of 1889. Indeed, until the middle of this century, many believed that the march of progress was such that uncertainty was a transient imperfection which, in time, would be eliminated by science and technology, thus rendering even insurance, or at least much of it, unnecessary.[4] Seemingly, although today the global village is overseen by a universe of computers, uncertainty is still there and, if anything, its impact has been underestimated.

In the 1980s current wisdom was that any risk could be insured at a price. The strand of folly in the wisdom, the assumption of certain underwriters that the price could be fixed without researching the risk, became apparent in the 1990s. People saw 'what happens when brokers of less than top draw quality are tempted to present bad risks to underwriters who are known to fly by the seat of their pants, particularly after lunch on Fridays'.[5]

---

[3] A. J. Vermaat, 'Uninsurability: A Growing Problem', Geneva Papers, No 77 (1995), 446–53, 447; M. G. Faure, 'The Limits to Insurability from a Law and Economics Perspective', *ibid.* 454–62, 458.

[4] O. Giarini, 'Insurability and the Economic Relevance of Insurance: A Historical Economic Perspective', Geneva Papers, No 20 (1995), 419–22; P. L. Bernstein, *Against the Gods* (New York, 1996).

[5] M. Mendelowitz, 'Reinsurance Dispute Resolution—Recent Trends and Recent Cases' (1993) 83 *BILA J* 23–33, 27.

Even so, underwriters at Lloyd's still pride themselves that for an honest proposer they can put a price on anything and do it in about three minutes, as the broker waits. However, the scale of some risks has changed. Before 1988 no single natural disaster cost the industry more than a billion dollars, but by 1994 there had been fourteen of them, and there have been more since. The Great Tooley Street Fire in warehouses along the Thames in June 1861 was a large 'red card' for the less professional players in the field of insurance. Some observers believe that recent disasters are having a similar effect.

Risk at Law

In respect of all insurance claims that come to court in England, legal costs amount to between 35 and 40 per cent of the value of the claims themselves. The decisions of the courts most welcome to insurers are those that settle doubt. In the case of liability insurance, the courts are regarded as one of the hazards in the risk. The current concerns of insurers include gradually developing diseases (GDD), childhood leukemia, lead poisoning, the effects of passive smoking, sick building syndrome, and the level of care and skill required of company directors. Almost any risk is insurable as long as its effects are reasonably predictable. An insurance journal's 'best decision of 1993' award went to a pollution case,[6] not so much because it decided against liability but because it settled doubts raised by the lower courts. The accolade of the year for worst court decision was shared among those of the lower courts on repetitive strain injury (RSI) because they were contradictory and left insurers unclear on the scope for liability.

The RSI cases are not good for the insured either. First, uncertainty about liability when things go wrong increases the cost of legal advice and the burden of litigation and, consequently, the cost of insurance. Secondly, uncertainty may limit the cover available. For example, an unexpected rise in legal costs—more claims and higher awards—was a major factor in the large loss on the underwriting account for employers' liability (EL) cover and led in the mid-1990s to threats of a cap on EL cover. Thirdly, in an extreme case, insurers may withdraw from an area of cover

---

[6] *Cambridge Water* v. *Eastern Counties Leather* [1994] AC 264.

altogether. A current concern of that magnitude centres on liability for clearing up pollution and, in particular, any change in English law which might have the effect of making current insurance policies pay for 'historic pollution', i.e. pollution perhaps many years in the past, when the current potential for liability had not been conceived still less rated. Insurers in England might well react to such a change as they have done in the United States and withdraw entirely from that market. The withdrawal there was forced upon them not only by unexpectedly large awards but also the difficulty of predicting the way the courts would construe contracts of insurance, thus making the risks impossible to rate. Whether of impending changes in the law or in the weather, uncertainty in any form is the bane of insurers.

Uncertainty in the law hurts the insured in other ways, however, ways that favour the liability insurer sufficiently for him to take account of them when assessing the risk. If the law is unclear and litigation in prospect, claims are more likely to settle at a figure acceptable to the insurer. In contrast with the RSI cases, for example, a decision that employers could be liable to employees for the effect of stress at work was bemoaned by some in the insurance industry, who wished that the claim had been settled out of court, for fear that the whole industry now be saddled uncomfortably with a single, and thus relatively certain, precedent.[7] If the case had been settled quietly out of court, other claimants of that kind would probably have got not only less money but less prospect of money. Generally, however, what concerns insurers most about the law is not so much what it is but that they know what it is.

Risk Prevention

Insurers have developed expertise in loss prevention— but in some areas rather more than others. For example, English insurers know more about fire risks and employers' liability risks generated by engineering than about the risk of disease. Currently there is a spattering of projects funded by insurers, projects ranging from designing systems to recognize signatures electronically to the

---

[7] See *Post Magazine* 1 Dec. 1994, 17 concerning *Walker* v. *Northumberland CC*, unreported.

ultrasound scanning of horses to catch tendon problems early which might otherwise threaten the (racing) career of the animal. They could do more. In Germany, the largest insurer has its own research centre with more than 100 engineers providing technical reports, studies, tests, training, and development.

Recently, minds have been concentrated by the weather. Weather losses have worsened and might get worse still. One insurer was quoted as saying that it is cheaper to insure a satellite in orbit than to get catastrophe cover in the Caribbean. Even so, a conference in 1993, 'Climate Change and the Insurance Industry', although attended by insurers, was organized not by the insurance industry but by Greenpeace. When Greenpeace suggested that insurers should join the lobby to persuade governments to enforce measures of prevention, a typical reaction among insurers was 'We are not a charity, we have to recognise that our shareholders want profits'. By 1996, however, the tune of the big insurers had changed and at a conference on these questions in Geneva in 1996 their voice was heard.

Another reaction is that the responsibility for safety lies not with insurers but with government. Insurers have their own priorities; market opportunities and conditions are high on the list. As we have seen (19 above), many markets are driven by price and the insured will buy the cover that is cheap today rather than that which is subsidizing research for improvements tomorrow. The insurer who spends little or nothing on loss prevention may be able to undercut insurers who do. Moreover, the lay person's perception of risk is subjective: above 6 ff. So, even when insurers do encourage research, the research may not be directed to the most urgent concerns of society and is more likely to be aimed at the short term than the long term hazard.

In general, research on prevention is not a priority, unless insurers perceive a sufficient common interest in pooling knowledge and sharing cost. An established and important instance lies in the work of the Transport Research Laboratory, which is now being run by the Motor Insurance Repair Centre set up at Thatcham and financed by and for insurers. Another is the risk appraisal initiative at Warwick University; this is conducted on an inter-disciplinary basis, supported by the subscription of a number of organizations representing a wide range of risk interests. A significant part of future research on prevention will be played by joint ventures. The common interest of insurers comes together in the most concentrated way, however, at the ABI, which represents nearly 99 per cent of the insurance industry.

Risk Control

Prominent in the work of the ABI is crime prevention. Notable among the ventures in crime prevention is the Arson Prevention Bureau, which was set up by the Home Office and the ABI in 1991 and which organized working groups such as a Fraudulent Arson Working Group. From this comes advice to the insurance industry, which in turn advises the insured directly or indirectly by the message that comes from the terms of the insurance contract. These are both to guide the insured in the paths of safety and to ring-fence the insurer's liability under the contract of insurance. All this concerns cover, a central part of the insurance drama, to which we return in Chapter 5.

3
Agents

Insurance Intermediaries

Insurance intermediaries are of two kinds, tied agents and independent agents, who, if registered as such, are called insurance brokers.[1] A 'tied' agent acts for insurers; at any one time the agent is allowed to be 'tied' to no more than one life insurer or six non-life insurers. In contrast, an independent agent is free to arrange contracts with any number of different insurers and is mainly the agent of the person seeking insurance, the client. According to the director general of the British Insurance and Investment Brokers' Association (BIIBA), 'Buying insurance is a little like buying bread. Tied agents . . . may sell you a loaf at a very attractive price, but it will be a standard, white, sliced pack of Mother's Pride. A broker will sell you white bread, brown bread, granary bread, wholemeal bread and even the more exotic croissants and ciabatta, all at the best possible prices'.[2] But are customers so discerning? One broker was quoted as saying that research among customers had shown that 'they don't understand insurance at all. We treat insurance as a commodity, just like selling beans or dog food. We use supermarket tactics like own branding and money-off vouchers to sell it cheaper.'[3]

The independent agent such as the broking firm is indeed a shop selling insurance; in the past it has been the standard retail outlet for insurance. Like the shopkeeper, the agent has an interest in selling the products which he has in stock at the time. However, although computer links between brokers and insurers have brought the 'just in time' practice of supermarkets to the stocking of insurance, the similarity does not go much beyond the shopwindow. It is easier to 'stock' a large range of insurance than a

---

[1] See further Clarke, *Law of Insurance Contracts*, chs. 7–9; R. W. Hodgin, *Insurance Intermediaries: Law and Regulation* (London, 1993), ch.1.
[2] *Post Magazine*, 10 Mar. 1994, 20.   [3] *Ibid.*, 23 Feb. 1995, 31.

large range of bread, as information no longer takes up shelf-space and does not dry up. Further, whereas most people can tell the difference between the bakery and the breadshop, it is sometimes difficult for buyers of insurance to tell the difference between agents and insurers. The 'direct' insurers bypass the agent and retail insurance directly to the public and, in response, some agents are not averse to letting the buying public think that they are insurers. This is a serious source of confusion. It has led innocent motorists to believe, the more so as it is sometimes true, that a mere call to the agent is enough to contract car insurance, and then to hit the road and someone on it, only to find that the cover is not yet in place.

Although the appearance has been attacked by the courts in the past, especially at Lloyd's (302 below), little has changed on the surface; and in the high street some agents pose as insurers by tacking 'direct' to the name of the agency. But the ignorance of the public about agents is matched, it seems, by the ignorance of some agents about the law. In law agents are fiduciaries with a duty of disclosure: 48 ff. below. Whether or not the agent is obliged to disclose that he is an agent and in no sense an insurer, it is arguable that the description 'direct' is an actionable misrepresentation. Clearly, it is a statement of fact about the agent's business. Buyers are drawn to 'direct' insurers to cut cost. What cost? The buyer is likely to answer that it is the commission which the agent usually charges for his services. The 'direct' agent might argue that, in context, 'direct' does not mean without commission but simply 'cheap'. The *Financial Times* has even doubted whether it is cheap, but, be that as it may, the truth surely is that the appeal is to the belief of the client that costs are being cut by cutting out the commission. If the 'direct' agent is getting commission, is this not misleading the buyer? The law interprets statements in context and regards them as relevant if they induce recipients of the statements to make contracts, to contract with X rather than with Y. An agent who sells 'direct' insurance without disclosing his role as agent is surely misrepresenting his position.

Agents Now and in the Future

If a person seeking insurance has perceived that he needs independent advice about what to buy, and that therefore he should turn to an agent, where should he go? He will find that there are brokers and brokers, large and small, local, national and international. The large international broker may put together complex schemes for new risks, selling these schemes not only to the insured but to insurers, perhaps with reinsurance already in place before the insurer has been booked. As one journal put it, 'many London Market brokers just do not speak the same language as their provincial counterparts'.[4] But it is the provincial broker that the average client needs.

The situation is far from static. On the one hand, the opening of a common market in Europe for general insurance will increase the value and importance of advice about insurance. On the other, many firms are unlikely to survive the competition. As one broker put it, the 'high profit, high reward, seat of the pants environment of the last two decades is over'.[5] Any outline of the current profile of any one of the firms may well be ephemeral. In 1994 a leading firm of solicitors in the field organized a conference. The title was 'The Next Decade for Brokers—Death of the Salesman?' As with the dinosaur, death it will be for brokers, as well as other agents, if they stand on past achievement and do not evolve with the changing commercial climate, by adding greater value and professionalism to their service. Already, some agents, mostly the larger brokers, have moved from sales into related areas such as risk management. The agent today has an identity crisis. He still wears the robe of advisor, although many members of the public do not understand that role and, rightly or not, may not want it. Like anyone with an identity crisis, the agent is sending conflicting signals to the potential client, who may well feel that this is one more element of confusion in the world of insurance and one that he can do without.

Regulation

An independent agent who is registered under the Insurance Brokers Registration Act 1977 can call himself a broker. With that title comes status and also professional regulation; see the Insurance Brokers Registration Council (Code of Conduct)

---

[4] *Post Magazine*, 14 Apr. 1994, 13.
[5] K. Davidson, 'The Future Role of the Broker' (1995) 87 *BILA Jo.* 26–8.

Approval Order 1994 (SI 1994 No 2569). Other agents, such as independent financial advisors (IFAs), agents tied to particular insurers, or employees of insurers, who are not registered as brokers but may be selling or advising about general insurance business, can carry on all these parallel activities—as long as they do not call themselves brokers. They can, however, choose a title, such as consultant. With a title such as that, in the perception of many people, comes as much status as they need, and, in practice, as little regulation as they have any right to expect. True, these agents are expected to observe provisions like those of the IBRC Code, set out in the Code of Practice 1989 (as amended in 1994) established by the Association of British Insurers (ABI); but there are doubts about how well the Code has been enforced.

In addition, whether insurance agents are registered brokers or not, common law rules apply. At common law, the independent agent is the agent of the insured, and the general rules of agency govern the question whether the insured is bound by the acts of the agent in relation to a third party, such as the insurer. These rules apply also to agents acting for the insurer.

The Nature of the Agent's Duty to the Client

Lawyers have commonly assumed that the agent's duties are based concurrently in both contract and tort, and stiffened by an added element of equity. From equity the agent gets duties to the client, called 'fiduciary' duties. From his contract with the client the agent has the duty to do whatever he has promised to do; that is a question of interpretation in each case. As for the achievement of the agent's promise, generally it will be inferred that he undertakes not to achieve it at all costs but to use best endeavours, reasonable care, and skill to that end. From tort the agent has a duty of care, and with it an obligation of reasonable care and skill similar to that implied from his contract.

As between contract and tort, in most cases the extent of the agent's duty to the client is the same. Between parties who have regulated their relationship by contract, courts today are reluctant to impose duties in tort which are more onerous than those imposed by the parties' contract. The agent is undertaking to do things for the client: the natural framework for this relationship is contract; that is how the courts see the situation and that is how it is presented here. When it comes to the client's *remedies* against the agent, however, it is still possible that the client will fare better in tort than in contract: see 62 ff. below.

Payment and the Problem of Commission

A curious feature of the contract between the agent and the client is that, generally, the agent is paid not by the client but by the insurer in the form of commission. This being so, the student of contract law may be wondering what the agent is getting from the client, and whether the agreement between client and agent lacks consideration and can be enforced as a contract at all. One answer is that if and when client C pays premium to insurer B, C pays agent A indirectly because the premium that C pays insurer B reflects the insurer's transaction costs, including commission payable to the agent. Clearly, that answer proves too little as regards cases in which agent A works for client C and no insurance is contracted. Equally clearly, the answer proves too much if it means that beyond the world of insurance anyone who contracts for any kind of service with B has a contract too with anyone else, including for example the employee, that B uses to carry out the service. However, courts are more astute now to find consideration than once they were, and there may well be a similar answer: if C provides A not with money but with the means of making money out of B, he thereby provides consideration for a contract between himself and A.[6] So it is with the proposer of insurance: he brings business to the agent, and that business carries the potential for profit for the agent via the insurer—even if no insurance and no commission comes out of that particular proposal.

The Quality of the Advice

Objectivity

The brokers' Code of Conduct (46 above) contains not only principles of conduct but also illustrations. The very first illustration requires brokers to give clients 'best advice': in the 'conduct of

---

[6] Thinking of this kind lies behind the court's assumption that the contract was enforceable in *The Good Luck* [1992] 1 AC 233.

business and in the choice of an insurer or investment' the broker must 'provide advice objectively and independently in the best interests of the client'. In practice, however, there are incentives that might work against best advice. A widespread suspicion among potential clients is that some financial advisers put their own interests first. The suspicion has been fuelled by certain features of recent practice.

First, until recently, brokers and other agents often advised people to take endowment insurance, described as 'the bread and butter of intermediaries and life offices', as a mortgage repayment vehicle, although some analysts doubt whether this is 'best advice'. Secondly, in response to the threat of competition from direct insurers, a group of brokers has tried to form what is in essence an insurance company, 'Broker Direct'. One obstacle to their endeavour lies in the understandable hesitation of some brokers to join, because they question whether, ethically, an independent intermediary could ever recommend a company in which his firm was a shareholder. Thirdly, given that some insurers will not grant an agency to a agent unless the agent can guarantee a minimum level of premium income, inevitably suspicion arises about the objectivity of advice. This problem has been alleviated, however, by the formation of a centralized broking operation to combine the forces of small brokers and give them the necessary bargaining power to remain centre stage. Last but not least, of course, some insurers pay more commission than others and this too makes the cautious client wonder about the objectivity of advice. The Consumers' Association has claimed that too many agents choose the insurer who pays the highest commission; and argued against commission differentials and in favour of a flat fee.[7]

A problem is posed by commission, as it raises a conflict of interests. The brokers' Code (46 above) now obliges brokers to disclose the commission on the insurance suggested to the client; but this does not tell the client how much (more or less) it would have been for some alternative cover which the broker has not suggested. Moreover, a survey by the Consumers' Association published in 1995 indicated that about half of the brokers visited refused to disclose commission—in breach of the Code. Anyway, brokers are under no obligation of disclosure as regards the

---

[7] *Which?*, June 1994, 31.

commission for certain kinds of cover. Disclosure is required for most financial products but not, for example, for term life insurance or critical illness cover. The effect is that some brokers are now focusing on unregulated products to defend their earnings, and one leading insurer admitted to helping them by launching 'appropriate' products. However, it is not clear that this is part of a general trend. On the contrary, some would-be retailers of insurance have seen the situation as a market opportunity and used the absence of commission on their part as a selling point at which to move into the insurance field. The effect on consumers, of course, is to heighten concern about commission. The effect perhaps is too much concern about commission and too little about what is more important in the end, the performance of the underlying fund or the suitability of the product.

Even when the Code applies, it does so as a matter of broking practice; it is not enforceable in law. The law, however, is neither irrelevant or toothless. Like any other agent, the insurance agent owes the legal duties of a fiduciary. These include not only a duty of care and skill (52 below) and a duty to act *bone fide*, i.e. what he believes to be the interests of his principal, the client, but also a duty not to place himself in a position in which his duty to the client may conflict with his duties to others—at least not without their consent. This is reiterated by Example (4) of the brokers' Code of Conduct. In practice, agents do not act solely for one client. Indeed, the agent may be acting not only for other clients but also for insurers.

A potential for conflict arises therefore not only with regard to commission but also when the agent has a binding authority from the insurer; although contracting for the client, the agent also acts as agent for the insurer. The best known and least objectionable instance of this is the temporary cover note for motor insurance. In individual cases the authority may well go beyond this and empower the agent to conclude the main contract within certain limits and to settle small claims—all on behalf of the insurer. In law, dual agency is lawful with the fully informed consent of the client. For the agent conflict between the interests of different clients is uncommon, but between those of the client and the insurer?

This question brings attention back to the receipt of commission. It is perfectly consistent with the fiduciary role of the agent, if the payment is received with the consent of the client. The corollary is that the agent is not allowed to keep *secret* payments from the insurer, because the general law of agency would see these as bribes. The same is true of any other material benefit conferred on the agent in order to induce him to act in favour of a particular insurer in transactions involving the agent's principal, the client. The practice whereby agents receive benefits in kind from insurers such as hospitality and free telephone calls, of which the clients might be unaware, is out of line with legal principle. It is irrelevant that nobody concerned has a corrupt or improper motive. This is still the practice, however, and with the apparent blessing of the Personal Investment Authority, which places a limit on how much benefit can be offered and received, but does not forbid it.

To make commission or any other benefit lawful, the consent of the client must be given in full knowledge of the actual or potential conflict and of its implications. The position in law is reinforced by an illustration in the Code, which provides that, if such a conflict arises, the broker should withdraw unless, after full disclosure, all relevant parties agree in writing that the broker should continue to act. Although it might be assumed that the client knew that the broker got commission from the insurer, the practice in the past was not to disclose the amount. The best that can be said of the practice is that it was an established commercial practice that conflicted with principle but was allowed because it was so well established. Nonetheless, agents protested when anyone suggested disclosure. Why? Is there good reason why the law should not require agents to disclose commission for all lines of insurance, and to disclose the full amount?

Objections have centred, first, on comparison with the position of direct sellers of insurance: if the agent must disclose what is paid by the insurer as commission, compulsory disclosure results in unfair competition unless the insurer's own sellers, who may be employed on a performance-related salary, disclose too. As the agents know well, that would be difficult; in particular, it would be difficult to assess the employee's performance component so that a fair comparison could be made. Secondly, some agents have doubted whether the client would appreciate the value and cost of the service provided by the agent. Would the agent understand that commission is just one element in the transaction cost of the policy? There has been a real fear that, in a market driven by price, the public will be driven to direct insurance and the agent will be driven out of business.

Is this not perhaps to 'protest too much'? Whatever the answer, the agents' protest did not impress the Office of Fair Trading, which declared that the availability of information of this kind was essential to competition. The *Financial Times* agreed and observed at the time (March 1993) that it was 'a measure of the failure of the practitioner-based regulation in the retail investment market that it should still be necessary to make such a self-evidently sensible declaration'. The outcome is that, since 1 January 1995, regulations have been in force to ensure that all costs associated with a life insurance policy must be clearly stated to the prospective purchaser. Non-life insurance is unaffected but disclosure of commission is required by the Code. Rule (7) requires that brokers shall, on request, disclose to any client who is an individual and who is, or is contemplating becoming, the holder of a United Kingdom policy of insurance, the amount of commission paid by the insurer under any relevant policy of insurance. Rule (9) of the Code provides that brokers shall disclose to the client any payment received as a result of securing on behalf of the client any service additional to the arrangement of a contract of insurance.

Standards

The agent must act with reasonable skill and care. To judge the agent's conduct, the courts have regard to the standards of the industry as set by the Codes. The brokers' Code (46 above) states that he must 'provide advice objectively and independently in the best interest of the client', in short, he must give 'best advice'. Moreover, since 1 January 1995, those selling certain life products have been obliged to set out in writing the reasons for their recommendations. Surveys, however, suggest that the codes are commonly ignored.

The Nature of the Advice

Usually the main thrust of the agent's advice concerns the

insurance that might meet the needs of the client and, perhaps, related matters of risk management. For a relatively standard risk, such as motor, for example, there are over 100 insurers and a bewildering choice of products on offer.

The policy suggested by the agent must be at a favourable rate, not necessarily the lowest rate; but there must be very good reasons for the agent to suggest the one that pays the most commission.

The insurance suggested must be with an insurer who is solvent, and who will pay reasonably promptly, not one who has acquired any sort of reputation for resisting claims which other insurers would not. This is not easy for the agent. To monitor the published accounts of insurers is burdensome and thus expensive; it may also be futile. Information concerning the financial health of insurers is available from the DTI, but recent events suggest that it is not always current or complete. This may partly explain why, although a BIIBA report in 1993 revealed that its members rated claims handling, problem-solving, and financial stability as the most important features of an insurance company, only 31 per cent of the brokers actually carried out any solvency assessment of insurers at all. Moreover, there has been some suggestion that some agents recommend cheap offshore insurers without warning the client of the risk. Nobody, however, is seriously suggesting that agents should not concern themselves with the solvency of the insurers they recommend. A check can be done relatively cheaply by employing a financial analyst or credit rating agency; a report on insurers offered recently by one leading agency cost only £200. Alternatively, a solution to the difficulty lies in collective action: BIIBA itself offers reports on a certain number of UK insurers. As European insurers can now sell their products in the United Kingdom it is to be hoped that BIIBA will soon imitate the equivalent body in Holland and offer information of this kind on insurers in the rest of Europe.

The insurance suggested must also meet the perceived needs of the client; and if the client asks about the meaning of terms, any advice given must be competent professional advice. This is important because, in the words of a management consultant brought in to look at the insurance industry, the 'customer must rely on an experienced and trained wizard to guide him through the maze of arcane language and apparently complex products', needlessly created by the industry,[8] and the agent is the guide. This may be especially important when insurance is renewed. Many insurers adjust terms, and some notify the existing insured not with a new copy of the entire contract, still less a new copy with the changes highlighted, but simply with notes of amendments; many people find this kind of presentation hard to understand without competent advice. In a world of word processors and rapid data transmission, this practice is very hard to justify, still less any reluctance by agents to help the client understand it. Some doubt, however, has been expressed in the industry and also in Parliament, in the All Party Parliamentary Group on Insurance and Financial Services, about the professional competence of agents to explain the products on sale. Indeed, that is one reason why some insurers have sought to devise simpler policies—they serve not only to facilitate quick sales but also to make policies easier for agents to explain when sold through agents.

Contracting Insurance

If the client accepts the advice of the agent about suitable insurance, he is also likely to instruct the agent to arrange it, i.e. to contract the insurance with the recommended insurer. As the agent of the client for this purpose, the agent's authority extends to all acts which are necessarily or ordinarily incidental to the execution of his instructions.

The agent's incidental authority extends to agreeing with the insurer the terms of the insurance. If the client does not hear from the agent to the contrary, he is entitled to assume that all is well and that the cover has been obtained or will be obtained in due course. If the agent is uncertain about the scope of his instructions, for example about whether a term insisted on by the insurer is acceptable to the client, he must go back to the client for further instructions. But if that is not viable and if the agent interprets his instructions reasonably and in good faith, the client is bound by the contract of insurance that the agent makes. Analogy with rules for other kinds of agent (company directors, mercantile agents abroad) suggests that the reference to good faith allows for honest

---

[8] *Post Magazine*, 30 June 1994, 19.

subjectivity in the agent's interpretation. However, those rules are based partly on decisions in old cases in times of poor communication. Moreover, good faith has no generally agreed meaning; see 231 ff. below. Today it should be stressed that, if there is the slightest reasonable doubt about the instructions and if there is time, the agent must seek clarification from his client.

Disclosure

The agent's incidental authority from the proposer extends to giving the insurer the information needed by the insurer to assess and to rate the risk proposed, i.e. the material facts: see 85 ff. below. If the agent fails to disclose material facts, the insurer is entitled to rescind the contract and refuse to pay claims. If the insurer does so, the agent will be liable to pay the client the amount of insurance money which would have been payable by the insurer, if the insurance has not been vitiated and if indeed the agent has not carried out his duty to the client. Obviously, the agent is obliged to disclose only those facts which he knew about the risk or which he should have found out. Less obvious, however, is what the agent should have found out: the law draws a difficult line between statements and omissions.

In one case[9] a broker prepared a proposal of motor insurance, which the client signed and which stated untruly that the vehicle was normally kept in a garage. The court held that the broker was entitled to assume that, before signing the form, the client had read it; and that the client assumed responsibility for the accuracy of what had been written. Indeed, the effect of the brokers' Code of Conduct is that the broker must make it clear to the client that the contents of the form are the client's responsibility and must ask him to check the details. The client does not, however, take responsibility for what has not been written, for what has been omitted. In other words, the completeness of the contents is the responsibility of the agent. So, in another motor case,[10] when the broker did not ask about and the client did not disclose the driving record of one of the named drivers, the insurer rescinded the contract and the broker was held liable to the client. The agent

---

[9] *O'Connor* v. *Kirby* [1971] 1 Lloyd's Rep. 454 (CA).
[10] *Warren* v. *Sutton* [1976] 2 Lloyd's Rep. 276 (CA).

must enquire about any material facts which he has reason to suspect are a feature of the risk proposed. On the one hand, the second case shows that the agent should enquire about the record of named drivers, as it is sufficiently likely that one or more of them will have had an accident. On the other hand, an English court is likely to agree with a decision in New South Wales that, unless there are grounds for suspicion, an agent does not have to enquire whether people working for a company proposing fire cover have a criminal record.[11] When it comes to disclosure of material facts, the pitfalls of pleasing the 'prudent insurer' are many (85 ff. below), and it is the agent's job to guide the client through.

Renewal

The agent's authority to contract insurance does not automatically extend to renewing that insurance.[12] Nor is the agent obliged to send a renewal notice or reminder. Of course, the client's instructions may include renewal, for example, an instruction 'to keep my Westminster property covered'. Moreover, if an agent has renewed a policy or sent reminders in the past, it is arguable that he is obliged to renew the policy again or, at least, to warn the client that it is about to expire.

Claims against Insurers

If an agent contracts insurance for a client, it does not usually follow from that alone that, if need be, he is also mandated to pursue claims, but authority is readily inferred from subsequent conduct. For example, as the agent usually cannot enter a claim without information about the loss, if the client gives him that information, authority to pursue the claim can be inferred. This aspect of his mandate may pose problems for the agent.

If a claim is disputed, the agent's interest is to handle the differences between insured and insurer while retaining the goodwill of both of them. The insurer may distrust the insured but

---

[11] *Fanhaven Pty. Ltd* v. *Bain Dawes Northern Pty. Ltd* [1982] 2 NSWLR 57 (CA).

[12] Cf. the practice at Lloyd's: J. Mance, 'Insurance Bokers' Negligence' (1993) 82 *BILA Jo.* 32–53, 39.

trust the agent, and the agent may well be aware of this. If the agent has unsubstantiated doubts about the honesty of the claim, however, the agent's duty in law is not unlike that of the barrister: to press the client's case to the best of his ability, in spite of the doubts, although the agent knows that the displeasure of the insurer may be incurred thereby. If the agent is a broker, Principle B of the brokers' Code requires the broker to place the interest of clients before all other considerations subject, however, to Principle C, which forbids anything that compromises or impairs the good repute of the broking profession, and to Principle A, which requires the broker to conduct business with utmost good faith.

If the agent expresses doubts about a claim to the insurer, the agent may lose the client but not, it seems, incur liability to the client. The effect of the Code seems to be that the broker is not in breach of contract. As regards liability for defamation, communications in good faith to the insurer attract the defence of qualified privilege. As regards actions for breach of confidence, the agent might rely on the defence of public interest. As a matter of business judgement, the agent might be inclined to 'pull his punches', but the law does not require this. When claiming for a client the agent owes no duty to the insurer except, of course, a duty not to be fraudulent and, possibly, a duty not to make careless misstatements actionable in tort.[13] On the one hand, the reliance placed in practice by some insurers on some agents may be used to argue that agents owe a duty to insurers actionable in tort. On the other hand, if their profession is really threatened with partial extinction, as some people have asserted, perhaps a court would hold that a tort duty would not be 'fair and reasonable': another liability might be the last straw that breaks the profession and, therefore, against the interest of the many members of the public who need agents. If the agent suspects that the claim is fraudulent, perhaps the best course is to pull out of the ring altogether and allow the insurer to draw whatever conclusion seems appropriate; the agent may lose the client, but at the same time the agent is likely to retain the confidence and goodwill of the insurer.

[13] *The Zephyr* [1985] 2 Lloyd's Rep. 525, 538 (CA).

The Agent's Liability

If the agent's advice to the client lacks the requisite care and skill, the agent is liable to the client both in tort, usually but not invariably the 'tort of negligent misstatement', and in contract, for breach of an implied term.[14] Liability in tort is of particular importance when the liability in issue is not to the client, who has a contract with the agent, but to a third person, who has no contract with the agent and must therefore base any claim against the agent in tort.

For any action in the tort of negligence, the claimant must establish that the defendant owed him a duty of care, broke that duty, and that, as a result, the claimant suffered loss of a reasonably foreseeable type. In general, no duty at all is owed to any person like the client of an insurance agent, as the client's loss is purely economic. A major exception, however, concerns 'negligent misstatements', such as negligent advice by an agent. Bad advice by the agent does not break the client's bones but leads to bad cover, and the loss to the client is usually the insurance money that would have been payable, if the duty had not been broken and the cover had been as good as it was supposed to be. This exception has recently been extended beyond advice to the case of a professional who undertakes work for a client and does not do it carefully or at all; and beyond the immediate client to a third person designated by the client.

The extension was the effect of the decision of the House of Lords in *White* v. *Jones*.[15] The decision concerned solicitors but applies to all 'professionals'. The professional for this purpose is not just a person who belongs to a recognized profession but any person who is an 'informed person': any person so placed that others might reasonably rely upon his judgement or his skill or upon his ability to make careful inquiry, and who takes it upon himself to give information or advice. Clearly, insurance agents are 'informed persons' and thus professionals affected by the decision. In general terms, the House ruled in *White* v. *Jones* that

---

[14] Implied at common law (the *Superhulls Cover case* [1990] 2 Lloyd's Rep. 431, 458) as well as under s. 13 of the Supply of Goods and Services Act 1982. See further *Henderson* v. *Merrett Syndicates Ltd* [1995] 2 AC 145, 184 ff.

[15] [1995] 2 AC 207.

D, the professional, is liable in tort to P, someone who C, D's client, wanted to benefit from P's professional services under the following conditions.

First, as is required of any duty of care, the loss or damage suffered by P must be reasonably foreseeable by D. Secondly, there must be proximity between P and D. Thirdly, liability must not be unfair or unreasonable on D. The key to the crucial second requirement, proximity, is an assumption of responsibility by D. Since *White* v. *Jones* the key cuts differently according to whether D has undertaken to give advice or to take action.

In the case of advice, proximity means that '(1) the advice is required for a purpose, whether particularly specified or generally described, which is made known, either actually or inferentially, to the adviser at the time when the advice is given; (2) the adviser knows, either actually or inferentially, that his advice will be communicated to the advisee, either specifically or as a member of an ascertainable class, in order that it should be used by the advisee for that purpose; (3) it is known, either actually or inferentially, that the advice so communicated is likely to be acted on by the advisee for that purpose without independent inquiry.'[16]

In the case of action on behalf of the client, the rule to be extracted from *White* v. *Jones* is painfully unclear. At least two different positions can be taken about the ratio of the case. First, there is the narrower common law position, the 'transactional' position whereby, in most instances, the rules for action are the same as those (above) for advice. Secondly, there is the 'Chancery' position of Lord Browne-Wilkinson, that the professional is a quasi-fiduciary: he owes a duty whenever he has assumed responsibility for a task knowing that P's economic welfare is dependent upon his carefully carrying out his task.[17] This is a wider rule than the first. 'Hell and Chancery', said Thomas Fuller, 'are always open'. The Chancery approach might lead, if not to damnation, then to open season on liability on a scale that would beggar not only belief but also many firms of professionals.

Finally, whichever approach is taken, liability is not regarded as fair and reasonable, and a duty will not be owed to anyone other than client C, if it results in conflict between D's duties to C and

---

[16] *Caparo Industries plc* v. *Dickman* [1990] 2 AC 605, 638.

[17] n. 15 above, 274.

D's duty to P. Nor would it be reasonable if the result is that D has to pay twice for the same loss. In *Verderame*,[18] for example, claims in tort were brought against the broker not only by C, the corporate client, but also P1 and P2, the sole directors and shareholders of C. The court held that broker D owed a duty, but to C alone. The effect is that D will not be liable very often to a person other than the client. Until now the only clear case concerning agents was when P was a substantial creditor of the client C and, as agent D well knew, P was to be an assignee of the policy and actively participated in giving instructions for the insurance. In this case, it was against the very possibility that a remedy against C would be worthless that P required insurance and assignment.[19]

Remedies

If the agent is in breach of a fiduciary duty, for example if he has an unacceptable conflict of interest between his duty to the client and his duty to the insurer, the client is entitled to rescind the contract of insurance with the insurer, which the agent has made on his behalf.

If the agent has failed to do what he promised to do—either failed altogether or done it badly—the client may seek compensation from the agent: action lies against the agent for damages for breach of contract. If the essence of the client's complaint is that the agent has acted (or advised) with insufficient care or skill, that is a breach of contract actionable as such. Also, however, it is negligence and action can be based in tort (58 ff. above).

The client can recover as damages an amount measured by his actual loss, provided that it is of a type that was or should have been reasonably contemplated by the agent (contract) or reasonably foreseen by the agent (tort) as a consequence of the breach of duty (contract or tort) that occurred. Contemplation is tested hypothetically at the time of contracting, and foreseeability is tested at the time of the act or omission which institutes the tort.

As regards the measure of damages, if the action is based on breach of contract, the client is to be put in the position he would

---

[18] *Verderame* v. *Commercial Union Assurance Co. plc* [1992] BCLC 793 (CA).
[19] *Punjab National Bank* v. *De Boinville* [1992] 3 All ER 104 (CA).

have enjoyed if the agent had performed his mandate. If the breach is failure to procure cover, the client can recover the amount of insurance money which he would have recovered from the insurer, if the breach had not occurred and the cover had been in place. If the action is based in tort, the client is to be put in the position he would have enjoyed if the tort had not occurred. In one case,[20] the client recovered consequential loss: the amount of a fine imposed by the court on the client who drove his car in the mistaken belief that the broker had got him motor cover. This is in line with the law of compensation but out of line with public policy, which generally rules out an indemnity for criminal penalties.

In most cases, the types of loss recoverable by the client and the damages awarded are the same, whether the action is based in contract or in tort. Let us suppose that the agent contracts cover but negligently fails to cover competitive motor sport, and that the client, believing the cover to be in place, competes, injures someone, and is liable. Whether the agent is liable in contract, as if the cover had been obtained, or in tort, as if the agent had not been negligent, the measure of damages payable by the agent to the client is the same: the amount of liability to the victim (and perhaps associated costs). This is true whether the cover required is available in the insurance market or not—on the assumption that, if the cover could not be obtained in the market and the client was aware of this, the client would have withdrawn from the competition.

Causation: Must the Client Check the Policy?

Trite law, contract law or tort law, tells us that the client's loss in this last case is recoverable only if it was caused by the agent's breach of duty. In at least two situations, the agent has an argument that the client's loss was the result, not of the agent's breach, but of the act or omission of the client.

First, if the client was so keen on the sport that he would have competed anyway, whether covered by insurance or not, it cannot be said that, but for the agent's breach of duty, the client would

---

[20] *Osman* v. *Moss* [1970] 1 Lloyd's Rep. 313 (CA): seen mainly as an action in negligence.

not have suffered loss in the form of liability to the victim. If it would have been caused anyway, it is caused not by the agent but by the client and the client's determination to race at all costs.

Secondly, the agent might argue that, if the client had read the policy, the client would have realized that the sport was not covered and withdrawn from competition; and that, therefore, the cause of the accident and associated liability is not the agent's original breach but the client's failure to read the policy, which is, in words well known to lawyers, a break in the chain of causation. This argument assumes that the client can be expected to read the policy and check the cover. Is that so?

Between insured and insurer, the insured must indeed read and check the policy, not as soon as it arrives but before too long (perhaps with the help of an advisor), and the insured cannot later plead ignorance of its contents. Between client and agent, however, the law is less clear because it is central to the normal mandate of the agent that the agent undertakes that the cover obtained meets the requirements of the client. In one case,[21] it was held that the client who failed to appreciate a flaw in the cover was negligent; however, this did not excuse the agent entirely: the client recovered from the agent, but some allowance was made for the client's negligence in the amount awarded to the client. Moreover, in that case, the client was a person of great experience in the field and quite different from the average client. Generally, however, the client can assume that the cover complies with his instructions, unless the non-compliance is obvious or concerns an aspect, such as a schedule of specified items, which the client knows better than the agent. The agent's argument that the cause of loss is the client's failure to read the policy is likely to fail.

Loose Ends: Limitation

Although the agent's duty is unlikely to be any greater in tort than in contract, the client's remedies are not quite the same. Conceptually, this is unsatisfactory and, practically speaking, it is potentially confusing. First, the discussion above assumes, as is most likely, that action against the agent is based on the tort of

---

[21] *Youell* v. *Bland Welch (No 2)* [1990] 2 Lloyd's Rep. 431, 461; affirmed [1992] 2 Lloyd's Rep. 127 (CA), which concerned reinsurance.

negligence. If the tort were the tort of deceit, different rules would apply. The claimant recovers all direct consequential loss, i.e. all loss unless the chain of causation was broken (58 ff. above). Secondly, the rules of time limitation are different.

If the action brought against the agent is for breach of contract, the limitation period is that of section 5 of the Limitation Act 1980, six years from the date on which the cause of action accrued. If the action is in tort, the period is one or other of the two specified by section 14A of the Limitation Act 1980. The first, like that of section 5 for actions based in contract, is 'six years from the date on which the cause of action accrued'. The second, however, is 'three years from the starting date'. Here lies the difference between contract and tort: sometimes the second (tort) period, although of only three years, will end later than the first (contract and tort) period of six years.

The six-year period starts when the cause of action 'accrues': when the client suffers loss as a result of the agent's breach of duty. In one case,[22] for example, action was brought in both contract and in tort against brokers in respect of insurance that did not pay because of misrepresentation and non-disclosure by the brokers who placed it. The claimants, the clients, argued that their action was in time, as the cause of action did not accrue until the insurance had actually been avoided by the insurer. The brokers, however, argued successfully that the action was time barred, because the cause of action accrued earlier, when the insurance, which was potentially voidable by the insurer, had been contracted. This was when the client suffered loss: financial loss, because the flawed contract of insurance afforded them lesser contractual rights and was less valuable than that which the brokers should have procured.

The three-year period for tort alone starts when the client has 'both the knowledge required for bringing an action for damages in respect of the relevant damage and a right to bring such an action': section 14A(5). Knowledge means knowledge of 'facts about the damage as would lead a reasonable person who had suffered such damage to consider it sufficiently serious to justify his instituting proceedings for damages against a defendant who

---

[22] *Islander Trucking* v. *Hogg, Robinson* [1990] 1 All ER 826; see also the *Iron Trade* case, n. 23 below.

did not dispute liability and was able to satisfy a judgment': section 14A(6). In one case,[23] for example, the 'damage' was that reinsurance contracts were voidable, so the question for the court became 'when did the plaintiffs have sufficient knowledge of the facts concerning the voidability of the contract as would lead a reasonable person to consider it sufficiently serious to justify the taking of proceedings?'.

The Problem of Performance

Although the agent's legal duties are fairly clear, in practice, they are not easily fulfilled. The average agent is under pressure. On the one hand, the agent must meet the legal standards of care and skill, and the agent who does not is more likely to be sued than agents past or, indeed, agents present in other countries such as Germany. This is partly the reward for past success: in England the market is more innovative and agent-driven and the agent is more involved in other people's deals. It is also a consequence of rules of English law which allow insurers to decline to pay on technical grounds: 181 ff. below. Sometimes the outraged claimant turns against the agent: 'the inevitable corollary of insurers' right [*sic*] to avoid liability on technical or unmeritorious grounds is that brokers are expected to advise, warn and protect their insureds against just such a possibility. The risk returns to the market through the medium of brokers' liability.'[24] Nor is there the consolation of an honourable martyrdom. Unfair to agents perhaps, but a Gallup survey published in *Moneywise* magazine in July 1994 indicated that 70 per cent of clients think their financial advisers put their own interests first.

The Problem of Time

In addition to the pressure of possible litigation, the agent is under market pressure which has led to falling remunerations. The pressure is not only from direct insurers but also from some 'indirect' insurers, who are now reducing the role of the agent by confining it to the initial introduction. The agent must sell more insurance to

---

[23] *Iron Trade Mutual Ins. Co. Ltd* v. *J. K. Buckenham Ltd* [1990] 1 All ER 808, 824.   [24] Mance, n. 12 (above), 40.

survive and, in particular, sell on price. But, if the agent were to seek to emulate the direct insurer by selling on the telephone, it would be difficult to offer best advice. Recently, faster and fuller response has been possible by means of networks and various computer programmes, including one which allows agents to compare insurance products. However, for the agent, the question remains: to what extent is it affordable to spend time giving advice without also making a sale?

A case very much in point, which is prominent in press criticism of 'mass marketed insurance products', is travel insurance. One insurer has been quoted as saying:

In the real world we know for a fact that 99.9 per cent of all holiday makers who effect travel insurance have no interest whatsoever in the cover provided. . . . They are far more concerned with their holiday. . . . We do not live in a perfect world and to carry out full discussion regarding [the travel cover] would make the cost of such insurance prohibitive.[25]

In these circumstances, the ABI has suggested that agents will comply with the Code if they give the customer a summary of the cover at the time of contract and send details later. But if, as sometimes happens, the summary mentions the general cover but not the conditions and exceptions, this does not seem to satisfy the ABI's own code on selling, which requires the agent to explain the cover in the round, including exceptions.

More important is the case of pensions. When the government announced that the State Earnings Related Pension Scheme (SERPS) was not sustainable in the long term, and encouraged people to seek private pensions, the result was the over-selling of personal pensions described by an insurance industry journal as 'just the latest of many instances over the years of greed getting the better of judgement'.[26] But, as the same journal asked, how many agents, faced with willing buyers, are going to spend a lot of their (unpaid) time trying to explain that they would be better off staying in the pension scheme they already have? The journal concluded that we do not have a culture where we seek out paid-for in-depth financial advice. The short answer is to change the culture. The observer is left with the impression that agents fear

[25] O. Hameed, 'The ABI Code of Practice for the Selling of General Insurance', (1993) 3 *Ins. L & P* 37–41, 39.   [26] *Post Magazine*, 16 Dec. 1993, 8.

that, if, like other 'professionals' in the private sector, they are to be paid for their services directly by the client on the basis of time spent, the client might decide to do without them. Indeed, in Germany until recently, whereas 75 per cent of business (by volume of premium) was by tied agents and 5 per cent was direct (and growing), only 15 per cent was done by independent agents. The English agent may well be relieved to hear, however, that he has been held up in Germany as the role model for counterparts in the common insurance market of continental Europe, on account of the greater independence and freedom of manœuvre that he enjoys! Moreover, a senior executive of the leading German insurer, Allianz, has argued that the effect of insurers marketing their products in other EU states will be that it will be harder for buyers of insurance to understand the products, so independent advice will be needed as never before.[27]

Solutions

Clearly, agents would benefit from better training. In 1993, a survey by the Consumers Association indicated that many agents did not understand the terms of the insurance they were selling. The insurance industry as a whole feels somewhat hounded by the Association. In this case, industry response varied from outright denial to implicit admission: if consumers want a better quality service they should be prepared to pay for it. Apparently they are not, at least in those sections of the market driven by price (such as motor business) where the agents' survival route is seen as cutting cost, and this inevitably affects the training of persons employed. Even so, legislation is in train which, with effect from 1 January 1997, will require all new brokers to pass certain of the examinations held by the Chartered Insurance Institute and, by the year 2000, the full associateship of the Institute.

In 1993, however, in response to demands from the floor at its annual conference the Institute of Insurance Brokers (IIB) launched a policy-wording analysis service because, it said, members of the profession were 'getting sued left right and centre because they are making mistakes'. Reliance 'on professional

---

[27] H. Schulte-Noelle, 'Challenges for Insurers in the Nineties', *Geneva Papers on Risk and Insurance*, No 72 (1994), 287–303, 294.

indemnity insurance is not', said the IIB, 'an answer to the problem' because of the spread of 'acute embarrassment and loss of client confidence'.[28] As with other problems faced by the insurance industry, such as loss prevention, the development of central assistance to members is part of the answer. So is central control—within the firm itself. The advent of the portable PC means that salesmen, whether in branch or on the move, can be equipped with the necessary data and a programme to facilitate advice; then their work can be monitored each night by the (head) office via a modem, to check whether best advice has been given.

Another solution favoured by some people who are not brokers is more and better regulation. The ABI has published a code of practice (46 above) but the IIB has been scathing of the ABI's monitoring of the ABI Code; and others have suggested that the Code has been more honoured in the breach than the selling. There is a real danger that a person of dubious competence can take the title of insurance consultant and take the public for a costly ride.

[28] *Post Magazine*, 13 May 1993, 3.

4

Contracting

Contract Formation

The rules of law governing the formation of contracts of insurance are the same as those which govern the formation of most other contracts. Those rules require the ritual matching of offer and acceptance.

In a simple case the person seeking cover (the 'proposer') considers the insurance available in some form of advertisement or brochure (invitations to treat). The traditional practice is that, with reference to the brochure or advertisement, that person then responds with a written proposal of insurance (offer) to the insurer, who accepts it or rejects it. If, however, the insurer rejects it but responds with new policy terms which differ from those expressed or implicit in the proposer's original offer, the insurer's response is a counter-offer, for the proposer to accept or reject. If the proposer rejects the insurer's counter-offer and comes back with a further proposition, he makes a further counter-offer, which the insurer may accept or reject, and so on. A further possibility, increasingly common today for standard risks such as motor insurance and house contents insurance, is that of 'direct' insurance. This is usually contracted by telephone with confirmation in writing.[1]

In each case the various communications are effective in law only on receipt; concerning the meaning of receipt (see 84 below). The exception is the communication of acceptance by post (or by any other authorized non-instantaneous mode of com-munication) which is effective when it is sent. This exception does not apply to telefax or, it seems, electronic mail. In late 1995 it became possible

---

[1] See Clarke, *Law of Insurance Contracts*, 11–1 ff. As regards the conclusion of contracts at Lloyd's, see Clarke 11–3.

to contract insurance on an 'insurance exchange' on the internet; this process is also outside the scope of the exception.

These basic rules, in their application to the formation of insurance contracts, work well. The insurer and proposer know where they stand, as long as the chosen mode of communication leaves them with a record of what has (or has not) been agreed. The greatest uncertainty, however, arises out of the rules special to insurance concerning disclosure: 80 ff. below. The effect and the effectiveness of the basic rules for the formation of insurance contracts rests on certain assumptions which must be addressed in turn: that the insurer is not bound unless he clearly indicates his intention (70 ff. below), that all the essential terms of the contract have been agreed (75 below), and that the apparent agreement is unconditional (76 below). First, however, we turn to the appearance of the agreement: its form.

No particular contract form or insurance policy is required by law; the exception is where the insurance is marine insurance, for which statute requires a policy: Marine Insurance Act, 1906 (MIA), section 22. In practice, most insureds are provided with a policy document of some kind when the insurance is first contracted. Insurers are making serious and welcome efforts to make the document intelligible to ordinary people. Whether this can ever be entirely successful, however, is doubtful: 121 ff. below.

One effort that is made by very few insurers is to reissue a policy document to gather up, compress, and consolidate the litter of amendments made on annual renewals since the cover was first contracted and the first policy document issued. The lawyer who has tried to read a statute subject to piecemeal amendments must surely be in sympathy with the puzzled policyholder, who tries to make sense of the paperchase left by his insurer. In a world of word processors, reissue should be easy. One objection, of course, is cost. However, the Code of Practice for Banks and Building Societies (clause 4.3) requires them to 'issue to their customers, if there are sufficient changes in a 12 month period to warrant it, a single document to provide a consolidation of the variations made to their terms and conditions over that period'. It is not clear why insurers cannot and should not do the same.

Expectations of Cover

The brochure or other advertising material put out by the insurer, like that of other suppliers of goods or services, is not intended as an offer which can become a contract simply by acceptance by the recipient. Just as other kinds of supplier may not want to supply all and sundry, the insurer too wishes to consider the kind of person that he insures. In theory, at least, the insurer is not obliged to quote (offer) in response to any and every proposer. Until the nineteenth century, for example, it was quite impossible to get life insurance for 'unhealthy lives', i.e. people with gout, asthma, and so on. Today professional footballers and publicans, for example, find it difficult to find affordable motor insurance. The right to pick and choose is a feature of the perfectly free market place, and that is what insurers want. This is a controversial point to which we return: 72, 149 ff., and 265 ff. below.

A feature of a free market is the possibility of negotiating terms of contract. Clearly, for most standard insurance risks negotiation is neither viable nor wanted by either side: standard terms reduce transaction costs and thus premiums. One view says that the market is still free because, although the proposer may not be able to change the terms offered by insurer A, he can still turn elsewhere for different terms from insurer B or insurer C. Many consumers, however, do not think that that is much of a choice on account of the time and expense involved. True, they may cut cost by using the comparative tables published by consumers' organizations, but it still takes time and then the 'best buy' cover may not be sold on every high street. Anyway, for some risks insurers offer similar terms or no terms at all, and that is no choice at all.

In California, home insurers have been required by law to offer earthquake cover; and Maryland has a statute forbidding insurers from raising motor premiums for drivers over 65 on account of their age. In England, the rating of risks, including that whereby some people or professions find it harder to get insurance than others, has been condemned as 'discrimination' by newspapers and pressure groups—but not by Parliament.

When it was suggested that, as a large percentage of household fires are caused by smoking, a lower premium should be offered to non-smokers, this was rejected by a representative of the Tobacco

Advisory Council as a discriminatory marketing gimmick. This objection got rather less sympathy than that of the Spinal Injuries Association, which complained of discrimination when disabled drivers were charged more for or refused motor insurance. The complaint, accepted now by the Association of British Insurers (ABI), was that some insurers do not understand the risks associated with disabilities and have thus been too 'careful' about taking on these risks. The practice has been been outlawed in principle by the Disability Discrimination Act 1996. The Act, which came into force in December 1996, makes it unlawful to refuse to provide or deliberately not to provide any service, but special regulations allow insurers to treat the disabled less favourably than others.[2]

Smoking is a negative factor, not only for fire and health insurance but also for motor insurance. One insurer uses non-smoking together with home ownership and marriage to identify better motor risks. This has been called 'lifestyle underwriting', whereby insurers identify good risks on sociological or psychological criteria. An obvious instance is the belief that people who are careful with their cars are careful with other things, so the person's motor history is relevant to household cover and vice versa. Another insurer draws conclusions from the proposer's job and loads premiums for people such as financial advisers, accountants, and doctors, because these professions are associated with stress. One newspaper, in its campaign against insurance discrimination, gleefully highlighted the case of a company which employed a certain actor in a television advertisement for its insurance, and then refused him motor cover. At the other end of the stress scale are not only retired people but also those who work on the land. Those with 'good' lifestyles and thus cheaper insurance may be happy about this; indeed, some insurers see this as a promotional opportunity and are quick to point out that, with cover like this, the good risks are not compelled to carry the bad. For example, one motor insurer targets owners of expensive cars over 25, who have at least four years no claims discount (NCD),

---

[2] The Disability Discrimination (Services and Premises) Regs. 1996. Insurers must be able to justify less favourable treatment on the basis of actuarial or other statistical information or other information on which it is reasonable to rely, such as medical reports. See also 256 ff. below.

underlining that the cover is exclusive in more senses than one. However, the corollary is that the bad carry the bad; this means, *inter alia*, that property and motor insurance is expensive in high-risk areas, which tend also to be where relatively poor people live, and this has been attacked as 'income-regressive'.[3] Moreover, sometimes these areas are where there is a high concentration of 'ethnic' groups and, once again, the cry is 'discrimination'. To a degree, therefore, rating becomes a political question which demands sensitivity of an industry that does not want government interference. The industry will insist that cover is available but, like the Ritz, for some citizens it may be barred by cost.

The idea of insurance as a kind of public calling and that the insurer has a responsibility and even perhaps a duty to provide cover (269 below) is one for which English law and English insurers are not yet ready. It is one thing to expect some insurer or other (or all of them collectively) to provide some kind of cover; it is another to say that a particular insurer must accept a particular risk. So, any realistic appraisal of English law must start from the double baseline of traditional contract law that there is no legal duty to negotiate a contract in good faith or indeed at all. But nor is there a complete vacuum. The market context is one in which there is a public expectation of cover; and in which the simple operation of the rules of classical contract law in a notionally free market may no longer be enough.

Expectations of Speed and Courtesy

If it cannot be maintained that a particular insurer is bound to accept a particular proposal, can any insurer simply ignore a proposal? If it is an offer of contract subject to classical contract law, the answer must be affirmative. In some parts of the world such as the United States, however, the position is less simple.

In the United States state law enforces an implied collateral promise to take prompt action on an application for an acceptable risk. If an insurer fails to accept or reject an application with reasonable promptness, and the proposer is thus led reasonably to believe that his application is acceptable, the insurer is considered

---

[3] See further K. S. Abraham, *Distributing Risk* (New Haven, Conn., 1986), 76.

to have accepted it.[4] In France, although, as in England, an insurer is not obliged to accept an application in the first place, if he does so and a relationship is struck and if later a limited modification is proposed (period of cover, range of subject-matter, etc.) by the insured, the insurer is bound by the change proposed, unless he rejects it within ten days: code d'assurances, Article 112–2. A similar rule is found in Switzerland: Versicherungsvertragsgesetz (VVG) Article 2. Most striking is art. 4 of the Insurance Act 1992 in Belgium:

If, within 30 days of receipt of the proposal, the insurer does not notify the prospective policy-holder of an offer of insurance, or that insurance is subject to certain inquiries, or a refusal of insurance, he undertakes to conclude the contract, in default of which damages shall be payable.

A similar rule is found in Finland for standard risks: section 11 of the Insurance Act 1994. Even in England, if the insurer indicates in any way that he will contact the proposer, if the proposal is unacceptable, a contract may be inferred from the insurer's silence;[5] and when, as is not unlikely, there is some dispute about what was said or done, the Insurance Ombudsman will give the proposer the benefit of doubt—even though in law it is for the proposer to prove the existence of the contract. Even so, generally in England consent cannot be inferred from silence alone.

One argument for a contract in these circumstances is that, if the proposer is prejudiced by the insurer's lack of response, the insurer may be estopped from denying that there is cover. If, indeed, the insurer is estopped from denying the formation of the proposed contract of insurance, there is some precedent for the proposition that the insurer is bound by it.[6] The obvious objection is that, generally, estoppel requires a positive representation by the insurer and cannot be based on silence. Occasionally, a 'duty to speak' has been inferred from the context, with the corollary that silence speaks,[7] but none can be inferred from the insurance context unless insurance is seen as a calling: 269 below.

---

[4] The seminal article is: F. Kessler, 'Contracts of Adhesion—Some Thoughts about Freedom of Contract' 43 *Col. LR* 629, 639 (1943). See further Clarke, n. 1 above, para. 11–2A3.

[5] See *Re Selectmove Ltd.* [1995] 1 WLR 474 (CA).

[6] See *The Henrik Sif* [1982] 1 Lloyd's Rep. 456.

[7] *The Stolt Loyalty* [1993] 2 Lloyd's Rep. 281.

A second, but related, argument might be built on key features of insurance contracting: the 'clear orderly and familiar procedure' and the 'prescribed common form'. In these circumstances, a promise might be implied, by analogy with the tender in the *Blackpool* case,[8] to give proper consideration and response to a standard proposal of insurance. Essential links in the analogy are an invitation to participate in a 'familiar procedure', that participation is in the business interests of all concerned, and that the prescribed common form is designed to suit the insurer. In the *Blackpool* case, the person who invited tenders but did not consider an eligible tender had broken the 'rules' and was liable. If the insurer leaves the proposal unanswered, here too the 'rules' have been broken, and if, as a result, the proposer suffers, the insurer should be liable—if not under an insurance contract implicitly agreed, then under a contract collateral to it which has been broken. The court in *Blackpool* wanted to protect ordinary commercial expectations, and to avoid a disjunction between the law of contract and such expectations; why not also the expectations of the proposer? Although the argument has strength, however, the precedent does not. A court determined to distinguish the *Blackpool* case could do so without difficulty. For example, the defendant there chose to deal with a limited number of people; and the orderly procedure only made sense if the defendant could be kept to it. One might almost say that the decision was based on essential business efficacy.

Nonetheless, it is submitted that there is sufficient force in these two points to drive the argument that, in certain cases, the insurer who does not respond to a standard proposal within a reasonable time will be liable to the proposer. In the end, however, the argument may well be blocked by the tradition of market-individualism. Only if the court can be persuaded that the insurance market is not a market like that for corn and other commodities will the argument make ground.

Terms Offered

Like any other contractual offer, the proposal must be unambiguous and complete. Ambiguity depends on interpretation in

---

[8] *Blackpool Aero Club* v. *Blackpool BC* [1990] 1 WLR 1195 (CA).

context. To be complete, the proposal must contain (expressly or by implication) all the essential terms for an insurance contract of the kind proposed.

One essential term concerns premium. So, when an advertisement 'guarantees' life insurance to anyone over 50 who writes in, that is not an offer accepted by Joe, aged 50, who writes in. Nor is Joe's response an offer because neither the advertisement or Joe's response contains a key term: the amount of premium. In law, what is being 'guaranteed' is not insurance but a subsequent offer of insurance at a premium, determined after the insurer has seen Joe's details, for Joe to accept or not. Generally, we can say, essential terms are of two kinds.

First, some terms are particular to the contract in question and to no other; these must be agreed because that particular contract cannot do without them. In the example of fire insurance, these are the identity of the parties to the contract (Joe and the insurer), the kind of risk (fire), the subject-matter at risk (Joe's house), and the amount of insurance (an estimate of the value of the house or of the cost of reconstruction).

Secondly, other terms are no less essential but are of a more general kind; so, if they have not been expressly agreed, they can be implied. For example, it is commonly inferred that fire insurance lasts for one year; that the amount of premium can be implied, as long as the risk is a standard risk and there is an ascertainable market rate; and that notice of any claim must be within a reasonable time.

In addition, terms may be implied which are not essential but are general not to the industry but to that insurer: the particular insurer's standard terms for fire insurance, such as a term about a right of access to the house after a fire. Like any other standard form terms, to be part of the contract they must be available for Joe to read on request. In England, that is enough: people are taken to know that insurers have standard terms and it is for the insured to enquire about them. Again, Switzerland provides a contrasting rule: the insurer must provide a copy if the contract is to bind the insured at all: VVG, Article 3.

Unconditional Acceptance

Like any other acceptance of a contractual offer, the acceptance, whether by insurer or proposer, must be unequivocal and unconditional. In practice, however, acceptance, notably acceptance by a life insurer, may be conditional.

A common example is an agreement for cover 'subject to payment of premium'. In that case either there is no contract and no cover at all or there is a contract but no cover until premium has been paid. The correct analysis depends on the correct construction of the agreement. Again, even if premium has been paid for life insurance, it may still be, for example, 'subject to satisfactory medical report'. The effect of this too depends on construction but, in this instance, courts are most reluctant to construe against any cover at all. Unless told otherwise, most people who pay premium expect immediate, although perhaps temporary, cover and in this situation are unlikely to withdraw the proposal during the period of investigation or look for alternative cover; meanwhile the insurer has the use of the premium money. So, acceptance of premium is strong evidence of contract and that some kind of cover has begun for, otherwise, the proposer, who might reasonably expect to get something for the money paid, is getting little or nothing.

In this sort of situation, Swiss law, for example, insists on interim cover: VVG, Articles 1 and 98. In England, the matter is left to the interpretation of the courts, but the courts are likely to see it as conditional cover, although the exact analysis might vary. One possibility is a preliminary or interim contract at the time of agreement, under which the insurer promises immediate but temporary cover pending the medical report, and to enter the main contract later, if the report is satisfactory. This is also the analysis of motor insurance and the familiar cover note, when some aspect of cover remains to be sorted out. Another possibility is a main contract from the beginning subject, however, to cancellation by the insurer later, if the medical report is not satisfactory. Further, note that, whatever the contract says, Parliament has given the proposer a right to cancel life insurance within a statutory cooling-off period: Insurance Companies Act 1982, section 75.

Renewal and Variation

When the period of cover ends, the insured may well wish to

renew it. People often forget when their cover ends, and this has led to the practice whereby insurers send reminders in the form of renewal notices. The renewal notice is an offer, which the insured can accept, usually by sending the premium required for the next period, or reject. However, although in some countries such as Switzerland (VVG, Article 20.1), the insurer is obliged to send a reminder when premium is due, this is not English law: the insurer is not obliged either to send the notice or, in general, to renew the insurance at all. To this we return: 149 ff. below.

A special case of renewal is life insurance. Strictly speaking, when the insured pays second and subsequent premiums the contract is not renewed but continued: provided that the insured pays premiums, the contract continues until the life 'drops' or a stated period of years has passed. The insured has a right to pay premium and to continue the cover, with the corollary that the insurer cannot refuse it because, for example, since the last renewal the insured has contracted a fatal disease. If the insured fails to pay premium on time, however, the insurance lapses.

A special case, both for life and other kinds of cover, *might* also arise out of the common practice of reminders. The insured could argue that the past practice of the insurer in sending renewal notices amounts to a waiver of the insured's duty to pay until the usual notice is sent, and that the past practice has lulled the insured into a sense of security of which the insurer should not be allowed to take advantage. The problem about this argument is that it must be framed as estoppel: insurer, you are estopped from pleading that my cover has ceased because you led me to believe otherwise; and that English courts are reluctant to infer estoppel from negative conduct. Failure to notify may be inconsiderate or discourteous, but the court is unlikely to censure the insurer by insisting that the insured is still covered. Nonetheless, an American court, observing a common practice among insurers, with a view to retaining and furthering their business and upon which the general public had come to depend, held that the insurer waived his right to require the insured to assume the burden of keeping track of dates on which premium was due.[9] The decision was a Pyrrhic victory for the public, as insurers responded with clauses to defeat it. The insured's case will be won in England only if the

---

[9] *Pester v. American Family Mutual Ins. Co.*, 186 NW 2d 711, 713 (Neb., 1971).

relationship between insurer and insured can be rid of the market image and seen as fiduciary, or at least one in which the insurer, like some brokers, has undertaken to see to the insurance needs of the insured in a more general way.

Flawed Consent

In 1732 Thomas Fuller described trade and commerce as 'cheating all round by consent'. Be that as it may have been then, a contract between A and B today is vitiated, if the consent of either, let us say B, is sufficiently flawed. The consent of B is flawed if B is fundamentally mistaken about the subject-matter, or if B is induced to contract on the basis of wrong information (misrepresentation) or insufficient information (non-disclosure) from A. This is true whether A is the insured or the insurer.

Mistake

Fundamental mistake is rare: it is hard to convince a court that consent was so flawed by mistake that the contract is void. There was once a case[10] in which life insurance was obtained by A by getting his friend's body examined for the required medical rather than his own which, in the event, proved to be on its last legs; but cases like that do not come up very often.

A corollary of the strictness of the law about mistakes is that the insured cannot get out of an insurance contract because of an uninduced mistake about its terms. Normally the insurer is entitled to assume that the insured read the policy and, if the insured did not understand it, sought advice. In the case of a genuine mistake about the policy terms, the insured may have a remedy against the broker, if there was one, for giving the wrong advice or getting the wrong policy: the broker is not entitled to assume that the insured client read the policy to check that the broker has carried out the client's instructions: see 61 above.

Misrepresentation

More commonly, consent is flawed by misrepresentation. Usually if there is misrepresentation, it is made by the insured to the

---

[10] *Obartuch* v. *Security Mutual Life Ins. Co.*, 114 F 2d 873 (7 Cir, 1940).

insurer; but it should not be forgotten that sometimes insurers, especially those inviting people to invest, have overstated the desirability of what they have to offer. Moreover, any person who publishes a false or misleading advertisement commits an offence under section 46 of the Consumer Credit Act 1974; some insurers have been prosecuted under this section on complaints brought by trading standards offices.[11]

An operative misrepresentation is a statement of fact by A which is one of the things that induces B to make the contract. To be factual a statement must be a statement about the present or the past which, as it appears to B, A is in a position (of knowledge, information or experience) to make. Moreover, a misrepresentation is nonetheless a misrepresentation if it is made innocently and in good faith. So, for example, if a fire insurer advises the proposer to insure the property in the amount indicated by an index of rebuilding costs, even an index prepared by an independent body of surveyors, and that amount turns about to be mistakenly high, the insured is entitled to avoid the insurance contract.

Further, B is entitled to assume that if A discovers that a statement, which although true when made, has become untrue between then and the time of contracting, A will tell him. If A does not, B's consent is flawed. The case can be seen not only as one of a statement which has become false by the time of contract (misrepresentation) but also as a case of non-disclosure, which is a special aspect of the law of insurance considered at 80 ff. below.

The remedy for misrepresentation, as well as for non-disclosure, is rescission. However, the view is widely held that, in many cases, the remedy is out of all proportion to the flaw in consent. Whereas in contracts generally rescission is often not much more than a nuisance for the innocent misrepresentor, for the fire insured, for example, whose misrepresentation or non-disclosure was perfectly innocent, it is a disaster because usually the contract is rescinded after fire loss has occurred and, without cover, the insured cannot be restored to the pre-contract position: to recover back the premium is all very well, but the insured is left with a damaged building and no insurance money for repairs. The risk of ruinous loss for an innocent mistake is infinitely more serious for the

---

[11] See further, A. G. Guest and H. G. Lloyd, *Encyclopedia of Consumer Credit Law* (London, 1975), para. 2–047.

proposer than is the risk of innocent misrepresentation or non-disclosure for the insurer and the pool. In England, the Law Commission (ELC) thought that insurers should not be allowed the drastic remedy of rescission for non-disclosure unless the insured had been himself dishonest or unreasonable. In Germany (VVG, Article 16(3)) rescission for non-disclosure is not allowed unless the insured was 'at fault'; and in other countries, too, the right of cancellation for non-disclosure is restricted, albeit in different ways. In England, however, the insurance rule has not been changed. For insurance obtained by innocent or careless misrepresentation, courts must be urged to make more use of their discretion under section 2(2) of the Misrepresentation Act 1967 against the rescission of insurance contracts for non-fraudulent misrepresentation. But there remains the parallel problem for non-disclosure, for which, it seems, section 2(2) gives the court no such discretion. It may well be, of course, that insurers, being aware of all this, waive rescission, but evidence of their practice is not available and every insured should view this uncertain state of play with concern.

Non-Disclosure

Insurer and insured owe each other a duty described as one of good faith. This is different from the general duty of good faith found, for example in German law and referred to in the EU Directive on Unfair Contract Terms: 230 ff. below. In English insurance law, the main application of the duty is the disclosure of information at the time of making or renewing the contract. Although the duty of disclosure is owed by both parties, it mainly affects the insured. The insured must disclose all information which, in the language of the MIA (section 18(2)), 'would influence the judgment of a prudent insurer in fixing the premium, or determining whether he will take the risk'; this is also the common law rule for non-marine insurance. If the insured does not disclose the required information, the consent of the insurer is flawed and, although not entitled to damages, the insurer is entitled to rescind the contract. Before looking more closely at the duty as it affects the insured, we shall look first at the corresponding duty of the insurer.

The Duty of the Insurer

The practical scope of the insurer's duty is unclear; but there is agreement that the insurer must disclose to the proposer any facts known to the insurer but not the proposer which reduce the risk. Is that all? Cicero, as jurist, might have thought not. Before selling corn in the market when supplies are low and prices high, the seller, he thought, should tell the potential buyer about the imminent arrival of supplies that would lower the price.[12] Pothier agreed.[13] Commerce, however, is more pragmatic and less high-minded, and English insurance law takes its tone from commerce; the insurer is not obliged to tell the proposer that similar cover is available around the corner at a lower premium. Nonetheless, can the insurer remain silent about the qualities of the cover itself?

Cover

If the cover proposed does not adequately meet the needs of the proposer, the insurer may well want to point this out to the proposer in order to extend the cover and increase the premium. However, failure to do so does not breach the duty of disclosure or any other duty owed by the insurer to the proposer, unless the proposer places his insurance needs in the hands of the insurer and the insurer's response falls short of what can reasonably be expected.[14] Usually, this kind of responsibility is the role not of the insurer but of the broker: 52 above. The common law tradition of 'buyer beware', much modified in sales of goods to consumers, appears to remain for those who buy insurance. This, perhaps, is because of the market tradition that the proposer, as the buyer of insurance, gets advice from a broker about what to buy; if not, the proposer takes the risk of buying inadequate cover. Today, however, this tradition needs to be reconsidered in view of the move away from brokers to direct contracting with insurers. If it is apparent to the insurer that the proposer has no broker and is not

[12] *De Officiis*, Book III, XII, paras. 50 ff.
[13] *Traité du Contrat de Vente*, Pt. II, ch. II, Art. III, 554.
[14] See, e.g., *Fletcher* v. *Manitoba Public Ins. Co.* (1989) 58 DLR (4th) 23 (CA Ont., 1989).

buying cover that really meets the proposer's needs, arguably, the position in law should be different.

The common law rule, that the seller of goods implicitly promises that the goods are suitable for the apparent purposes of the buyer, became section 14 of the Sale of Goods Act, but there is no corresponding statutory rule for services, such as insurance. In France it has been argued that a duty of this kind is to be found in all contracts for goods and services,[15] as part of a movement to efficient markets and openness in dealings. In Finland, the insurer is specifically required by statute to give the proposer the information needed to assist the proposer to assess the insurance required and to make a sound choice, 'such as information regarding forms of insurance, premiums and insurance conditions': section 5. At the very least, lawyers in England should ask whether in this respect the seller of the insurance should be in a position different from the seller of bread. The ABI, by its Code, and the Insurance Ombudsman, in his decisions, require insurers to bring conditions and exclusions to the notice of the proposer, but that is as far as it goes; and it is not the law.

Performance

Arguably, just as the proposer must disclose the 'quality' of the risk, including the 'moral hazard', so also the insurer should disclose more than most do about the quality of the 'product'; certain insurers have been censured by the Advertising Standards Authority for a misleading presentation of the benefits offered. The most important instance concerns life insurance sold as a financial product. In 1993 the *Financial Times* was moved to condemn the 'inadequate disclosure of surrender values' and the 'absurd practice' in the life industry of projecting returns on the basis of industry-wide costs instead of individual life offices' costs. It complained that lack of disclosure has long prevented investors from comparing the insurance industry's policies with a straightforward investment in equities, gilts, or the building society; and that many in the insurance industry appear incapable of recognizing that the widespread sale of poor products to the wrong people

---

[15] M. Fabre-Magnan, *De l'Obligation d' Information dans les Contrats* (Paris, 1992), para. 303 ff.

under the cloak of inadequate disclosure is undermining public confidence.

In recognition that consumers were not getting enough information about life products, such as surrender values and yield, in 1993 the Treasury ordered the SIB to draft new regulations. Since 1 January 1995, disclosure of commission has been required. In the present climate of general hostility to the way insurers have sold such products in the past and, in particular, in connection with pension transfer, it is arguable that regulations of this kind should be no more than a clarification of a more general duty of disclosure about what the proposer is getting for the money. In cases of inadequate disclosure the proposer should be entitled to rescission and to claim the premium money back.

The Duty of the Insured

In the landmark case on disclosure Lord Mansfield said:

Insurance is a contract upon speculation. The special facts, upon which the contingent chance is to be computed, lie most commonly in the knowledge of the insured only; the underwriter trusts to his representation, and proceeds upon confidence that he does not keep back any circumstance in his knowledge to mislead the under-writer into a belief that the circumstance does not exist, and to induce him to estimate the risque, as if it did not exist.[16]

The duty is said to be necessary for the protection of insurers. To claim under a policy, the claimant must prove insurance that covers the loss, to which the insurer has agreed by contract. If it appears that indeed the insurer has made such a contract, the claimant does not have to prove the reality of the insurer's apparent consent. The claimant does not have to prove performance at the time of contracting of the duty of disclosure. It is for the insurer who wishes to resist a claim (and rescind the contract) to raise non-disclosure by the insured as a defence and to prove it. More specifically, the insurer must prove that there has been a want of (a) disclosure of (b) a material fact (c) known to the

---

[16] *Carter* v. *Boehm* (1766) 3 Burr. 1905, 1909. Generally, see Clarke, n. 1 above, ch. 23.

proposer, who is usually also the claimant, at the time of contract. Even so, the insurer's defence will fail if the claimant proves that (d) the fact was known also to the insurer or (e) disclosure was waived by the insurer.

Disclosure

Disclosure is presumed unless the insurer proves otherwise. In the simple case of a proposal form, what is decisive is whether the material fact is mentioned in the form; courts are prepared to infer that, if the matter had been disclosed, it would have been done on the form and not in some other way—assuming that there was a place on the form for information of the kind in issue. In a less simple case, it depends on who the judge believes. In the past, courts have been more inclined to believe insurers than claimants. In a leading case, the experienced Scrutton LJ found in favour of the insurer, because, he said, it is 'inconceivable to me that the ordinary rate of premium should be charged [as it was] for a cargo as to which an underwriter knew' the relevant information.[17] Whether a judge of today, who is aware of some of the disastrous underwriting by certain insurers in the 1980s, would have quite so much confidence in the judgement of London underwriters we cannot be sure.

Disclosure must be to the right person, to the insurer. The proposer may have difficulty identifying the actual insurer (45 above) or communicating with him, but the law has developed to deal with this difficulty.

First, anyone in business who has a telephone, telex, or telefax, and who lets the numbers be known, represents to the world that any message that reaches one of those numbers during business hours will be dealt with properly and promptly. The same can be said of a postal or e-mail address. Hence disclosure takes place when the message reaches the recipient's number or address. Secondly, it is not necessary that the communication be sent directly to the insurer. It is enough to send it to an agent who has been held out by the insurer as an appropriate line of communication to the insurer; this includes the insurer's local agent. In that case, however, communication and disclosure take place not at

---

[17] *Greenhill* v. *Federal Ins. Co. Ltd* [1927] 1 KB 65, 79 (CA).

once but within a reasonable time after receipt by the agent, i.e. the time reasonably required for communication to the right person within the insurance organization. So great is the potential for confusion in the mind of the proposer that the Insurance Ombudsman has gone a step further than the law and treated *any* person who solicits or negotiates a contract of insurance as an agent of the insurer for purposes of this kind.

The Prudent Insurer

The rule of disclosure refers to the judgement of the 'prudent insurer', a hypothetical market model. However, prudence varies from one branch of the market to another. The prudent insurer's judgement differs according to whether, for example, the insurance is fire insurance or marine insurance. To find out in a particular case, the court receives evidence of market opinion; the court views that evidence with both respect and, occasionally, scepticism. Nonetheless, that is the evidence that determines what is expected by way of disclosure on the part of the insured; this aspect of the disclosure rule is harsh in several respects.

First, the proposer might well think that the questions put by the proposal form are the best guide to what the prudent insurer needs to know and, therefore, to the matters material to the risk. Indeed, if the insurer does ask questions, whether in the form or on the telephone, that is some evidence of materiality, but is that either conclusive or exhaustive of the information required? In some countries such as Finland, Germany, and the United States, there is a legal presumption along those lines, but not in England. The proposer here may complete the form with scrupulous care, but still find that there was something else material to the prudent insurer which, apparently, the insurer did not think to ask about but which, nonetheless, the proposer was expected to think of and disclose. The Insurance Ombudsman, whose jurisdiction permits him to do what is fair and reasonable, takes a different line; if the insurer does not ask clear questions about something, the insurer has waived disclosure of the matter. That seems fair and reasonable indeed, but it is not the rule of English law.

Secondly, mostly regardless of what is asked in the proposal form, if the prudent insurer in the market considers information material, it is irrelevant that the average proposer may have no idea that this is so. How many people who have just been allotted a company car and are seeking cover for their family car realize that, because the family car will be more available to be driven by their children, they must tell the insurer? Anyone who ventures into the realm of insurance must take a guide, such as a broker, or take a chance. This is a demanding rule which probably originated at a time when the insurer could avoid the contract only by proving that the proposer had withheld information fraudulently; to make that proof practicable, the law adopted an objective market view of what was material. Today, however, the legal boot is on the other foot, the insurer's foot, but again the Insurance Ombudsman has softened the effect on consumers. The Insurance Ombudsman has dropped the market test for one of what the reasonable proposer (or reasonable insured) would consider material; if the insurer wants to know more, it is for the insurer to enquire. Since 1984, this has also been the law in Australia: Insurance Contracts Act, section 21.

Thirdly, a material 'fact' includes opinion. The materiality of a medical opinion that the health of the proposer is unsound is not surprising. But the proposer may not expect that, as insurers are concerned with the character of the proposer, fact includes the 'fact' that X was being investigated by the DTI because in the *opinion* of the DTI X *might* have been guilty of insider share dealing—although that has not been and may never be established as a fact. The distinction drawn by the general contract law of misrepresentation between fact and opinion is unhelpful here. What counts is that the proposer knows something which, in the market view, is material. To say that it must be 'fact' adds nothing but confusion. The underlying rule on this point is harsh but simple: if the prudent insurer wants to know something, it is material and the proposer must disclose.

Finally, material information is any information which would influence the judgement of a prudent insurer at the time he contracts the insurance in the slightest degree. The rule in many other countries, that the information must have been decisive in the sense that, if the prudent insurer had been told, the insurer would not have made the contract or would have made it on different terms, is not the rule of law in England. In England, information is material if it would have had some influence, although perhaps no more than to confirm a contract of insurance that the particular insurer would have been willing to make anyway.

Information Known to the Applicant

Although, as we have just seen, English law does not excuse the disclosure of information which the proposer has but has no reason to think relevant, it does not require the proposer to disclose information which the proposer does not have at all. However, ignorance is one thing; forgetfulness another; the law does not excuse forgetfulness. Indeed, the proposer may well be surprised by what the law expects of the human memory. The information that the proposer must disclose includes not only information actually in mind when contracting or information which, if prompted, the proposer could recall, but also information which the proposer once knew but has completely forgotten or which the proposer never actually knew at all but which was known to the proposer's agents. No allowance is made for age or forgetfulness: the person with a bad memory is expected to have a good notepad or a good organization.

The proposer's agents are, first, any agent he has employed to contract the insurance; and, secondly, any agent employed for some other purpose but who receives, collates, or handles material information. The proposer may not know what information has come in; but, knowing that the agent is there to deal with the information, the proposer is expected to ask the agent about it. Moreover, when the proposer is a company, company knowledge may be composite. In one case,[18] one director contracted insurance for the company and the other director, who was also the chairman and main shareholder but took little other active part in the company, signed the cheques for premium. For the purpose of disclosure, the knowledge of the company was held to be the combined knowledge of both, so the contract was avoidable for non-disclosure of matters known only to the chairman. From another case,[19] however, it is clear that the knowledge would not include the knowledge of a chairman of the fraud he was planning on the company. The left side of the corporate brain cannot plead

---

[18] *Regina Fur Co. Ltd* v. *Bossom* [1957] 2 Lloyd's Rep. 466.
[19] *PCW Syndicates* v. *PCW Reinsurers* [1996] 1 All ER 774 (CA).

ignorance of what is known to the right—unless the right is not right at all but doing wrong!

Further, knowledge imputed to the proposer includes the accumulation of past experience. The proposer is taken to know what people in that position would know of their own affairs and of the world immediately around them. When insuring a car they are expected to know whether named drivers will use it for business or not. When insuring their lives after being advised to undergo medical treatment, they are not expected to know with any precision the name or nature of the condition, but they are expected to know that something is wrong—and to tell the insurer.

Information Known to the Insurer

The proposer is not obliged to disclose material information already known to the insurer. The proposer would be wise not to expect too much. The knowledge presumed of the insurer is less focussed on the particular risk than that of the proposer, whose risk it is. Further, although it might be thought that the insurer should have considerable general knowledge of the area of risk covered by the insurer's business, English law expects very little—either of what can be learned from the insurer's agents or from the insurer's own files.

As regards agents, like the insured the insurer is taken to know what is known, first, by any agent employed to contract the insurance; and, secondly, any agent employed to receive, collate, or handle information of the relevant kind. In this respect, the points of knowledge and the lines of communication are important: 84–5 above).

As regards accumulated data and general knowledge, since the early days of insurance each insurer has been presumed to be acquainted with the practice of the trade or context covered. For example, the fire insurer is taken to know that a corner shop might stock fireworks in early November; and the yacht insurer is taken to know that, if yachts are laid up for the winter in Spain, a certain level of theft and vandalism is to be expected.

Generally, however, the insurer is not expected to keep up with current affairs in Spain or anywhere else. On the one hand, he is expected to know of important events occurring at the time of contracting, and to make any connection between those events and the risk proposed. In one case, an insurer doing fire business in Ireland was expected to be aware of terrorists there who might set fire to anything English.[20] On the other hand, the insurer is not expected to recall events reported in the past, however prominent at the time, which appeared to have no bearing on the insurer's business at the time but which turn out to be relevant to a risk proposed later; in the leading case of *Bates Hewitt*,[21] it was merely three months later.

The Problem of Information Retrieval

Bates concerned information about the history of a notorious man-of-war which greatly increased the risk to that ship thereafter. Can we not expect insurers, as a matter of sound business practice, to collect and to accumulate information and experience, which not only is but also *might* be of importance in the future, in retrievable form? In *Bates*, Cockburn CJ thought not, and stated the traditional view of English law:

We should be sanctioning an encroachment on a most important principle, . . . if we were to hold that a party . . . may speculate as to what may or may not be in the mind of the underwriter, or as to what may or may not be brought to his mind by the particulars disclosed to him by the insured. . . . If we were to sanction such a course, especially in these days, when parties frequently forget the rules of mercantile faith and honour which used to distinguish this country from any other, we should be lending ourselves to innovations of a dangerous and monstrous character, which I think we ought not to do.[22]

That was said in 1867. Mercantile faith and honour may or may not have improved since then, but the means of collating, collecting, and recalling information have improved greatly. Moreover, that was said in a case of marine insurance. In England, commercial judges have tended to be very respectful of the law of marine insurance, in which so many of them excelled at the Bar, and perhaps rather too ready to pipe its rules ashore to regulate other branches of insurance. Most of the rules of law discussed in this book apply equaly to marine and non-marine insurance, but in other countries, such as the United States, the law keeps them

[20] *Lean* v. *Hall* (1923) 16 Ll.L.Rep. 100. [21] (1867) LR 2 QB 595.
[22] *Ibid.* 606–7.

apart. On this particular point, for a number of reasons, perhaps English law should follow that of the United States.

First, in many (but not all) respects, the non-marine insurer is in a better position through inspectors and technical expertise to assess the risk and to elicit material information. For the marine insurer, however:

> the subject of insurance is generally beyond the reach, and not open to the inspection of the underwriter, often in distant ports or upon the high seas, and the peculiar perils to which it may be exposed, too numerous to be anticipated or inquired about, known only to the owners and those in their employ; while [the fire risk] is or may be, seen and inspected before the risk is assumed, and its construction, situation and ordinary hazards are as well appreciated by the underwriters as by the owner. In marine insurance, the underwriter . . . is obliged to rely upon the assured, and has, therefore, the right to exact a full disclosure of all facts known to him, which may in any way affect the risk to be assumed. But in fire insurance no such necessity for reliance exists, and, if the underwriter assumes the risk without taking the trouble to either examine, or inquire, he cannot very well, in the absence of fraud, complain that it turns out to be greater than anticipated.[23]

This was the view of a court in Ohio in 1853; it was adopted by most courts of the United States in subsequent years, and in substance by the report of the Australian Law Commission (ALRC) in 1982. Moreover, modern technology aids the inspector. For example, fire insurers can buy an anti-arson financial referencing system. Assuming, as insurers do, that temptation rises when profits fall, this system enables the inspector to check key indicators affecting the moral hazard of a corporate proposer, such as published accounts, court judgments against the proposer and its executives; and then the same system presents the underwriter with an assessment of the quality of the risk. Again, most importantly, there is the Claims and Underwriting Exchange (CUE) (see 180 below), a database of proposals and claims that enables an insurer to look for contradictions between the two, and to effect a rapid check on the recent claims record of any proposer or claimant. Indeed, some insurers have admitted that, if they have access to CUE but do not actually use it until they want to resist a claim, they will face a strong argument of waiver.

---

[23] *Hartford* v. *Harmer* 2 Ohio St. 452, 472 (1853).

In other cases, it is true, inspection is less easy and can be carried out only from a distance by a tactic of 'wait and see'. In the case of legal expenses insurance for businesses, one leading insurer insists on a waiting period of 180 days before cover commences, so that, for example, any latent labour disputes come to the surface. Evidently, this kind of investigation is not viable when customers are clamouring for immediate cover: the inclination will always be to grant cover and rely on the law of non-disclosure to 'rewrite the risk' later, if it turns out to be bad.

The second reason against the marine rule is that today's technology has made it relatively easy for the insurer to store information in vast quantities and to retrieve it at speed. For example, software is now in use which enables any accredited employee of the insurer to call up the claims history of any policy-holder, with images of all original documents and thus without the paperchase through the insurer's different departments that was necessary in the past. Of course, the data must be there; but today one composite insurer is planning a 'data warehouse' of 200 gigabytes which is expected to reach a terabyte within three to five years—all this to analyse market data, and with satellite 'data marts' for the use of particular departments. Surely, a data mart for the underwriting department is an obvious and easy extension of the main warehouse. English law, however, is based on precedents from a Dickensian world of paper and pink ribbon, and still allows the insurer to plead ignorance of information on file. In other countries the law has kept pace with progress. In the United States and in Canada, for example, if the insurer fails to look in his files, hard or soft, he has waived the information which they contain.[24] So it should be in England today.

The third reason is an extension of the second. If the implication of CUE is that insurers can be expected to collect information about the persons they insure, they can also be expected to collect information of a less personal or particular kind which is, nonetheless, relevant to their business. Indeed, today, insurers do not even have to collect much of the information themselves, but can access it, as required, via Nexis or the internet.

---

[24] *Columbia National Life Ins. Co.* v. *Rodgers*, 116 F 2d 705 (10 Cir., 1940), cert. den. 314 US 637. *Coronation Ins. Co.* v. *Taku Air Transport Ltd* (1991) 85 DLR (4th) 609, 623.

Whether or not the English courts were correct to allow a marine insurer to plead ignorance of marine affairs in 1867, this is scarcely justifiable today. A century or so later, the rational rule is said to be that the rule that minimizes 'the joint costs of a potential mistake by assigning the risk of its occurrence to the party who is the better (cheaper) information-gatherer'.[25] The inclination against a rule that discourages or impedes the search for information is seen, for example, in recent decisions of the Canadian Supreme Court. The Court held that a liability insurer should have been aware of the dangers of asbestos at a time when these dangers had become a matter of notoriety in the press, both technical and general;[26] and that an aviation insurer must scan the public records of accidents that might have a bearing on the risk proposed.[27] Cockburn's law of 1867 in *Bates* (note 22 above) is out of date.

A health insurer, for example, can expect the proposer to know (or to find out) whether the proposer's parents had arthritis; but it is the insurer who is better placed to discover whether Fenland farmers, such as the proposer, are more likely to suffer arthritis than other people. Further, if the insurer says that the proposer should have told him that a great-uncle (who died before the proposer was born) had arthritis, any sensible allocation of the burden of expense and responsibility suggests that the insurer should have to show that the information was important: 86 above. Cockburn's law of 1867 is inefficient, as it deprives insurers of incentive to acquire available information by investigating risk, because they know that, if a risk turns out to be worse than it seemed on a superficial presentation, they can fall back on rules of disclosure framed in 1867 to avoid the contract. Clearly, this is not good for the insured and, to the extent that insurance is to spread risk and that insurers have a significant role in that, it is not good for society. Moreover, for insurers to plead ignorance in this way does not do much for the public perception of insurers.

---

[25] A. T. Kronman, 'Mistake, Disclosure, Information, and the Law of Contracts', 7 *J. Legal Studies* 1, 4 (1978).

[26] *Canadian Indemnity Co.* v. *Canadian Johns-Manville Co.* (1990) 72 DLR (4th) 478.

[27] *Taku Air*, n. 24 above.

Facts that Diminish Risk

Information suggesting that the risk is less great than might otherwise appear does, of course, affect risk; but it has been long established that the proposer does not have to mention it to choose the insurer. The proposer may choose to do so in order to argue for a reduction in premium but is not obliged to.

Waiver

In the 1940s commentators were concerned about long proposal forms. The chance of an innocent but inaccurate answer by the proposer increased with the number of questions in the form. Since then practice has moved from a catechism, in which the proposer has been asked too much, to quick cover, for which he is asked too little but which can still be avoided later on the ground that he has not provided information—information which the insurer did not ask for and which the proposer did not know was required. However, the proposer does not have to disclose information the disclosure of which has been waived by the insurer. This frequent and sometimes fertile line of argument for the insured against the insurer takes more than one form.

Waiver of All Information

One possibility is that the insurer waives the requirement of any information of a certain type. For example, the cargo insurers would like to know about the safety record of the ship and of the shipowner, but, for practical reasons, disclosure of this information is waived by the common standard forms for cargo insurance. The reason is that, usually, the insured sender of cargo has no idea which ship will carry his cargo, still less its record; moreover, carriers often reserve the right to change the ship at the last moment. The insurer cannot and does not expect the insured to disclose what he cannot reasonably discover.

More contentious is the view of the Insurance Ombudsman that the insurer who asks no questions at all may waive disclosure altogether. On the face of it the law is quite different: 85–7 above. Whether that view can be sustained in a court of law may depend on why the insurer did not ask questions. If the reason lies in the way the insurer has chosen to market the cover, there is force in the Insurance Ombudsman's view that the insurer has waived disclosure. Waiver might be inferred in the case of the travel insurer who finds it expedient to sell cover through travel agents or Post Office counters; the property insurer who sells through building societies; the motor insurer who covers those who hire; and, indeed, any insurer who sells by telephone. These sales share the feature that, knowing that the less the formality and fuss the more likely people are to buy, the insurer deliberately forgoes any real opportunity for enquiry into the risk in the interests of market share. By contracting in this way, surely, the insurer takes the risk in every sense. Even if the proposer actually asks himself whether he should tell the insurer something, he may well be permitted to assume that an insurer who asks no questions expects no answers; and the court might assume that, expecting a certain percentage of poor risks, the insurer has adjusted the premiums accordingly. On the contrary, if proposers were to start to tell assistants in the travel agency about their hernias, they would be unlikely to get much encouragement. Further, if the insurer did not ask because the insurer conducted his own investigation of the matter, this proposer might also be entitled to assume that the insurer was not interested in what he might have to say. In that situation, moreover, the insurer may find it hard to prove reliance on what the proposer said or did not say and may thus lose the right to rescind.

Waiver of Certain Information

Subject to what has just been argued, the general rule is that omission to ask questions about the risk is not waiver. For waiver, the law requires a positive representation on the part of the insurer. However, if the insurer asks questions about some things that may amount to waiver (by omission) of other related things. For example, to ask about fires in the property to be insured over the last five years but not before that is to waive information about any fires that there were before that. So too, a health insurer who asks about basic factors, such as age, sex, location, occupation, and smoking habits, but does not require medical tests waives, surely, any material information that the tests would have revealed. This appears to be a feature of much direct insurance contracted on the telephone. Like fast food, the direct insurer offers the proposer what the proposer wants, quick and cheap insurance with minimum fuss. But the insurer also gets what he wants, more customers. Who should bear the risks of indigestion?

When I go to be checked by my doctor, I want to be in and out of the surgery as quickly as possible, and to be told that all is well. The doctor knows that; it is also what the doctor wants to tell me, not only to make me happy but because the waiting room is full. Yet, no responsible doctor would overtly prune the list of his patients to cherry pick the strong and decline the weak. Nor would that doctor cut short the investigation and grant me a clean bill of health, and later, when cancer is found, disclaim responsibilty because I did not disclose that I was passing blood. Direct insurance is a marketing method made possible by modern technology which has been brought to insurance mainly because it cuts the costs of the insurer and gives the direct insurer a competitive edge. Contract law generally is that the risks of the medium (e.g. delays in the post) are born by the party that chose the medium. Although the first telephone call comes from the customer, the medium is one publicized by the insurer. The insurer calls the tune and chooses the instrument; and it is the insurer, surely, who takes the risk of information adverse to the risk insured that inquiry would have revealed. In the language of current law, the insurer has waived disclosure.

Waiver of Available Information

If information has been disclosed to the insurer which puts the insurer on enquiry, then it can be said that the insurer, who requires the rest of the information, could and should seek it out; and that, if the insurer does not, disclosure of the rest has been waived. Waiver of available information can occur in at least two ways.

First, the proposer volunteers some information which is not complete information on the matter but is sufficient to alert the insurer to the possibility that there is more to be had. For example, if, having been told that the proposer has been ill, the insurer obtains the proposer's permission to consult the proposer's doctor, but does not, the insurer cannot plead non-disclosure of information which consultation would have revealed. Again, a landmark case from 1759 was that of insurance on 'Fort Marlborough' located, as the insurer knew, in a potential theatre of war. It was Lord Mansfield who held that it was for the insurer to enquire about the defences and the likelihood of successful attack.[28]

Secondly, disclosure may be made by reference, so that, if the proposer gives the insurer the opportunity to consult documents such as the proposer's records, or refers the insurer to a document to which the insurer has access, the proposer is considered to have disclosed the contents of all the documents concerned.

The Time of Disclosure

The duty of disclosure must be performed at certain points in the contractual relationship: initial contract, renewal, variation of contract—times when the parties, mainly the insurer, have a decision to make and information is needed in order to make that decision. The duty is limited to information which is material to the decision to be taken and which has not already been disclosed.

The insurer may also like to be able to review and to cancel the cover at other times, if he finds that the risk is turning out to be greater than expected; generally, English law does not allow this once the insurance period has begun. This is a problematic point to which we return: 136 ff. below.

Disclosure or Investigation: Whose Line is it Anyway?

Most commentators outside the insurance industry agree that in most cases the obligation of disclosure is too difficult for most insureds, whether advised by a broker or not, and that the law is due for reform. As a rule of contract law, the rule requiring disclosure is an unusual one born of particular times and circumstances which no longer prevail. The time was the middle of the eighteenth century and the midwife was Lord Mansfield in *Carter* v. *Boehm*.[29] The circumstances were those of policies,

---

[28] *Carter* v. *Boehm* (1766) 3 Burr. 1905.
[29] n. 28 above. See further J. Oldham, *The Mansfield Manuscripts* (Chapel Hill, NC, 1992), 450–1.

which contained few warranties, which were written on marine risks by underwriters—underwriters who were persons of general business experience but who often knew much less than the proposer about that kind of risk, and risks which often concerned ships and merchandise far away from England. In these circumstances, understandably enough, an effort was made by the judges of a trading nation to nurture and encourage the business of marine insurance and to protect the underwriters. English insurance law was developed at that time to facilitate trade between persons experienced in such matters. A rule suitable for the insurance of a ship on the other side of the ocean is not necessarily the right rule for insurance on the life of a human body the other side of the insurer's desk. This was why, in the United States, by the end of the last century the Mansfield rule was limited largely to marine risks. The corollary of the American viewpoint was that such a strict rule should not apply to other risks, notably, but not only, fire risks, which the insurer could inspect or investigate.[30] The exception which 'proves the rule' is reinsurance: the proposer of reinsurance is obliged to put before the reinsurer all information on which he wrote the underlying risk, and the reinsurer, who like the marine insurer is usually not well placed to conduct a personal investigation of that risk, is not obliged to do so: that would be a pointless duplication of the activity and expense of the proposer.[31]

In 1980, a report of the ELC (no 104, paragraph 4.43) concluded that the law was 'inherently unreasonable'. In 1982, the report (paragraph 175) of the ALRC recommended that 'a new balance should be struck between the underwriter's need for information and the insured's need for security in relying upon insurance'. In Australia, the law was reformed; in England, it was not.

The Power of Precedent

'No proposition of insurance law can be better established', said

[30] See D. F. Cohen, T. E. DeMasi, and A. Krauss, '*Uberrimae Fidei* and Reinsurance Rescission: Does a Gentlemen's Agreement Have a Place in Today's Commercial Market?', 49 *Tort & Ins. LJ* 602–22, 609 (1994).

[31] See S. W. Thomas, 'Utmost Good Faith in Reinsurance: A Tradition in Need of Adjustment', 41 *Duke LJ* 1548–97 (1992).

Cockburn CJ[32] in 1867 of the Mansfield marine rule, and that, perhaps, is why he cited no authority. But the Mansfield rule which he had in mind and which he applied was not the Mansfield view at all. The real Mansfield view, excavated by Hasson[33] a century after Cockburn CJ got it wrong, put much more responsibility for obtaining information on the insurer. Indeed, Hasson finds that Mansfield eventually developed not just one view but two. The first view, pronounced in 1787, is what is now the American rule (104 below), that to vitiate the insurance the non-disclosure must be fraudulent. The second Mansfield view, dating from 1817, is that information *exclusively* known to the proposer should be disclosed to the insurer but that information which the insurer, 'by fair inquiry and due diligence, may learn from ordinary sources of information need not be disclosed'. Of course, the proposer will be advised to be frank about matters which ordinary sources of information might not reveal and, if in any doubt at all, to presume ignorance on the insurer's part. Nonetheless, the Mansfield of 1817 put the main onus of enquiry on the insurer and, today, that position is significantly nearer the current rule in the United States than the rule in England, which owes its origin to the Cockburn error. Even now, to throw out the latter would be to overturn the tablets neither of Moses nor of Mansfield. Cockburn's version is based on a very selective reading of the judgments of Lord Mansfield. Be that as it may, however, it is the Cockburn version that has come down to us today, and which puts the main responsibility for information on the proposer rather than the insurer.

Reform

If the English rule, in its Cockburn version, is to be changed, what should it become? The possible answers to be discussed here are (a) the Australian rule by reference to the reasonable insured; (b) the Swiss rule, which requires of the proposer a reasonable response to the insurer's questions; (c) the Law Commission

---

[32] *Bates*, n. 21 above, 604.
[33] R. A. Hasson, 'The Doctrine of *Uberrima Fides* in Insurance Law—A Critical Evaluation', (1969) 32 *MLR* 615–37.

proposal by reference to a reasonable insured such as the proposer; (d) the French rule based on proportionality; and (e) the American rule whereby the contract can be avoided only in cases of wilful concealment.

The Australian Rule: The Reasonable Insured

Australia (ICA, section 21(1)) and Belgium (Act of 25 June 1992, section 5) have opted for a rule which requires disclosure of what would appear material to the reasonable insured. In Ireland, too, there has been a move in the direction of a test like this.[34] It leaves the onus of information with the proposer but in a more manageable form than the current English rule. However, the ELC thought such a rule too inflexible and preferred a qualified version of the test: 101 below.

In spite of the ELC, a test of this kind is the one adopted by the insurers themselves in their Statement of General Insurance Practice for non-commercial cases (section 2(b)): insurers are not to refuse claims for non-disclosure of information 'which *a* policy-holder could not reasonably be expected to have disclosed' (emphasis added). Some insurers think that that should be enough to silence critics. Perhaps it should, except that applicaton of this criterion depends nonetheless on the discretion, goodwill, and good faith of the insurer. The experience of lawyers, of course, is that it is rarely satisfactory to put one party in the position of deciding whether to use legal advantage to pull out of a contract; and that what is true of most other people is also likely to be true of insurers.

The Swiss Rule: A Reasonable Response to Questions

A related solution is that the duty of disclosure be limited to a full and frank response to the insurer's questions, as understood by the reasonable insured. A rule of this kind has been in force in Finland since 1994 (Insurance Act 1994 section 22), in France since 1990 (Loi 89–1014 of 31 December 1989), and in Switzerland for much

---

[34] B. C. Greenford, 'Non-Disclosure in Ireland' (1994) 4 *Ins. L & P* 39–41, 41.

longer (VVG, Article 4.).[35] In England, such a rule might be enacted as the new reformed rule of law or as the (main) application of a (wider) rule like the Australian rule (99 above) which refers to the reasonable insured. Or it might be introduced by the courts as a qualification of the current English rule, whereby the proposer still had the current wide duty of disclosure in principle but, in practice, the insurer was taken to have waived the duty on matters about which the insurer did not ask questions. When the insurer does ask questions, to a limited degree this is the law already (94 above); however, this kind of solution has been criticized as 'a myriad of exceptions to an unwanted principle rather than an improved principle'.[36] Moreover, the Swiss rule would leave the proposer who fails to answer the questions in breach of duty and, unlike, for example, the American rule (104 below) whereby the initiative lies very largely with the insurer to get his questions answered, neither the Swiss rule nor an English rule modified to have the same effect would give any such incentive.

In many instances, the effect of the Swiss rule would be that the scope of the duty would be determined by the proposal form. To make any such solution workable, however, first, the 'form' should not be taken literally, but should be taken to include any questions put to the proposer, provided that, as a reasonable person, the proposer should have realized that they concerned rating the risk, and that they were such as to lead the proposer to suppose that no further rating information was required of him. Secondly, as a reasonable person, the proposer would not be entitled deliberately to conceal other obviously material information: to this extent there would remain a residual duty of disclosure. Thirdly, although there would be a presumption that the insurer's questions were material, the insurer would be entitled to rebut the presumption; similarly, a proposer would be entitled to ignore questions of such generality that they made a nonsense of the rule—because these give insufficient guidance about the kind of answer required. An example given by the ELC is: 'Are there any facts which you, as a reasonable man, consider might influence the judgment of a prudent insurer . . .?'.

---

[35] See further, B. Viret, *Droit des assurances privées* (3rd edn., Zurich, 1991), 96 ff.   [36] C. Wells, 'If It's Broke, Fix It', [1993] 11 *Int. ILR* 355, 356.

This is the kind of solution originally put forward by the ELC in a working paper, but withdrawn later in the face of objections raised by insurers. One objection was that, if the form were to determine the scope of the duty of disclosure, forms would have to become far more lengthy, detailed, and complex. The retreat of the Commission left some unanswered questions. First, might not proposers prefer a long form to the short shrift they can be given under the present law? Might they not prefer higher transaction costs (the expense of accurate completion of long forms) to be shared by all insured persons to lower costs at the 'expense' of the few who find out, too late, that they are not covered after all? Might not those aware of the current burden of disclosure like to be relieved of the cost of trying to accumulate all the information required? Is it not possible that more detailed questions would lead to better underwriting and *reduce* the overall cost of cover?

A further objection to the solution was that the purpose of proposal forms is to elicit information of a standard nature and not to circumscribe the nature of the risk *in all respects*. Once again, this appears to be an argument partly based on cost: standard questions are cheap; tailored and focussed questions are not. The forms, however, have evolved in the context of the current rule requiring a wide range of disclosure; their role is less a practical reason for maintaining the status quo than a consequence of it. In short, this may be one of those cases when second thoughts are not better than first: the retreat of the Commission from a reform that appears to have worked in other countries may well be a mistake.

The Commission's Reasonable Insured of that Kind

The ELC fell back on a qualified reasonable man test: reference to the reasonable man of *that* man's education etc., so that the standard would depend, for example, on whether the insured was in business or was a consumer.[37] A qualified test of this kind would go some way to providing for those who needed special protection, such as persons of different education, culture, language, and

[37] See Law Commission, Working Paper no 73 (1979), paras. 60–61.

social and commercial experience. This was accepted in principle by the Report of the Australian Law Reform Commission; the Report (paragraph 180–2) went on to object, however, that the test would collapse into a subjective inquiry because there might be almost as many reasonable proposers as there were insureds, and, consequently, uncertainty. Indeed, from the start, the ELC conceded that, to avoid excessive uncertainty, legislation would have to give 'guidelines'; and later it recommended objective categories of reasonable men: Report no 104, paragraph 4.51.

The effectiveness of a solution of this kind depends on achieving the right balance between fairness, which inclines to particularization, and certainty, which prefers large categories. The ELC was confident that the judges had enough experience of the application of such standards. If, as appears, the categories of reasonable men would be like those inhabiting the tort of negligence, that is true—but not reassuring, in view of the amount of litigation generated in tort. From a commercial viewpoint, the judges are experienced because the law is such that they get practice—too much practice. The very degree of disagreement about the viability of this test is not reassuring either.

Every society has to decide the level of special provision for the handicapped. Ramps for wheelchairs are one thing, but special rules of law for the 'legal legless' another. Even in the United States, the illiterate have not been excused from being bound by their signature. Nor are they in England where, in general, the law does not excuse those with handicaps of which they are aware—if there is something they can do about it. The general rule of contract law is that the blind signatory bears the risk that the contents of the document are not what the other party states. In tort, the driver who starts his car and at the same time starts to feel faint must stop; diminished capacity, of which the driver is aware, does not carry a diminished duty of care. Equally, the person asked to fill a form for insurance must also stop and take advice— or take the consequences. The argument that the confused and inexperienced immigrant, whether to England or to English law, should be excused local law is, surely, the thin end of a wedge of confusion of another kind. Subsequently, although revived in Hong Kong where some allowance is made for language difficulties, solutions of this kind were dropped from discussion papers issued by the DTI.

The French Rule: Proportionality

In France, the rule (Code d'assurance, Article 113–8 and 113–9) is that, in the case of wilful misrepresentation or non-disclosure of material information, the contract is nullified; but that, if they are not wilful, the insurer pays that proportion of the claim which the premium paid bears to the premium that would have been paid if the insurer had been given full and correct information. A qualified version of this kind of rule is found elsewhere, for example in Denmark (Insurance Contracts Act 1930, section 16(2)), Finland (Insurance Act 1994, sections 24 and 25), and Ontario (RSO, 1980, c.218, section 265).

The attraction of the French rule, on the one hand, is that it departs from the 'all-or-nothing' approach for which English law has been criticized. It softens the consequences of breach in some proportion to the seriousness of the case. On the other hand, an objection to the rule is that the putative premium may be hard to assess in the absence of tariffs, such as are found in France, or without dependence on evidence from insurers, which the insured would find difficult to contest or to contradict. However, in practice, English insurers, as well as the Insurance Ombudsman, do something very similar: they waive rescission of the contract and pay the claim, but minus the putative extra premium they would have charged if full disclosure had been made. A further objection is that French law does not allow for the insurer who, if fully informed, would not have accepted the risk at all or would have accepted it subject to conditions. This is true but, in the present climate, will any representative of the industry stand up and say that no section of the industry will take the risk? In a few cases, certainly, but only those of proposers with really bad histories or dangerous occupations. In these cases, the French rule is indeed arbitrary and unfair to insurers. So, if such a case arises in Finland, the version of the rule there allows the insurer to rescind. The objection has most force in respect not of outright rejection but of acceptance subject to conditions. Still, French opinion sees this as the lesser of the evils and favours the retention of the rule. Indeed, if the French rule is seen less as an attempt to guess the terms of the contract, if there has been disclosure, than to be fair to the parties in the face of non-disclosure, this second objection loses some of its force.

The American Rule

Although a rule of disclosure of some kind is found in many European countries such as Belgium, Finland, France, and Germany, for non-marine insurance, the law in some parts of the United States and Canada comes close to doing without one. The rule there is that the insurer can avoid the contract on account of information undisclosed by the proposer on two conditions. The first is that the information was not discovered by the insurer's own investigation of the risk. The second condition is that the odds of discovery were tipped against the insurer by wilful concealment, i.e. fraud, on the part of the proposer. This rule puts the burden of investigation largely on the insurer, except that, unless there is reason to doubt the veracity of what the proposer has actually disclosed, the insurer is entitled to rely on that without further investigation. There are a number of objections to the American rule; that may be why the ELC, although apparently unaware that such a rule could be found in Canada and the United States, rejected it more or less out of hand.

The first objection lies in difficulties of proof. Proving the proposer's knowledge, and hence fraud, is said to be so difficult that the American rule is for practical purposes one that abolishes the duty of disclosure altogether. Abolition leads to an unacceptable level of 'cross-subsidization', i.e. higher premiums for the many to compensate for sharp practice by the few. This, it is said, is unfair and leads to adverse selection, which encourages fraud and increases the number of (bad-risk) fraudsters in the pool and, as premiums rise as a result, to 'unravelling' whereby good risks leave the pool altogether and efficient insurance becomes impossible. In the United States, however, commentators are more sanguine both about the insurers' ability to prove fraud from circumstantial evidence and the courts' ability to identify states of mind from objective indicators. Whether or not this is a sufficient answer for Americans, it is not self-evidently so for the English and certainly does not satisfy English insurers; see 168 ff. below.

Further, the danger of cross-subsidization has been raised again at a second level. Critics argue that the general pool of insureds should not be obliged to carry those who, when contracting insurance, are not fraudulent but careless about the accuracy or completeness of their disclosure. Defenders of the American rule answer that insurers are better able than insurance buyers to spread the risk of loss caused by non-disclosure and misrepresentation.[38] Just as the insurer assumes the risk of carelessness during the insurance period, so also the insurer assumes the risk of carelessness before it begins. Just as careful (and lucky) drivers help to pay for the losses suffered by careless (and unlucky) drivers, they also pay for the extra risk posed by a proposer who, in response to a question about convictions during the previous five years, overlooked that a conviction for speeding five years ago was just inside that period. This is unlikely to lead to adverse selection and unravelling; most insured drivers surely are risk-averse and would prefer to pay a little more to cover careless contracting by the pool than find themselves uninsured.

As it stands, the English rule puts the cost of acquiring information for the insurer about the risk on the proposer. The American rule saves the proposer that as a direct cost and puts it on the insurer, together with the cost of the insurer's not having the information; the insurer then passes these costs on to the pool. Of course, it will cost the proposer of motor insurance very little to check indorsements on a driving licence for the exact date of a conviction. It will cost the proposer for liability cover a great deal, however, to have an environmental audit to ensure that there is no toxic waste under the property to be insured. Sometimes the cost of requiring the proposer to obtain information outweighs the benefits. Even in the less extreme example of fire risks the American rule, which encourages the insurer to combine questions with an inspection of the premises, may be more efficient, as the insurer is better able to assess the risk than the proposer or anyone that the proposer can reasonably employ for this purpose. In contrast, the English rule is positively inefficient, as it encourages the anxious proposer, if aware of the rule, to double-check his property lest one day he has to claim and the insurer pleads non-disclosure.

Another objection to the American rule is that insurance in England is often contracted without questions because insurers rely on the duty of disclosure. But this practice is a consequence of current law rather than a reason for it; and still less is it a

---

[38] See T. R. Foley, 'Insurers' Misrepresentation Defense: The Need for a Knowledge Element', 67 *S. Cal. LR* 659–87, 681 (1994).

justification for it. It is a practice that has served insurers in ways that are not self-evidently good for the proposer or anyone else. As the Report (paragraph 183) of the ALRC observed, for 'reasons of cost and competition, proposal forms are often kept to a minimum. Relevant questions concerning the moral risk are not asked in case they should embarrass a prospective insured. The adoption of direct marketing techniques has increased the pressure for brevity and simplicity.' The practice has enabled insurers to sell more cover at less cost while, for the minority of insurances giving rise to a claim, insurers still have the possibility of using the law of non-disclosure to rerate the risk with the benefit of hindsight. The practice is scarcely a justification of the present law. Indeed, the objection may prove a little too much. If it is good to save the proposer the embarrassment of questions, is it not even better to save the proposer the embarrassment of self-examination and disclosure to strangers, which the current English rule requires?

A third and last objection to the adoption of the American rule in England would be the associated need to change not only the law of non-disclosure but also the law of misrepresentation in order to maintain the current and important trend to keep them in line. This is true, but, for some, this would be not only a price worth paying but a further gain in the modernization of English law.

Conclusion: More Questions

The ELC was persuaded that underwriters need to rely on disclosure by the proposer. But insurers know full well, as the ELC recognized, that the people who have to make disclosure have little or no idea what they ought to disclose. Apart from what is said in response to specific questions, do insurers really rely on what the proposer does or or does not tell them? Or do insurers really rely on being able to raise a defence of non-disclosure if and when a claim is made? Are they really covering themselves against the possibilty that later they will not want to cover the insured? And does this mean that the rule discourages investigation by insurers which might have enabled a better evaluation of the risk and, perhaps, better risk management?

As regards effective investigation, the difference between the ELC's solution, and the American rule, is one of degree. The

ELC's solution would allow rescission not only against the fraudulent proposer but also the careless, and leave the burden of investigation largely with the proposer; in contrast the American rule puts it more squarely on the insurer. Where agreement is most evident is in opposition to the current English rule. Typical is the startled reaction of an American court, when a rule like that was put before it. That, said the court, 'would, in effect, be to place the burden of underwriting decisions upon the insured and not the insurer. This would turn the relationship between the insured and its insurer on its head and nullify the duty of an insurer to act reasonably to protect its own interests'.[39] Ultimately, a judgement must be made about the burden of investigation.

The present English rule in favour of the insurer came about because an insurance contract is different: because, as Lord Mansfield said, it is a contract upon a speculation. As an economist today might say, a prominent feature of insurance contracts is that the characteristics of the buyer affect the costs of the seller; that is, a high-risk customer will cost more than a low-risk customer.[40] In some risk situations, a creditor can take security or require a performance bond. But insurance is one of the situations in which heavy measures of that kind are not viable. Still the question remains whether insurance is really *so* different from many other kinds of contract in which there is a risk of non-performance, in which one party is depended on for payment or other kinds of performance—the factory that will grind to a halt without the flow of cash or components—that the current rule of disclosure is justified for the protection of insurers. Is the insurance industry so important to society, as it was perhaps at the time of Lord Mansfield, that it merits special protection—not only from the fraudulent in society but also from the careless and the ignorant? As information is valuable, generally the law does not oblige people to hand it over without compelling reasons. The insurance rule of disclosure is totally exceptional. Perhaps it can still be justified today for unknown risks; environmental damage liability comes to mind. But if, as appears for better known risks

---

[39] *Insurance Co. of North America* v. *US Gypsum Co.*, 870 F 2d 148, 153 (4 Cir., 1989).
[40] See S. A. Rea Jnr., 'The Economics of Insurance Law', 13 *Int. Rev. of Law & Econ.* 145–162, 153 (1993).

such as fire, the difficulty of investigating risks is much less than in the maritime world of Lord Mansfield, and if, as this book argues, the present law undermines the sense of the security which people rightly seek when buying insurance, it is for those who would retain the present law to make a convincing case for its retention.

The case for retention might run like this. Although the insurer is better equipped to investigate risks, it does not follow that the insurer should bear the entire burden of investigation, as that is not the cheapest approach; and, if indeed the insurer must bear that burden, it will be passed back to the insured in higher premiums. For many aspects of the risk, the best and cheapest investigator is the honest proposer who already has the information in head or at hand. Currently, the insurer is saying, 'you tell me about the risk, and I shall give you cheap(er) insurance but you must take the risk of non-disclosure'. The trouble with this arrangement, of course, is that the insurance is cheap, at least for the majority who make no claims, because the insured are largely unaware of the risk of non-disclosure or, if they are, of what they should disclose and, therefore, they do not incur the full cost of compliance with the duty. Moreover, the cost to society is not kept down because the arrangement provides the insurer with less incentive to manage risk and with a route of escape if there is a claim.

Better, it is submitted, would be a change in the law which allows the proposer to reply, 'alright, I'll be your investigator but you must tell me exactly what you need to know'. This, of course, is something not unlike the Swiss rule, and the American rule. Significantly, it is submitted, it is also close to the current Statement of Practice here in England; the proposer is alerted to the duty of disclosure, and the risk of non-disclosure is limited to matters the insurer has asked about, together with any other information that is 'palpably material'. Palpably material is the American description of information, which is in the proposer's possession and which the proposer should have known was material, but which the insurer had no reason to suspect and thus did not ask about. The famous example, that of the man who contracts life insurance without telling the insurer that he is about to fight a duel, tells us that it will not arise very often.

Agents: The Problem of Identity

Commonly the insurance contract is concluded through an agent on each side. On the insurer's side, the agent's role should be straightforward and his advice reliable; often it is not. In principle, whether the insurer is bound by the acts or omissions of these persons is a question governed by the law of agency. An outline of relevant rules is as follows.[41]

The insurer is bound by all the acts of the agent within the scope of the agent's actual authority as agent. Actual authority may be express or implied. If the insurer instructs an agent to conclude a contract with a particular person on particular terms, the agent has express authority to make that contract. If the insurer appoints an agent to a particular job or position in the insurance company, the actual authority of the agent depends on the actual relationship between the agent and the insurer—about which the average member of the public knows and can learn next to nothing. If the agent has a job with the insurer, however, the proposer is entitled to assume that the agent is authorized to do what is *usual* in a job of that kind: that the agent has implied authority to make any contract of the kind usually made by a person in that position. Further, if the agent does not have actual authority, express or implied, to do an act, the insurer will still be bound by the act if the insurer has let it appear that the agent had authority, and the proposer reasonably relied on the appearance of authority. In other words, if there is disparity between actual authority, on the one hand, and implied or apparent authority, on the other, it is the latter that counts.

Evidence of what is usual can be found in the codes of practice for intermediaries. Generally, however, the proposer is entitled to assume that agents, through whom everyday insurance is contracted, are usually authorized to issue interim cover and to receive premiums, but not to make the main contract of insurance: that is decided by someone higher up in the insurer's organization. The agent may be the one to inform the proposer of the decision, but it is not his decision. Importantly, however, such agents are authorized to pass communications to and from the insurer: to 'receive the proposal and put it into shape'.

[41] See further, Clarke, n. 1 above, ch. 8.

If the agent's role is to 'put the proposal into shape', the reasonable proposer may well think that, as the form is the insurer's own form and has been put in front of him by the insurer's own agent, it is part of the agent's job to help the proposer to complete it—as it undoubtedly is with forms in other walks of life and, as regards insurance, in other countries, such as Germany[42] and the United States.[43] Indeed, in Germany contract terms purporting to change this position have been struck out as unfair. In particular, the proposer may think that if there is any inaccuracy or omission in what is written on the form, of which the agent was or should have been aware, the insurer cannot later complain. Such a case was *Bawden*,[44] in which the insured's proposal of accident insurance did not state that he only had one eye; if he thought about it at all, he would have thought it did not matter, as it was obvious to everyone, including the agent, that he only had one eye. The Court of Appeal, clearly, thought likewise and rejected the insurer's defence of non-disclosure. But it is not entirely clear that the court would do so today. This is the result of a later case, the troublesome decision in *Newsholme*.[45]

In *Newsholme* the proposer gave the agent the right information, but the agent wrote it into the form wrongly. The Court of Appeal held that the agent completed the form as agent not of the insurer but of the proposer; that, therefore, the agent's knowledge of the correct information was not attributable to the insurer; and that the insurer was entitled to rescind the insurance contract. This decision is confusing, impractical, and out of line with principle. It is confusing because it does not correspond to the reasonable expectations of those involved. It is impractical because it envisages an agent with a revolving head, whose role changes from one moment to the next. If *Newsholme* is right, what, for example, of the agent who first notices the inaccuracy in the form when the agent gets back to the office? Is awareness to be attributed to the insurer because the agent has left the proposer and is back in the

---

[42] e.g. BGH 18 Dec. 1991, IV ZR 271/91, VersR 1992.217. See also M. Müller-Stüler, 'Broker v. Tied Agent: Some Aspects' [1996] *IJIL* 151–7.

[43] *Union Mutual Life Ins. Co.* v. *Wilkinson*, 13 Wall 222 (1872).

[44] *Bawden* v. *London, Edinburgh & Glasgow Assurance Co.* [1892] 2 QB 534 (CA).

[45] *Newsholme Bros.* v. *Road Transport & General Ins. Co. Ltd* [1929] 2 KB 356 (CA).

place of employment? *Newsholme* is out of line because it has left this bit of insurance law high and almost dry, out of the general course taken by the rest of the law of agency. General agency law takes a different view of the apparent authority of agents: 109 above. The appearance to the world of proposers, surely, is that the agent is acting for the insurer, who is bound by all that his agent does for the proper completion of the insurer's form in the furtherance of the insurer's business. To eliminate any trace of doubt left by *Newsholme*, a New Zealand statute now spells out that 'as between the insured and the insurer' an agent like this is 'at all times during the negotiations' the agent of the insurer: Insurance Law Reform Act 1977, section 10.

If, however, the agency reasoning in *Newsholme* is ignored, the decision itself can be accommodated. The proper place for all these cases is under the rule that the signatory of a document, which is part of a contract or leads to one, is bound by the contents of the document signed, unless that person has made a reasonable mistake about contents of which the other party is or should be aware. Although importance is attached to the certainty of transactions based on signed documents, courts also seek to protect those who, without being careless or gullible, have trusted those with whom they deal. If the proposal cases are seen in the light of these rules, both *Bawden* and *Newsholme* can be made to fit the mould and to make sense. Mr Bawden was entitled to think that his form was in order, because he was entitled to assume that the agent had taken his handicap into account. Mr Newsholme, who signed his form without reading it and hence without discovering the inaccuracies, was not. If, however, the inaccuracy had been such that, in any event, Mr Newsholme would not have realized that anything was wrong with the form, he would have been in the same legal position as Mr Bawden: entitled to rely on the agent and to assume that full and accurate disclosure had been made to the insurer.

Agents: The Problem of Advice

If people are sold unsuitable insurance, it may not cut their finger or crack their mirror but it can make a large dent in their fortunes. One problem recognized by insurers and brokers alike is the variable quality of the insurance advice offered by those they employ at the point of sale to the public. Currently, more and more insurance is sold through outlets mainly concerned with something else, places such as banks, whose staff lack the knowledge to explain the products. Nor can people be sure that parallel advice sought from brokers will be any better: 64 above.

One form of 'interference' which insurers have had to endure concerns the way that insurance, in particular life insurance, is sold. The industry's fight to retain the right of self-regulation has been undermined by its poor public image after the pension 'scandal'. A survey published in 1994 indicated that 76 per cent of those who deal with them do not expect complete honesty from financial sales people. 'Few disinterested observers', said the *Financial Times* in May 1994, 'would argue with the Treasury select committee's assertion that the British retail financial services industry has for too long been characterised by incompetence and mis-selling.'

The industry is now resigned to some form of government regulation of selling but there is disagreement on means. Although some want extra-legal control by the Personal Investment Authority (PIA) others would prefer statutory control, as is the case for example in France. The *Financial Times* in March 1994 stressed that it is

in both the public interest and the interest of the insurers that urgent action is taken to restore order to the industry's sales activities. This cannot wait for legislation, not least because ministers are clearly wary of the political pitfalls in taking on responsibility for monitoring those who are busy mis-selling endowment policies and personal pensions. The short-term priorities must therefore be to make the best of the PIA and to ensure that the new disclosure regime . . . provides information in a form that allows the consumer to make worthwhile choices. If the industry is forced to compete on the basis of price and quality instead of the means of distribution, much of its act will be forcibly cleaned up as consumers penalise inefficient producers. In the longer run [however] full statutory support for the system is probably desirable and may well be inescapable.

The newspaper called for the Treasury to come out from behind 'the protective shelter of the SIB' and again called for legislation. A year later, all was still not well. *Which?* criticized the standard of selling by financial advisers and called for tighter controls, and in November 1995 the ABI published a report by management consultants, Price Waterhouse, which conceded that public confidence in the life sector had yet to be restored; nor has it since.

To train a new recruit costs upwards of £35,000. The task of training those who sell insurance is made harder and more expensive by the high turnover of staff. In 1994, it was reported that more than 50 per cent of sales staff in UK life offices leave within their first year of service and that some insurers have a retention level as low as 20 per cent. The problem persists.

5

Cover

A Large Role for Small Print

What the insureds want for their money during the insurance
period is cover—the assurance that, if the insured event (the peril)
occurs, they will get something 'for' it, and that is usually money.
The insureds want the circumstances and degree of cover to be as
wide as possible; people commonly assume that it is wider than it
really is. When they are disabused, they complain about the
insurer's small print—which they have probably never read. Most
people do not read their policies until they want to claim, if then,
but the law on that is clear: they cannot plead ignorance of the
terms of their insurance contract. If they do read the contract
terms but do not understand them, they must get someone to
explain them.

What insurers want is a clear idea of their exposure, of the
circumstances in which they must pay, and some idea of the likely
amount. This is in their hands. Partly it depends on information
and research: 38 ff. above. Partly it depends on the contract
cover—the terms and the quality of the drafting. Nonetheless,
according to the Deputy Chairman of Lloyd's, many insurers are
prone to underwriting business with little knowledge of the
subject-matter, and on wording that is unclear.[1] Whether or not
that is true of the market outside Lloyd's, it is not a practice which
he or any other underwriter would condone.

For insurers, the role of the contract terms is, first, to mark the
boundaries of cover in accordance with established categories of
risk and thus with data on past losses. Secondly, terms are aimed
at better risk management on the part of the insured. Against
'thieves that break through and steal', for example, discounts are
available to those insured who fit their vehicles with tracking
devices or their premises with CCTV. Moreover, insurers may

---

[1] R. Hiscox, 'Why So Much Insurance Litigation?' (1996) 90 *BILA Jo.* 1–2, 2.

specify the kind of locks on doors and windows; and, to encourage people actually to lock the doors and windows, theft cover may be conditional on forcible entry. Against 'moths and rust that doth corrupt', contracts for collectables, for example, from vintage port to vintage motor cars, may specify the atmospheric conditions of storage.

A prominent example of all this is motor insurance. To cut claims, like the government, insurers would like to cut speed. Drivers under surveillance, whether by a police car or by a video camera, slow down. This inspired one insurer to require the installation of a 'black box' data recorder in a fleet of vehicles with a bad claims record; the record improved dramatically and everyone was happy—except the drivers. But, if they complained about 'big brother', the insured employer could blame the insurer while still enjoying lower premiums. The box also enabled the insurer to apply a low mileage discount without having to trust the insured to monitor the mileage. Life insurers, too, would like to fit a black box to human bodies: to offer lower premiums on life or health insurance for those who do not drink (alcohol) or smoke; but, as things are, the insurers feel that too many insureds cheat and that they cannot afford to police them effectively. The black box in vehicles does just that. The contract condition, requiring the box, combines effectively the two most common ways in which insurers seek to combat 'moral hazard' in the form of risk compensation, i.e. the tendency of the person insured to relax and increase the risk. The first way is to impose safety measures, in the case of the black box, purely psychological measures; and the second, with the incentive of lower premiums for less mileage, is to reduce exposure to risk. Whatever the contract condition, clearly, the drafting of the contract is of prime importance.

Defining Cover: Insurance Contracts

Standard-form contracts are important in the control and alloca-tion of risks, risks of all kinds. Standardization of terms is such that insurance contracts have long been described in both England and the United States as the archetype of 'contracts of adhesion', tantamount to private or delegated legislation.[2] In the United

[2] e.g. V. P. Goldberg, 'Institutional Change and the Quasi-Invisible Hand', 17 *J L & Econ.* 461–96, 484 (1974).

States private legislation is perceived as undemocratic and, therefore, to be made subject in some way to the democratic process—if not to the consent of the people then, the next best thing, to the consent of the courts. Courts seek to determine what the weaker contracting party could legitimately expect by way of services according to the other's calling, and to interpret the contract accordingly.

Although the response of courts to contracts of adhesion has been largely hostile, standard-form contracting has advantages too. It reduces transaction costs and increases the speed with which, in the case of insurance, cover can be made available and the accuracy with which risks can be rated by reference to past records. 'The predominance of standard forms', argued Slawson,[3] 'is the best evidence of their necessity. They are characteristic of a mass production society and an integral part of it. They provide information and enforce order.' Insurance policies, he concluded, are the 'extreme illustration' of the standard form. This claim was made back in 1970 and the writer drew an analogy between mass-produced insurance and mass produced cars. The trend since with cars, however, is for makers to offer varieties of a basic model in order to customize the car and give the owner a sense of individuality. Equally, the use of computers both to calculate risk and to process words has enabled the insurer to customize insurance to a greater degree and at lower cost than before. Moreover, Slawson's claim was made in the United States where, through legislation and the influence of the Insurance Services Office, standardization has been more extensive than in England and other countries. In England today, insurance contracts are still in standard form, but there are many forms. In future the cost of training staff to meet higher standards of advice may reduce the variety and discourage innovation; or, on the contrary, the development of software may lead to the rapid production of insurance tailored exactly to the individual, without destroying the pools of risk. This remains to be seen.

Words: The Rules of Interpretation

To construct a clear contract, the insurers' basic materials are the

[3] D. S. Slawson, 'Standard Form Contracts and Democratic Control of Lawmaking Power', 84 *Harv. LR* 529, 530 ff (1971).

words of the English language. They must understand their materials and, more to the point, they must be aware of how their words will be understood by others: the insured to whom the chosen words must be intelligible and the courts which, ultimately, decide how they will be understood by the insured. So, the rules for writing contracts are much influenced by the rules for reading them—the rules of interpretation applied by the courts. When reading a contract, the courts' overriding objective is said to be a search for the intention of the parties. To this end, the courts apply the same rules to all kinds of contract which, in summary, are applied to insurance contracts as follows.

Rule 1: Words are to be understood in their ordinary sense, that is in accordance with the dictionary meaning of the word. However, the word is to be understood not in isolation but in the context of the contract, and with certain traditional canons of interpretation, namely:

(a) If particular words have a generic character, more general following words are construed as having the same character (*eiusdem generis*).

(b) The express mention of one thing may imply the exclusion of another related thing (*expressio unius est exclusio alterius*).

Rule 2: In the event of inconsistency in the ordinary meaning of words in different parts of the contract, the court prefers the meaning that best reflects the intention of the parties; for example, preference is given to that part to which the parties gave actual attention.

Rule 3: If it appears that the words have been used in a special sense, either (a) as previously defined by the courts or (b) the sense used in a particular commercial context, the words will be interpreted in that special sense.

Rule 4: If, after application of Rules 1 and 2, the words are ambiguous and Rule 3 is of no assistance:

(a) the words will be read with reference to any evidence of the purpose of the contract, which was not apparent from the contract itself; and

(b) the words will be construed *contra proferentem*, that is, against the insurer and liberally in favour of the insured.

In the application of Rule 4(b), the insured's interpretation of the words is preferred if it is a reasonable view, whereas the insurer's interpretation of the words, if different, will not be adopted unless it is the only reasonable view. As an American judge put it, if the insurer uses a 'slippery' word to describe cover, 'it is not the function of the court to sprinkle sand upon the ice'. If 'the limits of coverage slide across the slippery area and the company falls into a coverage somewhat more extensive than it contemplated, the fault' is its own.[4] Note, however, that words are not ambiguous just because they are complex or because lay people are not sure what they mean; if lawyers can find the meaning of words, those words are not ambiguous: see Rule 3.

Somewhere between Rule 3 and Rule 4, the Rules begin to look less technical, to be tools for 'creative' interpretation by a court determined to see a particular result. Nonetheless, it should be underlined that, unless the meaning can be described as absurd, the court must give it the interpretation indicated, however much it dislikes the result. A poignant illustration of sharp drafting requiring painful decisions is found in accident insurance that covers 'dismemberment within 90 days of the injury'; and in American cases in which the surgeons struggled to save a leg and, in one case only after 100 days, gave up and amputated.[5] Some courts have found that a clause that compelled the choice, to cut within the insurance period or to struggle to save it, was gruesome, unconscionable, and to be disregarded. English courts would probably agree with other courts that felt that it was not their role to rewrite the contract; that lines have to be drawn somewhere and, if clearly drawn, should be respected. However, the line between a meaning which is merely unreasonable and must be applied and one which is absurd and can be avoided is hard to draw.

Somewhere between Rule 3 and Rule 4, nonetheless, is indeed another rule, Rule 3(a), a rule against absurdity. Rule 3(a) is that, if the application of Rules 1 to 3 produces a result that is so very unreasonable or inconvenient as to be absurd, that result will be ignored. For example, one of the purposes of reinsurance is to protect the reinsured from exposures which he cannot bear, and

---

[4] *Jamestown Mutual* v. *Nationwide Mutual*, 146 SE 2d 410, 416 (NC, 1966).
[5] K. S. Abraham, *Insurance Law and Regulation* (New York, 1990), 83 ff. The purpose of the clause is to limit disputes over causation: *ibid*. 86.

which might otherwise imperil his solvency. Against this background, the contention of a reinsurer that the reinsurer was not liable until the reinsured had, literally, 'actually paid', perhaps many millions of pounds, was dismissed as being without any warrant in common sense or experience[6] and thus absurd.

Words: The Problem of Comprehension

Comprehension by the Court

The value of precedent (Rule 3(a)) is that the insurers drafting the contract can predict the effect of their words, not only particular words, but underlying ideas. Moreover, if they use 'old' words and phrases, insurers can assume that words interpreted in one sense by one court will be understood in the same sense by another court. When courts come to new words and phrases, however, they tend to employ what psychologists call a heuristic stratagem, by which they strive to relate the new issue to previously established patterns of experience and thought. So, in the task of interpretation, the court looks for an analogy with precedent or, at a conceptual level, with an established concept. A clear illustration of this is provided by the courts' construction of the requirement of many insurance contracts that the insured should take precautions to prevent loss; see 139 ff. below.

Comprehension by the Insured

The rules of construction work in favour of both the insurers and the insured insofar as the rules discourage disputes, inhibit wishful or 'creative' argument, and permit the parties to predict the effect of the insurance contract. If such certainty is achieved, however, it may be at a cost to the insured. The rules of construction being lawyers' rules and some of the language lawyers' language, the insured may not know exactly what the contract means and, therefore, may have to pay for professional advice to find this out. What is plain to insurers and, perhaps, to the judge may not be plain at all to the insured.

---

[6] *Charter Reinsurance Ltd* v. *Fagan* [1996] 2 Lloyd's Rep. 113 (HL). Note, however, the reservations of Lord Mustill: 118–19.

Worse still, the insureds may walk the fool's paradise of believing that their policy clearly means one thing when, in law, it means something else. What could be plainer than the motor policy with cover 'from 1 January 1996 to 1 January 1997'? Just as a holiday in France booked from 1 July to 1 August would be from the morning of 1 July to the evening of 1 August, might people not reasonably assume that linked travel cover 'from 1 July to 1 August' is for the same period? If they were to check with a competent broker, however, they would find that the cover does not begin until the *end* of the first day in July—because the law needs a rule about this and that is what the courts have decided. The ignorant may be in a state of bliss but, as the ferry to Calais founders, they may also be in a state of another sort—uninsured. It is all very well to say that the insureds should always check with their broker, but that is not justification enough, if people do not know when to do so.

Again, more might be done by insurers to avoid some of the stranger definitions of English law. If a word has a technical meaning in criminal law, the interpretation is usually the same in an insurance contract (Rule 3(a)) but this is a presumption and one that should not be applied automatically. In one case,[7] a Boeing 747 aircraft was quietly and efficiently hijacked in the air by two terrorists, who were in radio contact with others on the ground. The insurer argued before the court in New York that the loss of the aircraft was not covered, because the hijacking was a 'riot'. This argument would surely have been laughed out of court, but for an English precedent for a quiet riot of only three people,[8] and perhaps the New York court was too polite. Having expressed 'deference' on matters of insurance law to the 'ancestral authorities on the old mysteries', the court dismissed the argument. The 'notion of a flying riot in geographic installments cannot be squeezed into the ancient formula'. Riot cannot be 'conducted by mail, by telephone, or as in the present case, by radio'. The court preferred what it saw as the common sense and popular idea of riot, which connoted some degree of tumult. In England, the common law has been changed by section 1 of the Public Order

---

[7] *Pan American World Airways Inc.* v. *Aetna Casualty & Surety Co.* [1975] 1 Lloyd's Rep. 77 (US CA, 2 Cir., 1974).

[8] *Motor Union Ins. Co. Ltd* v. *Boggan* (1923) 130 LT 588 (HL).

Act 1986. We now need twelve people to have a riot and although, obviously, tumult is more likely with the statutory dozen than the common law trio, a quiet riot by a disciplined football team is still possible, if not in reality at least in law. In practice, however, some insurers take their line not from the law but from the police: if the police describe an actual event not as a riot but as for example 'a series of incidents of disorder', the insurers pay.

Another word which people find strange and which, in times of climate change, people are more likely to be concerned about than 'riot' is 'subsidence'. Claims by householders have been refused because what occurred, said the insurers, was not 'subsidence' but 'settlement'—even though the dictionary says that 'subsidence' is 'a gradual lowering or settling down of the earth'. Distrust and anxiety in the public over terms such as these, fanned by the press, have encouraged the selling of 'security of wording', of 'easy-to-read' policies, written in 'plain English'. And is that not how it should be? Should not all insurance contracts be in plain English and easy to read? Unfortunately, it is submitted here, although the language of these policies makes an immediate impression, like music for easy listening, it is unlikely to stand the scrutiny of time.

The Myth of Ordinary Meaning and Plain English

English contract forms are often used abroad, if not always understood. 'Perhaps those whose native tongue is not English have been unduly encouraged by the supreme status accorded to the language of Shakespeare to acquiesce in a degree of inaccessibility', which is hard to justify.[9] But are they sufficiently understood in the land of Shakespeare itself? Evidently not, but there is nonetheless a widespread belief that they could be and should be; that insurers and lawyers have heeded too much the warning of Oscar Wilde that to be intelligible is to be found out; and that their documents should be demystified and brought out of the inner sanctum of the few and made both available and intelligible to the many ordinary people in the street. Indeed, the belief is not new. It was St Luke (chaper 11, verse 52) who said: 'Woe unto you, lawyers! for ye have taken away the key of knowledge: ye entered not in yourselves, and them that were

---

[9] F. D. Rose, 'Review of O'May, *Marine Insurance*' (1994) 110 *LQR* 494–6, 495.

entering in ye hindered.' Today, there is a movement for demystification, in tandem with the assumption that there is such a thing as 'ordinary' or 'plain' English; and that this English is used and understood by ordinary people, and should be used in their contracts. Even if we accept another assumption, that ordinary English and plain English are the same and refer from now on (hereinafter?) only to the latter, the notion of plain English is a myth in more than one sense of that ordinary (?) word.

English that is plain should be plain to all but experience soon shows that it is not. Often enough, words are commonplace precisely because they are not precise but contain several shades of meaning. Moreover, to write plain English we must first tame the emotive power of words; and then we must overcome the limits of words. It may be an impossible task. 'He who knows does not speak, he who speaks does not know.' Silence, of course, is a golden luxury that the insurer and, still less, the insured cannot afford. Our linguistic outfit may be treacherous, but it is also indispensable; and what is needed is not so much a new 'plainer' use of words but better means of controlling the words we have got.

To control the use of words, we must first understand the limits of words as a medium of expression, the scale of the task. In 1994 the most learned judges in the land were divided on the meaning of the word 'influence'.[10] Of all the cases closed by the Ombudsman in 1995 about 50 per cent concerned one category alone, disputes between insurer and insured about the meaning and scope of cover. In late 1996, English health insurers still could not agree even among themselves on the meaning of 'disability'. The potential of the insurance contract to confuse to the point of driving the parties to the end of the disputes procedure seems undiminished. The prose of the recent past provides little encouragement for those who put their faith in plain English. Further, recent American legal history shows that there are none so blind as will not see, and that no language, English or American, is plain to the court determined to find ambiguity and thus do its idea of justice. Much depends on the attitude of the reader, and of the court.

---

[10] In *Pan Atlantic Ins. Co.* v. *Pine Top Ins Co.* [1995] AC 501.

The Limits of Dictionaries

In practice, sooner or later, the search for plain English for ordinary people leads to the dictionary—of which people tend to expect too much.

First, the dictionary may not give an answer that ordinary people would regard as plain. Dictionaries cannot be trusted blindly; they have to be used with care. Stories abound of misuse. For example, 'the spirit is willing but the flesh is weak' was once translated into Russian as 'the vodka is good but the meat is rotten'.

Secondly, the dictionary may not give an answer that ordinary people would think ordinary. In the supermarket tomatoes are found among the vegetables because that is where ordinary buyers expect them to be; but in the dictionary they will find them with fruit because that is the view of the botanist and, naturally, that is what they 'are'.

Thirdly, dictionaries are frozen in time and out of date before they are published. One of the virtues of the English language is that it accommodates changes in the speech of ordinary people and has not been nailed down by any '*Académie Anglaise*'. Some dictionaries, however, are still giving primary meanings of words that are a century out of date. That was why a court recently applied an 'ordinary' meaning of 'insurance' which differed from that in the dictionary.[11] That is why one publisher of dictionaries no longer purports to produce the definitive definition, and has joined a university department to create a database of the use of English, which has over 200 million entries and, in the early stages of its evolution, was being expanded at the rate of one million entries per week. The plain meaning itself, it has been suggested by a leading authority in the United States,[12] is 'incapable of responding without lag to a world that changes faster than language'.

Fourthly, words cannot be properly understood without some regard to their context. Simon Hoggart, a well-known journalist

---

[11] *Re NRG Victory Reinsurance Ltd.* [1995] 1 All ER 533.
[12] F. Schauer, 'Statutory Construction and the Co-ordinating Function of Plain Meaning' [1990] *Sup. Ct. Rev.* 231–56, 252. More general objections come from E. A. Farnsworth, ' "Meaning" in the Law of Contracts' 76 *Yale L.J.* 936–65, (1967).

writing about an even better known politician, John Prescott, said ruefully: 'As we know, his grammar is all over the place, his syntax and vocabulary entirely haphazard, but—thanks to his body language and emotional energy—we always know exactly what he means.' But when his language must be reduced to writing, the 'readers of Hansard don't have that assistance'. Only to a limited degree can dictionaries help with context by listing common phrases. Some words, such as 'building' and 'goods', have such a fringe of meaning, a penumbra of uncertainty, that no technical definition alone will ensure precision. Nonetheless, these words can usually be understood if they are seen in context, in relation to other words to which, in context, they are opposed or with which they are associated.

The Language of Precedent

When people want to give very precise instructions to computers, they use either numbers or special languages. There is no plain English for computer programmers. However, this is not to suggest for contracts the language of mathematics. As Glanville Williams once observed, Euclidean geometry 'starts from notions of points and lines which, having no size, are not objects of sense; thus the figures constructed from these notions are not objects of sense either'.[13] Nonetheless, for precise and predictable communication, technical language is unavoidable and, of course, problematic. When the law attributes to some clause in a contract a meaning which it does not bear in plain English, because it has been held to have that meaning in the past, there is a risk of defeating the intention of the parties, who thought it would mean something else. Against that consideration there is a legitimate desire among lawyers for certainty. When a clause has been held to have a particular meaning, disputes will be avoided if it is held to have the same meaning thereafter, especially if those who make contracts can rely on that and the courts, in their turn, rely on that. There is a circle, but a circle of understanding from which the insured, who is not a lawyer, may be excluded.

Like travellers to foreign parts, people who come to the world of insurance must not expect the natives to speak (their) English. If people do not understand the proposed contract, their only proper course is not to complain but to seek an interpreter, such as a

---

[13] G. L. Williams, 'Language and the Law' (1945) 61 *LQR* 293–303, 300.

broker or even the insurer himself. If brokers get it badly wrong, they may be liable to the insured. If insurers get it wrong, they may be estopped by their own interpretation of their own contract and the court will make the contract mean what the insured was led to believe it to mean: 128 below. This seems to be the best compromise on offer between certainty and comprehension. At the end of the Code of Practice for Banks and Building Societies is this statement: although terms 'will be expressed in clear and straightforward language', 'the precise wording of some contract must, of necessity, be in technical or legal language'. Insurance likewise. The Insurance Law of New York (section 142) requires that policies 'use words with common and everyday meanings to facilitate readability and to aid the insured or policy holder in understanding' the cover, *wherever practicable*. Plain English must be sought, but not at the cost of precision.

There is a difference between clarity and precision.[14] Surely, we have a kind of wisdom when we know that you do not know. The danger of the pursuit of plain English is the fool's paradise, in which the plain English believe that they understand their insurance policy and that they have cover when perhaps they do not. Plain English is a convenient point of reference or *lingua franca* for persons of comparable intelligence and training who *want* to agree with each other, such as draftsmen and, sometimes, judges; but that role does not qualify plain English as a general means of communication or rule-making between persons of different intelligence, background, and training, who are dealing at arm's length and who may not always want to agree. Perhaps the best position is a compromise: to leave technical terms in insurance contracts and append an explanation of those terms. This seems to have the merit of making the terms intelligible to lawyers (in the main contract) and to others (via the appendix) without destroying the flow of the contract and hence the contextual sense of the terms.

Unexpected Effects

If application of the ordinary meaning of the words under Rule 1 (117 above) leads to an unreasonable result, courts have stated

---

[14] On this somewhat technical distinction, see J. Stark, 'Should the Main Goal of Statutory Drafting be Accuracy or Clarity?' (1994) 15 *Statute L Rev.* 207–13.

that generally they must give effect to that meaning nonetheless. Words that come before the Insurance Ombudsman or before a court applying the EC Directive on unfair terms in consumer contracts, however, will be subject to a test of fairness: 117 above. Moreover, as we have seen, Rule 3(a) (231 ff. below) is that, if the application of Rules 1 to 3 produces a result that is so very unreasonable or inconvenient as to be absurd, that result will be ignored. These exceptions apart, the terms of a contract cannot be defeated simply because they are unreasonable. In general contract law, the judges, led by Lord Denning, got around this with a rule that did indeed defeat terms because they were unreasonable by calling them something else—'unusual' or 'un-expected'. Is there any lesson here for insurance contracts?

The enquiry must start from the Rules of Interpretation, in particular Rule 1, which gives primacy to ordinary meaning. In England, there appears to be no rule like that in the United States, that the contract must be construed in line with the insureds' reasonable expectations,[15] unless, of course, their expectations coincide with the ordinary meaning. The American rule is that the insureds are bound by what they did read of the contract or can realistically be expected to read, and only in conformity with that is the rest of the contract enforced; it is enforced only in conformity with the reasonable expectations of the insureds, together with any other relevant features implicit in the overall transaction. As regards the overall transaction, just as people buy goods they buy promises of a less tangible kind. The reasonable consumer depends on the insurer to sell him a policy that works as it was meant to, in much the same way that he depends on someone who sells him a television set.

For example, in *Kievet*,[16] 'accident' cover was sold to a man of 48, who later suffered an accidental blow on the head which triggered latent Parkinson's disease. The insurer defended the man's claim, pleading an exception of 'disability or other loss resulting from or contributed to by any disease or ailment'. This

---

[15] *Smit Tak Offshore Services* v. *Youell* [1992] 1 Lloyd's Rep. 154, 159 (CA), as regards commercial insurance. The Insurance Ombudsman, however, has shown some sympathy for the argument in non-commercial cases. See also Clarke, *Law of Insurance Contracts*, 15–5B.

[16] *Kievet* v. *Loyal Protective Life Ins. Co.*, 170 A 2d 22 (NJ, 1961).

defence failed. The court noted that people would expect this kind of accident to be covered and, moreover, that, if it were not covered, the insurance would be of little use to a man of 48: if the exception were read literally, any disability or death resulting from accidental injury would in all probability be in some sense contributed to by the infirmities of age, and thus excluded. To make the policy 'work', the court construed it in line with the policyholder's reasonable expectation that an 'accident' policy covered what most people would regard as an accident.

Put like this, surely, the argument takes a form that should at least get a hearing in England because, even without ambiguity, the English court construes in accordance with the main purpose of the contract as it appears from the contract itself: Rule 4(a) (117 above). Where the American form of the argument would run into difficulty in England is the point of focus on the expectations of just one party, the insured, to determine the purpose of the insurance, rather than the expectations of both. The role of the English court is not to rewrite contracts but to expound and apply existing law to contracts as they have been agreed by the parties— both parties.

A further difficulty in England is an ingrained belief in gradualism and pragmatism, which tends away from wide generalizations and abstract principles. Argument with reference to reasonable expectations *tout nu* is too stark, too general, too exposed. Our courts feel agoraphobically uneasy with wide rules like that. The argument would also suffer from association with the violence done to insurance contracts with such a rule by some of the more immoderate courts in the United States. It is but a small step from the purpose of the insurance contract before the court to the purpose of insurance contracts generally and, therefore, from the expectations of the parties before the court to the expectations of the court itself. Nonetheless, two more modest and more selective versions of the argument for a rule of reasonable expectations can be made in England; and there is conjecture about a third.

First, as we have seen in Rule 2 (117 above), if there are words of the contract inconsistent with other words of the contract, the court prefers the words that best reflect the intention of the parties. These will be those, for example, that the parties have specifically adopted rather than printed words in standard form. More to the immediate point, the preference will be for the words which best give effect to the purpose of the contract. Given that a dominant purpose of the insurance contract is to provide cover, if the insured reasonably expects to be covered for the loss in question, it should not be too hard to persuade the court to uphold that expectation. For example, if one part of a liability insurance contract indicates that the insured's negligence is covered, but another part indicates otherwise, the courts have shown a clear preference for the former.[17]

Secondly, if the insured's expectations are not only reasonable but actually induced by the insurer, the contract will be construed in line with those expectations. If, for example, the insured do not understand the extent of the cover, they may well ask the agent of the insurer, whose role it is to explain the terms. General contract law states that, if party A tells party B that a term of their proposed contract means X, although it really means Y, it will be treated as meaning X, if B has acted reasonably in relying on what A told him. Clearly, insured B is entitled to rely on what insurer A's agent tells him about A's contract of insurance. So, if the agent tells B that a certain kind of loss is covered by the insurance, whereas on a strict application of the rules of interpretation it is not, the loss is covered because the insurer said so and is estopped from denying it.

Thirdly, the duty of disclosure between the parties to an insurance contract is mutual: 81 ff. above. So, the insurer owes to the insured a duty to disclose all matters which would affect the judgement of the insured in deciding whether to make the contract at the premium demanded. This cannot be taken entirely literally; for example, insurer X is not obliged to disclose that similar cover costs less from insurer Y. More sustainable, surely, is the contention that the insurer should tell the insured exactly what the insured are getting for their premium money, i.e. the scope of the cover. Or, in the words of the American *Restatement 2d of Contracts* (1979), section 211(3), which applies to all standard-form contracts, including insurance contracts: 'Where the other party has reason to believe that the party manifesting . . . assent would not do so if he knew that the writing contained a particular term,

[17] *Woolfall & Rimmer Ltd* v. *Moyle* [1942] 1 KB 66, 76 (CA). See also *Forsikringsaktieselskapet Vesta* v. *Butcher* [1989] 1 AC 852, 895, 909.

the term is not part of the agreement.' The Association of British Insurers' (ABI) Code of Practice for all Intermediaries (other than brokers) requires that exclusions be brought to the attention of the insured. The brokers have a similar rule of conduct; and this is also the standard required by the Insurance Ombudsman. French law (Code d'assurance, Article L112–4) seeks a similar result by requiring that exclusions be printed in prominent typescript. The argument here is that the English law about disclosure indicates a result in line with the ABI Code so that the reasonable expectations of the insured about the cover offered are not frustrated.

The Use of Words: Terms of the Contract

The form of the contract varies but, in substance, the terms in which the words and phrases are used can be grouped according to their function. For example, motor insurance might cover (a) the private motor vehicle A653 JEB against loss, damage, or theft, unless (b) used for business, provided that (c) reasonable steps are taken to maintain the vehicle in an efficient condition. Moreover, (d) any theft claim against the insurer may be conditional on notice to the police and to the insurer within forty-eight hours of discovery of the theft.

In this example, term (a) is called the description of the risk; it defines cover in positive terms of two kinds, the subject-matter (vehicle) and the perils insured against. Term (b) is called an exception (or exclusion), and also serves to define cover; however, it does so in negative terms: it qualifies the literal reading of term (a), that the cover extends to all kinds of use. Term (c) also qualifies the scope of cover, but in a different way and is called a warranty. Term (d) has nothing to do with the scope of cover, but is designed, in part at least, to make the contract less burdensome to the insurer; terms of this kind are often called conditions and are considered later (182 below). Terms (a), (b) and (c) must be looked at more closely now.

Term (a), as regards subject-matter, is case-specific and there is little to be said about it here, except this: if the registration number of the vehicle is changed, the risk insured is still the risk described and cover continues. If, however, the vehicle is modified to a degree that takes it out of the original contract description, for the purpose of the insurance, the vehicle originally insured no longer exists—just as if it had been destroyed. Cover ends, unless perhaps the vehicle is returned to its original form: that depends on whether, as regards the effects of the change, the importance to the insurer of the contractual description of the vehicle is such that it is more like term (b), an exception, than term (c), a warranty.

Term (a), as regards perils insured, is also important. Any claim against the insurer for insurance money must establish that the loss was caused by one of these perils: 157 below. Common perils such as theft have been defined by the courts and are given their technical meaning: 120 above.

Term (b) has this in common with term (c), that both may operate to defeat cover, even though there is no causal connection between the relevant circumstances and the loss: 133–4 below. This may be why both (b) and (c) are sometimes called conditions. However, there is an important distinction between them. If an exception, term (b), operates to stop cover, the effect on cover is not permanent but only suspensive. Thus, although the effect of term (b) in the above example is that damage to A653 JEB during business use in June is not covered, damage to it on holiday in July is covered. If, however, the brakes are out of order in June, unless they were repaired as soon as reasonably possible, that is a breach of warranty, term (c), and the effect is that the damage in July is not covered. Breach of warranty terminates cover automatically and for ever. To make matters worse for the insured, a warranty broken slightly is broken nonetheless. In one case,[18] Lord Wright held that the insured who warranted that he had paid £285 for his vehicle but had paid £271 was in breach of the warranty. To know whether a term is an exception or a warranty is sometimes difficult but always important.

Exceptions

Exceptions, which insurance law sometimes calls exclusions, are terms excluding cover for certain risks or an unacceptable aspect of the risk that is covered. An example of the first might be cover for houses in Holland except against floods. An example of the second is cover against (the cost of) cancellation of a wedding, but

---

[18] *Allen* v. *Universal Automobile Ins. Co. Ltd* (1933) 45 Ll.LR 55.

with an exception for cancellation because bride or groom have changed their minds!

The more complex the case, the more appropriate it is to see exceptions as part of the overall structure of cover. Cover, like any other contractual undertaking, may be drafted entirely in positive terms. In a lease, for example, the landlord may promise to let the first and second floors of the (two-storeyed) house. Alternatively, the lease may be drafted in a combination of positive and negative terms, for example, a promise to let (all of) the house, except the ground floor. In general contract law, it has been strongly argued that the effect of the contract is the same in each case, and that, in the alternative draft, the exception (of the ground floor) is definitional rather than exclusionary of liability for breach of a broader promise. This is the view of such clauses in France, for example, and it is the better of the two views in England. The sculptor, who chips bits off a chunk of stone, is doing the same kind of work as the potter, who builds his shape from clay. The work of the insurance draftsman, whether it is done like the potter or the sculptor, should be viewed as a whole. The role of the exception, therefore, is to define the boundary of the risk insured: A653 JEB is covered, but not when used for business.

In general contract law the importance of the point is that, if exceptions are classifed as terms excluding liability under the Unfair Contract Terms Act 1977, the court can strike them out to the extent that they are unreasonable. That might have been equally important to insurers and their contracts, but it is not; insurers persuaded Parliament that their contract 'exceptions' should be outside the operation of the Act. Insurers have now to be more concerned, however, as the classification may affect whether their 'exceptions' can be censured under the EC Directive: 230 ff. below.

Warranties

The warranty has a distinct role in the insurance contract but, unless they have learned the language of insurance law, to lay people and to lawyers alike the word 'warranty' is confusing. An insurance warranty is sometimes called a 'condition'. For that reason the lawyer may well think it important, which it is, and that it is very much like a sale of goods condition, which it is not.

If a sale condition is broken, it is such a significant part of the sale that the buyer has been substantially deprived of what was contracted for. An insurance warranty is not part of what the insurer contracted for, not what the insurer mainly wants out of the transaction; what the insurer wants is premium. Hence, the insurance warranty is said to be 'conditional but not promissory', whereas the sale condition is both.

Moreover, if a sale condition is broken, the effect in law is that the promisee has both a right to damages and an option to terminate the contract of sale which, unless that option is exercised, remains in being. If an insurance warranty is broken, the breach terminates the insurance contract; however, it does so not at the insurer's option but automatically by operation of law; and breach does not give the insurer any right to damages. The insurer wants the warranty, not for any net benefit he may derive from contracting the insurance but in order to circumscribe the relationship with the insured—to limit the risk and thus to reduce the burden or extent of the insurer's own promise of cover.

If, then, the insurance warranty is not a sale condition, our lawyer might take it at 'face value' as something not unlike a sale warranty. Again, that would be a mistake. A sale warranty is a promise collateral to the main purpose of the sale of goods contract. If a sale warranty is broken, it is not such a significant part of the sale as a condition but nonetheless the promisee (buyer) has been deprived of one of the things contracted for. An insurance warranty is not at all part of what the insurer contracted for, which was simply and solely premium.

Moreover, if a sale warranty is broken, breach gives the buyer a right to damages but does not entitle the buyer to terminate the contract. As we have seen, however, breach of insurance warranty terminates the contract automatically, and does not give the insurer a right to damages. So, clearly, the insurance warranty is not a sale warranty either. With perversity of the traditional English kind that holds May Balls in June, English insurance law calls a term of this kind both a condition and a warranty, although in the language of the general law it is neither.

In the end, our lawyer will find that the insurance warranty is best thought of as a 'condition precedent', but still one that must be distinguished from the condition precedent of general contract law on two counts. First, the general condition is one which must be satisfied before a contract comes into existence. In contrast, an insurance warranty has no role until a contract of insurance has come into existence, a contract of which it is part. Secondly, breach of the general condition must be proved by the one who seeks to rely on the contract. A troublesome development in France is that some courts have held the same for insurance contracts, for example, that the insured whose goods have been stolen must first prove compliance with any anti-theft measures required by the insurer.[19] Although Lord Goff has defined the insurance warranty as a 'condition precedent to the liability or further liability of the insurer',[20] which might suggest that English law is similar, it is not. It is not for the insured to prove compliance with the warranty. Breach of warranty is a defence to a claim against the insurer which must be proved by the insurer.

Exceptions, Warranties, and Causes

As warranties are 'conditions precedent' to cover, breach of them terminates cover, even though there may be no causal connection between the warranty (or its breach) and either the loss or the risk of loss. Although the purpose of warranties is to circumscribe risk, the assessment of risk is a matter for the insurer and, if the insurance contract says clearly that something is a condition precedent to cover, that is how it is interpreted by the court, whatever anyone else thinks about the relevance of the condition to the risk insured or of the relevance of its breach to loss. Thus, in a leading case,[21] an erroneous statement about where the insured vehicle was kept was a warranty, and there was no cover, even though the place where it was actually kept was probably safer than the place stated; and, in another leading case,[22] Lord Blackburn said that, if a warranty of temperance in a life contract was broken, the cover would be defeated even though the insured died in a road accident when cold sober.

Exceptions differ from warranties in that, generally, excepted events do not excuse the insurer unless they cause the loss. Thus,

---

[19] e.g. *Paris 9 Nov. 1994*, BTL.1994.875; idem in Belgium: Antwerp 15 Oct. 1993 (1994) 29 ETL 368.
[20] *The Good Luck* [1992] 1 AC 233, 263.
[21] *Dawsons* v. *Bonnin* [1922] 2 AC 413.
[22] *Thomson* v. *Weems* (1884) 9 App. Cas. 671, 685.

an exception of riot does not excuse the property insurer unless it is proved that the loss was caused by a riot. As this may be hard to prove, insurers sometimes convert it to a 'temporal exception', excepting damage 'occasioned by riot': if a riot occurs in the neighbourhood *at the time* of the loss, a connection is presumed and the insurer excused without having to prove the actual cause of the loss. To insurers this is reasonable enough. They are less concerned with a causal connection between riot and loss in a particular case than with a statistical connection between riot and loss over a large number of cases. Their records tell them that when there is a riot there is also a lot of damage to property. As insurers see it, once a riot occurs risk insured has entered a new category.

To the insured, this may not seem reasonable at all. As casual observers, people do tend to assume a causal connection between results and possible causes that are close in time and space. As insurance claimants, they are more inclined to see the fallacy of the assumption, but, if a temporal exception defeats their claim, to be told about categories of risk is more likely to lead to enlightenment than to satisfaction. The Australian Law Reform Commission (ALRC) has condemned temporal exceptions as harsh, and in New Zealand, by the Insurance Law Reform Act 1977 (section 11), the law was changed to require a causal connection. In Australia, however, the ALRC also accepted the insurer's point of view about categories of risk and rejected a proposal for change as an unjustified interference with the market. Indeed, if the exception is to retain a role in the definition of risk insured, New Zealand may have pruned the common law too hard. For example, take the common motor-insurance exception of business use. If a vehicle is to be insurable (more cheaply) for private use only, the exception of business use must except damage *while* on business rather than damaged caused by business. However, although the business exception may seem reasonable enough, the temporal exception can have unreasonable results. For example, motor cover may also cease 'while the insured is intoxicated'. That seems fair enough at first sight but, on a literal construction, that would mean no cover for his wife shopping by car while the insured is drunk around the corner in a pub. Clearly the court will construe temporal exceptions strictly.

Problem: Distinguishing between Exceptions and Warranties

As we have just seen, it is important to know whether a term of the insurance contract is an exception or a warranty. The first step is to see if the contract itself classifies the term. Thus, a 'warranty' that the building insured will not be unoccupied for more than thirty days at a stretch is a warranty; but an unlabelled term that insurance does not cover any loss, if at the time the building has been unoccupied for thirty days or more, has been held to be an exception. Generally, the courts respect labels like 'warranty' but, of course, labels can be confusing. As we have also seen, both exceptions and warranties may be called 'conditions'. The confusion is 'the worse confounded' by the profusion of labels for exceptions: 'terms delimiting risk', 'exclusions', 'temporal exclusions', or 'limitations of risk'. Although labels are important, they are not always decisive.

The second step is to identify the branch by its fruit: if the contract spells out the effect of the term and, the effect of exceptions and warranties being quite different (133–4 above), that indicates which it is. A controversial but clear case is the 'basis clause': the courts have ruled that, if any statements made by the insured in a proposal form are stated to be the 'basis of the contract', they become warranties, even though the statements are not recorded in any document, such as the policy, of which the insured has a copy. This rule has been described as an objectionable trap, and a major mischief in the law of insurance. Reform has been recommended by the Report (No 104, paragraph 7.5) of the English Law Commission (ELC) and the use of the basis clause is contrary to the ABI's Code of Practice; but the law has not been reformed and it is unclear to what extent the statement of practice is actually observed.

If there is still no answer, the third step is to seek the essential nature of the term. Generally, if the term is concerned with circumstances which give rise to a *temporary* increase in the risk, it is an exception. Thus, if a van is insured for business use (only), it is off risk when driven to the golf club (unless for business); but once the van is back at work and none the worse for the excursion, the insurance resumes. If, however, the term concerns circumstances in which there is or might be a *permanent* increase in the risk, it is a warranty. Thus, if reasonable steps have not been taken to maintain the van insured in an efficient condition (road-worthiness), as the contract requires, that is a breach of warranty. Once the warranty has been broken, the insurance cover ends, even though the van is later restored to a roadworthy condition.

One reason for the last case is that, although the insured did attend to the van in the end, the insured now appears to be the kind of owner that the insurer may not want to insure—at all or not without reconsidering the level of premium. The risk may or may not have changed, but the insurer's perception of the risk has changed and, through the warranty, the insurer has contracted for a right to reconsider. From this point of view the warranty makes good sense. From the insured's point of view, however, warranties like that undermine the security of cover. The dilemma is the problem of 'moral hazard': how far can the insured be allowed to 'play Russian roulette' with the risk? This raises the more general question of risk management.

The Problem of Aggravation of Risk

In the past, the role of insurance has been not to rein in human activity and endeavour but to encourage it. Of course, if people put a match to their own insured property, the fire is not covered—not because they have broken a condition or warranty but because, in insurance law, fire deliberately started is not a fire risk. But if the fire arises out of a new and experimental process, English law is reluctant to let the insurer off risk because the insurer had had no warning of the experiment. In England, the insured must mention any plans of that kind when cover begins or is renewed, but, between those times, they do not have to telephone their insurer every time they plan something new. 'If a person who insures his life goes up in a balloon, that does not vitiate his policy. . . . A person who insures may light as many candles as he please in his house, though each additional candle increases the danger of setting the house on fire.'[23] That was said

[23] *Baxendale* v. *Harvey* (1849) 4 H & N 445, 449, 452.

by a court in 1849. Then, as now, the insured may be a fool but, unless also a knave, the fool is covered.

Even so, insurers prefer that their insured do not take up hang-gliding or start selling camping-gas from a paint shop. English insurers may well prefer the German rule for non-life insurance (VVG, Articles 23–25) that insureds are not allowed to increase the risk in any way without the consent of the insurer and that, if they do, the cover ends at once in respect of any loss 'influenced' by the increase, as well as any subsequent loss if the insurer so elects. More attractive still perhaps to the insurers is the corresponding French rule (Code d'assurance, Article L.113–2–3.) that, if the risk is materially increased during the insurance period (whether or not through any act or omission of the insured) by circumstances specified in the policy, the insurer is entitled to terminate it or demand a higher premium. A similar rule is found in Switzerland too (Versicherungsvertragsgesetz, Articles 28 and 30) but, in practice, it is softened by contract terms in favour of the insured.

The French rule has been attacked in France itself as an unreasonable burden for the insured. It would also be opposed in England. The ELC Report (paragraph 5.50) concluded that it may be appropriate to the relatively long-term cover found in continental Europe where, for example, Germans may contract motor cover for as long as ten years at a time, but not to the shorter periods of cover usually found in the United Kingdom. Moreover, one of the very reasons for insurance from the insured's point of view is certainty, including certainty of cost—so much so that, recently, one insurer has been offering businesses a fixed premium for three years, because research confirmed that stable insurance planning was a selling point. Further, anything like the French rule goes against the grain of the classical contract, which is distinct and discrete rather than relational: 146 below. The English tradition is that the rules of engagement must be fixed at the time of contract.

On all this the law of insurance has conflicting objectives: to promote compensation and loss-spreading by the insurer without encouraging foolish conduct by the insured. Once the insurance period is running, English law puts the first objective ahead of the second. Whereas the law does not allow the insured to gamble with the insurer (20 above), it does require the insurer to gamble to a degree on the insured—in the interests of the latter or of society at large in some degree of certainty of cover and compensation. In the case of compulsory motor insurance, for example, this is evident not only in England (Road Traffic Act 1988, sections 14(1) and 151(1)) but also, for example, in France (Code d'assurance, Article R211–13–3) and other countries: certain defences cannot be raised by the insurer against third parties to whom the insured motorist is liable.

Even in England, however, an intermediate situation should be noted when insurance is contracted a relatively long time in advance of the period of cover: an express warranty may be introduced which makes it a condition of cover that the risk has not increased at a specified date between the contract and the commencement of cover. Moreover, with 'candles' in mind, some English insurance contracts require notification; for example, motor insurance may require notification of any modification to the vehicle. This is the kind of policy specification sanctioned in France. Just what the insurer thinks he is entitled to do in response to notification is not always clear from the contract, but it is fairly clear that the English courts will respond unfavourably to any attempt by the insurer to end or modify the contract before the renewal date. As we have seen, the English tradition inclines against a contract term or rule of law that makes the activity of the insured during the insurance period dependent on the will and whim of his insurer. The tradition stands in contrast with that in France, that the level of risk should not depend entirely on the will and whim of the insured. However, the difference is less marked than it might first appear. To some extent the entrepreneurial freedom of the insured in England is illusory because his activities can be hedged in by warranties undertaken at the commencement of the insurance period.

One of the main measures to stop the insured 'playing with fire' is the continuing warranty. If anyone wanted to insure a theatre in the nineteenth century, there was a ban on illuminated scenery, fireworks, and the discharge of firearms; and today fireworks can still be warranted out of shops that do not specialize in such merchandise. A more general example is a warranty that the insured has a working fire alarm, not only when cover begins but throughout the insurance period. Again, in the 1970s some insured householders discovered that they could raise cash by dropping mirrors; insurers responded with clauses requiring reasonable care during the period of cover. Breach of the clause must be proved by insurer but, although courts construe them strictly, the clauses are applied: see 140 below.

In the absence of a well-drawn continuing warranty the insurer may have to shoulder an unexpectedly heavy burden of increased risk for the full course of the insurance period. If the insurer does have a well-drawn continuing warranty, however, the insured may suddenly be without cover without their knowledge—like the fairytale king without clothes and without awareness of his exposure. Better sometimes the corresponding French rule, which encourages renegotiation and, if new agreement on premium cannot be reached, gives the insurer his freedom and gives the insured time to find alternative cover.

The Prudent Uninsured: Reasonable Care

Insurers sometimes talk as if the insureds have a legal duty to 'act as a prudent uninsured'. In law, they have no such duty unless the contract imposes one in very clear terms. Whether the insured *should* have a duty of that kind is a matter for debate: 216 ff. below. What is clear is that, not surprisingly, insurers would like the insured to have one and try to impose a duty by contract. Equally clearly, the courts resist care conditions by construction against the insurer.

Suppose that an employer is careless about fencing his machinery so that a worker's hand is trapped in a welding machine. What is the use of the employer's liability insurance if the carelessness defeats cover? As a judge put it in a leading case, that would mean that 'the underwriters were saying: "We will insure you against your liability for negligence on condition that you are not negligent." '[24] The response of the courts has been that it is one of the purposes of insurance to cover the carelessness of the insured, and so, whenever possible, any condition requiring care by the insured is construed so that it is breached only by extreme carelessness i.e. by something close to recklessness. In another leading case, Diplock LJ said: 'What, in my view, is reasonable

---

[24] *Woolfall*, n. 17 above.

. . . is that the insured should not deliberately court a danger, the existence of which he recognises'. Any breach of the condition

must at least be reckless, that is to say, made with actual recognition by the insured himself that a danger exists, and not caring whether or not it is averted. The purpose of the condition is to ensure that the insured will not, because he is covered against loss by the policy, refrain from taking precautions which he *knows* ought to be taken.[25]

The result, of course, is that the greater the carelessness the smaller the chance of cover for the employer and of compensation for the employee. From the viewpoint of people at work, the courts' construction achieves a compromise which, it seems, is better than would be the effect of a literal interpretation of the condition. From the viewpoint of the law student, the result is interesting in the way it is achieved. It shows how courts cope with new issues, what psychologists call a 'heuristic stratagem', by which the thinker seeks to relate the new issue to established patterns of experience and thought. In other words, in the task of interpretation, the court looks for an analogy with precedent or with some familiar or established concept.

To decide whether the insured has 'taken precautions', as required by many of the clauses aimed at making the insured more careful, the court reasons in the (more familiar) way it does in tort when deciding whether the defendant has been negligent. First, the court sets the standard of care required according to the sort of person the insured purports to be, i.e. according to the knowledge and skill that can be expected of a person of that sort. When it comes to handling liquid petroleum gas (LPG), higher standards will be expected of an employer in a factory than of a holiday-maker in a caravan. Then the court assesses the degree of care to be expected of an insured of that sort; this depends on the situation in which the risk arose. The more likely the loss the more care is expected, which in turn will depend, in liability insurance for example, on the danger of the operation or, in all-risks or transit insurance, on the attractiveness of the goods to thieves. The more serious the consequences of loss the more care is expected, which in turn will depend, for example, on the kind of human injury in prospect or the value of the goods. The more viable

---

[25] *Fraser* v. *Furman (Productions) Ltd* [1967] 1 WLR 898, 906 (CA).

(cheap and available) the precautions the more that can be expected of the insured in that direction, which in turn will depend on the location of the insured and the resources at his disposal.

In any one case, however, the court's thinking may be influenced by more than one established pattern of legal thought. The 'tort thinking', just described, may be coupled with that of 'overriding breach', sometimes called 'wilful misconduct'. This is conduct which is *prima facie* uninsurable, or which, in other branches of the law, rules out contractual defences. To the English judge, wilful misconduct implies that the person was aware that he was taking a risk. If an insurance case is approached from that frame of reference, the insured is more likely to be censured, and less likely to be covered, if he deliberately 'courts danger' than if he gives the danger no thought at all; something of this can be seen in the words of Diplock LJ (see the text to note 25 above). Again, when the court has to decide whether loss was 'accidental' a similar strain of thought is seen. In *Dhak*,[26] the court held that death caused largely by drinking too much alcohol was not accidental, because the deceased, a well-qualified nurse, would have been well aware of the danger and must have taken a calculated risk.

Typical of tort thinking is the leading case of *Sofi*.[27] A condition in a householder's policy required the insured to 'take all reasonable steps to safeguard any property insured and to avoid accidents which may lead to damage or injury'. One January, the insured and family set out for the Dover ferry on holiday. In a case measuring twelve inches by six inches in the locked glove compartment of the car was valuable jewellery. The reason, as the insured had previously told the insurer's agent, was that, having had a burglary at home, he felt the jewellery would be safer with him than at home. Being early for the ferry, they stopped to have a quick look at Dover Castle. The car park was unattended. What were they to do about their things? Having discussed the matter, they took their money and travellers cheques, but left everything else in the car. On their return fifteen minutes later, they found that the car had been ransacked. The insurer argued that the insured was in breach of the condition; that the insured should either have taken the jewellery with him to the Castle or left one of

---

[26] *Dhak* v. *Ins. Co. of N. America* [1996] 1 Lloyd's Rep. 632 (CA).
[27] *Sofi* v. *Prudential Assurance Co. Ltd* [1993] 2 Lloyd's Rep. 559 (CA).

the party behind in the car. In the response of the Court of Appeal, we see something of the 'heuristic' approach and the template of tort. The gravity of the risk (thieves like jewellery) and the triviality of the occasion (a casual unscheduled visit to Dover Castle) counted against the claimant. However, the small chance of theft (short absence from empty park in January) and the difficulty of taking adequate precautions counted in his favour. On balance, held the Court, the insured might have been careless but had not been reckless; he was not in breach of the condition of care, and his claim against the insurer succeeded.

Premium Incentive

A common belief is that if the premium charged goes up or down with the claims record of the insured, that will discourage claims and encourage care by the insured. The insurer cannot play with the premium, however, if the insured is in a stronger bargaining position than the insurer, or if the insured can pass on higher insurance costs to his customer. Nor will the insured respond with more care, if he does not think it will make any difference because, for example, the pool in which he is rated is so large that good risk management on his part will have no effect on his premium. A common example is the motorists' 'no-claims' discount (NCD), but it has been doubted whether it has much effect on how carefully people drive or, even, whether 'experience' rating of this kind in general insurance is very scientific.

First, there is too little up-to-date information on the insured to be a guide to future claims. If rating is perceived to be inaccurate, and thus unfair, it inspires in the insured discontent and a quest for cheaper cover rather than repentance and a mending of ways. Secondly, to match premiums with suffcient accuracy to risk may not be economic. To have a significant deterrent effect, liability insurance premiums must in some way indicate to the insured the cost of each activity but, to achieve this, the insurer has to draw insurance categories narrowly; and that is simply too costly.

If and when premium incentive does have an effect on the insured, it can be used in more than one way. One is to rate, for example, fire risks according to the design and construction of the building insured and, in this way, insurers have long had an influence on the choice of design and materials. Once a building has been built, another way is to reduce premium if the insured take certain measures to prevent loss or if they bear the first layer of risk (excess). These 'excess' provisions (also called 'deductibles'), whereby the insured pay the first layer of loss have two functions. First, they reduce the insurer's administrative costs because, proportionately, the smaller the claim the larger the cost. Secondly, they are an incentive to the insured to avoid loss altogether. They must, however, be marketed as such; otherwise people tend to perceive them as a punishment. They are best presented as a self-generated premium discount. Not only does this make them more acceptable to the insured, but also, as the insurer sees it, they emphasize the line between the wise and the thoughtless, between those who regard insurance as a maintenance contract and those who seek simply to protect their assets.

Risk Management: Advice

After the fire at Windsor Castle in 1994, the chairman of the House of Commons Public Accounts Committee claimed that, if the Castle had been insured with the industry and subject to conditions, there might not have been this 'wretched fire'. Conditions are just one aspect of risk management; another, more general and 'strategic' form, is planning and advice. The role of the insurer in managing and preventing the risks, the chairman said, is of such importance that it is now widely assumed. Sadly, it was not and is not always so. In 1918 some insurers refused life cover to asbestos workers. Recently the Court of Appeal concluded that a defendant company knew or should have known of the harmful effects of asbestos on workers as early as 1925. Yet, other insurers were still covering these workers in the 1960s, as if asbestos and its dust made no difference and, later, came to court and denied knowledge of the hazards.

Today, risk management is a service that many insurers offer to preserve market share. Some of their customers are so large that, were it not for their expertise in risk-management, insurers would have little to offer them that could not be done by self-insurance. When the contingency occurs, too, modern insurers may provide more than money but services of one kind or another: not only a courtesy car while the car insured is under repair but care and advice concerning the loss itself and future prevention. An economist has described insurance as a prism with three sides: risk-transfer, information-exchange, and services.[28]

This picture is striking, but far from perfect. At one end of the spectrum, insurance is but one aspect of a package of services on offer. For example, a credit package offered to small businesses might include credit information on other companies, debt recovery including the legal costs, and debt insurance for incorrigibly bad debts. At the other end, the insurer might offer insurance uncluttered by advice of any kind, except perhaps what is implicit in the policy conditions. Somewhere in between is the liability insurer, for example, who offers a twenty-four hour executive helpline, with access to solicitors for advice to executives about their legal obligations; and the life insurer who offers bereavement counselling to the surviving relatives.

The movement of insurers into risk management and services, in particular advice about risk at the point of contracting, raises the question whether, if they give careless advice, they are liable to the insured for the consequences. Of course, one consequence may be the loss covered by the insurance. However, insurance covers only the immediate consequences of the peril insured, and there remains the possibility of liability in contract or tort for consequences that are more remote.

Liability for Careless Advice

If this inquiry starts from the baseline of general contract law, it seems that there is no duty of care between people negotiating contracts. Against that conclusion is *Esso Petroleum Co. Ltd* v. *Mardon*.[29] But although some have dismissed that decision as a quirk of legal history, in which Lord Denning led the court to anticipate the operation of the Misrepresentation Act, Treitel accepts the decision: since the Act it is still precedent for the case in which the defendant had superior knowledge and experience.[30]

If the inquiry starts from the baseline of insurance law, insurers in breach of the duty of disclosure and, therefore, of the duty of good faith are not liable in damages either on that ground or on

---

[28] R. Schmidt, 'Considerations on the Significance for Insurance Law of the Consequences of Economic Studies', Geneva Papers no 74 (1995), 74–82, 77.
[29] [1976] QB 801 (CA).   [30] Op. cit. 323.

the basis of any breach of a duty of care. This was decided in *Westgate*.[31] However, that case did not concern risk advice but a very different situation. If the inquiry starts again from the baseline of principle governing actions for negligence, an action by the insured seems possible. According to the well known general guidelines for the existence of a duty of care, the loss must be a reasonably foreseeable consequence of the failure alleged. Secondly, there must be 'proximity' between the parties which, in turn, is often fused with a third requirement that the imposition of a duty of care must be fair and reasonable. If the claimant's damage is physical rather than economic, just as doctors may be liable for careless advice about preventing illness, risk managers including insurers, surely, should be liable for negligent advice having foreseeable physical consequences; that is fair. Courts which have held a fire brigade liable for negligence in the heat of a fire are unlikely to hold back from a similar decision against risk managers in the business of preventing fire and with plenty of time to investigate the risk and reflect on their advice. If, however, the foreseeable consequences to the claimant are not physical but purely economic, the general rule is that a duty would not be fair, unless it is also a special case called 'negligent misstatement'.

For such a duty, the law requires a voluntary assumption of responsibility by the insurer. In *Westgate* there was none.[32] Generally, however, an assumption of responsibility will be inferred when advice is given by the insurer; he knows why the insured wants the advice and that it is likely to be acted on by the insured. Given the greater expertise of the insurer in matters of risk management and the mutual concern with controlling the risk, it is not only likely and reasonable that the insured will act on the the advice, but it may well be a condition of the insurance.

The inquiry from the baseline of principle is confirmed by the analogy of precedent. A duty is owed by the surveyor of a house to the purchaser of a house, and by an architect who certified the quality of building work, so it would be surprising if a duty were not owed also by an insurer who advised a purchaser or occupier about fire or theft precautions. In conclusion, surely, the insurer's advice on risk management is an assumption of responsibility

---

[31] *Banque Financière de la Cité* v. *Westgate Ins. Co. Ltd* [1990] QB 665, 801, affirmed on other grounds: [1991] 2 AC 249. [32] *Ibid.* 275.

which carries with it a duty of care. If that is part of the service expected of the insurer from the start, part of what the insured is paying for, the advice will be in performance of a contractual duty in which a similar duty of care and skill will be implied. Otherwise it will be based in tort.

The Insurance Relationship

The paradigm of classical contract law is the executory contract. Generally, however, most contracts are performed almost as soon as they are concluded or very soon afterwards; and the longer the period between conclusion and execution the less typical they become. Purely as a matter of duration, insurance looks like one of the latter. But duration as such is not what matters. What matters is whether the period is such that the contract in question enters a different 'relational' category for which different rules of law might be appropriate. Typical relational contracts are franchising, employment, partnership, lease, management, licensing, research and development, and charterparties. If a relational contract were simply one involving not merely an exchange but also a relationship, then insurance would be relational; but that alone is not what counts here. Here a relational contract is a long contract which gives rise to certain problems, notably unexpected changes, which have to be solved as they arise by 'relating' with the other party. In the element of the unexpected the insurance contract is archetypical: the insured event is not expected. When it comes to the solution, the response to the unexpected change, however, the opposite is true. A key characteristic of the insurance contract is forward-planning and the retention of risk in the way initially allocated by the contract by one party, the insurer. The very purpose of insurance is the transfer of risk of the unexpected from one party, the insured, to the other party, the insurer—and left there, as initially agreed. For insurance, therefore, there is no question of adaptation such as price adjustment mid-term; that is the antithesis of insurance. But there is still the question, what is mid-term?

Fire insurance is usually for a term of a year and is not changed during that period. At the end of the year, however, English insurance law says that that is not the middle of any longer term but the end of the term, and that, if there is to be a further insurance period at all, that must be the subject of new agreement and, therefore, of any amount of 'adjustment' in comparison with the previous contract. However, long-term relationships also include those in a series of discrete contracts of a broadly similar kind, among them certain kinds of insurance such as health insurance. At the end of the year they may be mid-term in the sense of mid-series, but insurance law has no special rule. Insurance law treats them as discrete, like the sale of soap: fixed terms for the fixed period and, after that, a new fix.

In practice, the line between insurance periods is cut less clearly. The contract of insurance may contain some provision for continuity. For example, the contract may provide for renewal on the basis of a relatively objective reference to the 'table of rates then in effect'. In some policies, however, subjective factors have been brought; for example a string of factors including 'current loss experience . . . and such other factors as [the insurer] may determine from time to time'. These leave the insured with little security. Should anything be done about this? Are there any lessons for insurance law in general commercial law or practice?

Flexible Friends; Measures for the Unexpected

To deal with the unexpected during the period of contract performance a number of measures have emerged for contracts generally. One is the use of implied terms. This seems to have little relevance to insurance contracts; apart from a few basic terms (above 75), there is virtually no implication of terms.

A second is to adapt performance without formal or explicit agreement to vary the original contract. Parties simply do it. If the adaptation is unilateral, English contract law has enforced the change by the device of estoppel or waiver. An important example is found at the point of claim, when the insurer relaxes some of the claims' conditions. This also occurs during the insurance period, if and when the insurer waives breach of a continuing warranty. However, this is a matter entirely for the discretion of the insurer and free of influence either of the law or of the insured.

Thirdly, like other contracts, insurance contracts sometimes refer to a 'standard'. An instance of this is the reference to a premium TBA (to be arranged), when commercial cover is extended under a Lloyd's policy; the shipowners who decide to send their ship into dangerous waters are entitled to cover under their existing insurance on payment of an additional premium. This is less, however, initial contract provision for future uncertainty than a standard option that the insured chooses to take and pays for. Still, this might be seen as an instance of the device, more important in contracts generally, of 'planning for flexibility' by reference to standards such as a Consumer Price Index.

Fourthly, as in contracts generally, a provision for arbitration is sometimes found in insurance contracts to settle disagreement about a claim. These have been enforced, although sometimes they put the insured claimant at a disadvantage: 200 below. This is what contract theorist Macneil called 'Direct Third-Party Determination of Performance'.[33]

Fifthly, flexibility is seen in the 'rules' for members of clubs. Insurance clubs, like football clubs, have rules of no fixed duration and contain provisions for change. Clubs resemble the 'firm', such as a joint venture or something yet more integrated. The immediate interest of the club form of mutual cover is that, although a degree of provision is sought by carefully drafted rules of association, outstanding matters, which might arise during the period of cover, may be delegated to the decision of some kind of directorate.

Mostly, all these measures are the creation of contract and the work of the parties. Should the law make other or better provision for flexibility in relational contracts? McKendrick is one of several who argue against the thesis that relational contracts require special rules of law or special resort to the courts to have contracts adapted.[34] The parties must do the best they can with contract terms for forward planning.

The tradition of insurance law and practice is that insurers respond in the way exhorted by McKendrick. Insurers draft their contracts with a view to the immediate insurance period in its entirety. They seek to limit the impact of the unexpected by hedging their commitment with warranties extracted at the time of contracting, warranties 'controlling' the risk (138 above) and terms

---

[33] I. R. Macneil, 'Restatement (Second) of Contracts and Presentiatation', 60 *Va. L Rev.* 589–610, 594 (1974).

[34] E. McKendrick, 'The Regulation of Long Term Contracts in English Law', in J. Beatson (ed.), *Good Faith and Fault in Contract Law* (London, 1995), ch. 12, 312 ff.

of various kinds that seek to influence the conduct of the insured (216 ff. below). The suggestion made for other kinds of contract, a suggestion of deliberate and allegedly 'productive' ambiguity to permit flexible interpretation later, is unhelpful for insurance in view of the tradition of strict construction *contra proferentem* and the fundamental desire for certainty. Sharp edges may be uncomfortable, but people know where they are. So, it seems that, for insurance contracts, there is little to be gained by any kind of framework for flexibility during the insurance period.

However, tradition must accommodate change in society and in the requirements of insurance. For example, it may be that more widespread health and long term care insurance will require more use of reference to a standard, and perhaps to a referee. The practice of the mutual insurance clubs suggests that this might work. Moreover, the integration of European markets will lead to some harmonization of law, and the English lawmaker may reflect on the merits of the rules found, for example, in France (137 above) whereby aggravation of the risk entitles insurers to reconsider their commitment during the insurance period. Meanwhile, however, for those who wish to change or terminate an insurance relationship the focus of attention is the point of renewal.

Rights of Renewal

In theory, insurers are bound strictly by the contract and the risk that they have assumed. For them the moment of release comes at the end of the insurance period: they are not obliged to renew at all or on terms. Even in the United States courts have upheld the 'absolute right' of insurers to reconsider on renewal, and have done so even when refusal was devastating for the insured: for example, the case of the private investigator who needed a licence for his profession but could not get one without insurance,[35] and of health insurance and the insurer who, as the price of renewal, demanded a massive (489 per cent over two years) increase in premium[36]—a kind of 'constructive' refusal. More likely than refusal, however, is the case of the insurer who does want to renew

[35] *Harding* v. *Ohio Cas. Co.*, 41 NW 2d 818, 823 (Minn., 1950).
[36] *Compton* v. *Aetna Life Ins. & Annuity Co.*, 956 F 2d 256 (11 Cir., 1992).

but on different terms. In theory, each party to the insurance contract is entirely free to negotiate terms for the next period of cover.

In practice, neither side is entirely free to spurn the other at the point either of contracting or of renewal. For their part, insurers may be under moral or political pressure to contract. When *Which?* complained about the difficulty some people had in getting motor insurance, it was significant that the industry's defence of itself did not appeal to freedom of contract; on the contrary, there was tacit acceptance that cover ought to be there—somewhere, albeit on the industry's terms. The industry accepts a duty to provide compulsory cover, if only to ward off government interference. For their part, the insured, considering the renewal offered, are not entirely free to take it or leave it. Not only do we find the commonplace inequalities of information and skill, but the insureds' hands are partly tied by fear of the effect of refusal on their 'record' and, therefore, on the willingness of other insurers to grant them cover then or in future. What can the current law do for them?

Duress

For contracts generally, it is arguable that the law of duress has become the principal means of regulating renegotiation or renewal of contracts. Duress may consist not only of threats of physical violence but also 'economic' duress, something more subtle, which has been been described as illegitimate pressure. Commercial pressure, however, is usually legitimate. To end a relationship by non-renewal might amount to commercial pressure, but it is not illegitimate. For economic duress between parties already in a contractual relationship, the duress usually takes the form of threatened breach of contract, which gives the victim very little practical choice but to do what is demanded. Moreover, illegitimate pressure requires an element of bad faith, i.e. the deliberate exploitation of the difficulties of the other party. In the case of the insurer who threatens non-renewal of insurance, however awkward that may be for the insured, there is no illegitimate pressure of the kind that the law calls economic duress. This doctrine is of no assistance.

Good Faith

The relationship between insurer and insured is said to be one of good faith, with reciprocal duties throughout the contractual relationship at a level appropriate to the operation in hand: see 80 ff. above and 168 ff. below. In particular, the duty of disclosure, most prominent prior to contract formation, revives whenever the insured has an express or implied duty to supply information to enable the insurer to make a decision. Hence it applies when insurance is first contracted or renewed. It is, however, no more than a duty to offer information, if required. A party has no duty to receive information or, in any other way, to consider renewal of insurance which that party does not want to renew.

In some legal systems there is a general contractual duty to (re)negotiate in good faith but this is not even current general contract law in England. Even so, insurance parties do not deal with each other as market duellists at arms' length but in a 'contractual environment' of other extra-legal norms and influences.[37] For insurance, as we have noted, there is some social and commercial 'influence' or pressure to persist. Moreover, whereas in the past the insured may have been kept at a respectful distance by the broker, today there is the rise of direct insurance whereby insurer and insured come 'face to face' on the telephone. Above all, insurers have more involvement with their insured through greater risk management. Even so, not even a qualified duty of renewal can be built on the insurance doctrine of good faith. This doctrine does not help the insured either.

Estoppel

The expectation of (renewed) cover may leave the insured exposed. Perhaps this is why in some countries there is a rule not unlike estoppel, whereby the cover is renewed automatically unless the insurer acts positively to stop it. In the United States there are also decisions of the federal courts to that effect;[38] and in California the Insurance Code (section 678.1) requires insurers to

---

[37] S. Deakin, C. Lane, and F. Wilkinson, 'Trust or Law? Towards an Integrated Theory of Contractual Relations between Firms' (1994) 21 *J Law & Soc.* 329–49, 340 ff.   [38] Clarke, n. 15 above.

continue certain classes of commercial insurance unless they have given the insured notice of their intention not to renew at least forty-five days before the end of the insurance period. In Australia, too, insurers are required to give the insured notice not later than fourteen days before expiry whether they are 'prepared to negotiate to renew or to extend cover': Insurance Contracts Act, section 58(2). If they do not, and if the insured has not obtained alternative cover before the expiry, the insurance continues for an equivalent period on the same terms, except that no premium is payable at all unless a claim is made. In both Australia and California, the insurers who decline to renew or are prepared to renew only on conditions disadvantageous to the insured are required to give reasons for their decision. This is an important improvement over the English common law, as it helps the insured to explain the non-renewal, which of course they must disclose, to alternative insurers.

In France, there is no such rule of law, but there is enforcement by the courts of contract terms, whereby renewal is automatic unless one party objects.[39] In German law there is a similar rule (VVG, Article 8), under which any objection must be made before the end of the previous insurance period. The purpose is both that of the insurer to retain business and that of the insured to provide against unintentional omission to renew and a gap in cover. This practice should be seen, however, in the light of the legal obligation (not found in England) which requires the insured to notify the insurer *during* the insurance period of a change in circumstances which increases the risk: see 137 above.

In principle, such terms could be enforced in England. No disputed instance appears to have been reported. However, a rule of automatic renewal has attractions. It is a theme of this book that, as it is in the nature of Man to be careless, it is (still) an important purpose of insurance to provide for that; surely, one of the most common instances of carelessness is to overlook renewal dates—unless reminded by the insurer. People depend on them and, in general terms, insurers encourage dependence. An important situation arises when, for the convenience and advantage of the insurer, insureds have been persuaded to pay premium by

---

[39] Y. Lambert-Faivre, *Droit des Assurances* (9th edn., Paris, 1995), 202 ff. See also Code d'assurance, Art. L.112–2, al. 2.

direct debit. It must surely be the duty of insurers, if they do not intend to trigger the debit, i.e. if they do not want renewal, to advise the insured. Moreover, when there is no debit instruction to the bank, if the usual notice of renewal does not come, but nor does any other advice from the insurer, why not automatic renewal, at least for a limited period?

In England, it has been said,[40] the 'great enforcer of morality in commerce is the continuing relationship, the belief that one will have to do business again with this customer'. But in the case of insurance, as we have seen, once the insurance period is over, the only safe view of current law is that is not so. The parties do not have to do business again. They do not have to renew the insurance at the end of the insurance period.

Where Next?

What counts, it seems, is not the state of the law but a state of mind: how much the insurer wants to retain the insured's business. Generally, there are powerful forces for continuity, which encourage the parties making an insurance contract to see it as the beginning of a relationship that may last beyond the next *Which?* report that says another insurer is cheaper.

The first insurance period may have been preceded by 'invest-ment': the insurer surveys the risk, the insured complies with conditions, for example, as regards security or fire prevention. The conclusion and performance of any contract may involve 'sunk costs' and, in insurance as in many other cases, the amount of cost invested by each side is not obviously disparate, and each party to insurance contracts bears the risk of the initial 'invest-ment'. Even so, it costs each side, especially the insurer, less to continue the relationship into the next insurance period than to look for a new partner. It is no surprise that one of the larger motor insurers has been advertising that it believes 'in relation-ships that last'. Like the banks, which have been wondering if the closer 'relational' banking found in Germany might be better than the more conservative and less committed banking practised in England in the past, insurers are taking a longer view that leads to closer relations with the customer.

[40] M. Mayer, quoted by S. Deakin *et al.*, n. 37 above.

Cost could also be a factor for continuity with the insured. Too few buyers seem to be aware that those who are prepared to enter into a longer-term relationship with their insurers will often benefit from fidelity discounts and can expect the service to improve, especially in the case of a claim.

If there is to be a longer relationship that looks beyond the immediate insurance period, what will it be like ? The answer to this question, it will be submitted later (307 below), lies less in the law than in attitudes, less in the marketplace tradition of getting a bargain than in trust; for this a framework is in sight—good faith, not in the narrow sense of common law but in the spirit of co-operation that characterizes the version of good faith that has now crossed the Channel from Brussels.

6

Claims: Taking the Drama out of the Crisis

The Claim

In the event of certain circumstances stated in the contract of insurance, the insurer promises to pay money (or money's worth) to the insured. General contract law calls this promise a promise to pay subject to a condition precedent—the occurrence of the stated circumstances. Insurance law calls this promise cover, and calls the circumstances the insured event or the peril insured. To get the insurer to pay the money promised, it is for the insured to make out a claim against the insurer by showing that the peril has occurred.

First, he must notify the insurer that he has suffered loss which, he believes, is covered by the insurance. Later, he must prove his claim: that he has actually suffered loss proximately caused by an event (or peril) covered by the insurance. If he proves this on the balance of probabilities, the insurer is liable to pay the claim unless the insurer can establish a defence.

The insurer's defence is likely to be that the real cause was something other than an insured peril (for example, an exception), or that the insurance contract was ineffective (for example expired or vitiated) or that the claimant has not followed the correct procedure (for example that notice was too late).

Insured Loss

Insurance law distinguishes between indemnity insurance, which pays on the basis of the actual value of what has been lost as a result of the peril insured (for example fire), and non-indemnity or 'contingency' insurance, which pays a sum on the occurrence of a specified event or contingency (for example death) on the basis not of any assessment of the value of what has been lost (the life) but of the amount stipulated in the contract. The amount stipulated depends simply on the amount of cover purchased.

In the case of non-indemnity insurance, the law is little concerned with the extent of loss. The claimant widow has 'lost' her husband. That is a general reference to the contingency, in that example the death. In the case of indemnity insurance, the law is very much concerned with the extent and nature of loss. The insured loss is the immediate effect of the peril on the thing insured—i.e. the subject-matter of the insurance, the car, the factory. Here, insurers speak of both loss *of* the car, which has been stolen, as well as loss *to* the car, which has been dented and which the insured retains but which has been damaged. In this book, unless otherwise indicated, loss refers to loss in both senses.

Insured loss, which is immediate and proximate, must be distinguished from less immediate 'consequential' loss to the insured, which is not covered unless the policy says it is. Loss insured under a motor-insurance policy covers the dent to the vehicle but not the dent in the insured's business profits because he cannot use it while it is being repaired. The dent to his pocket is not covered unless it is specified as the loss insured—usually referred to as 'business interruption' or 'consequential loss' cover—either in the contract of motor insurance or, more likely, in another contract of insurance altogether.

Insured loss must also be distinguished from other less tangible and less predictable effects on the insured. Tort damages may be awarded against a wrongdoer in respect of distress and suffering caused to the victim; a wrongdoer is in no position to contend that he should pay less because his victim was too soft. The insurer is not a wrongdoer. His position is that he is not bound to pay more than he has agreed to pay; and the usual interpretation of the contract of insurance is that he has not agreed to pay for this or any other kind of intangible loss because it is hard to predict and to rate. Insurance indemnity is confined to 'material' loss.

The exception is liability insurance, under which the insurer covers the insured's liability to others for the insured's torts and, of course, that liability may well extend not only to physical damage but also to distress and suffering. These are perhaps more predictable because they depend less on the sensitivity of the victim than on that of the court; as long as the award of the court is made not by a jury but by a judge, the insurer has some confidence that he can rate the risk profitably.

Caused by a Peril

The price of cover depends on the insurer's assessment of the likelihood and extent of loss from the peril insured. Assessment requires prediction on the basis of present data and past records. Records are useless without consistency in the categories of both cause (peril) and loss. Assessment, it has been said, requires a close connection between the peril and the loss, to exclude the more remote and more imponderable consequences; and this explains the basic rule that the insurer pays only for immediate or proximate loss. The explanation, however, tells only half the story. Less immediate 'consequential' loss can also be covered and is available on the market, but as a distinct category of loss at a distinct and higher price. So, the tight rule of remoteness, that limits recovery to loss that is proximate, is less a consequence of the requirement of predictability than of the way insurers classify and rate risk.

The close connection may be mechanical (cause x always leads to loss y) or statistical (if x, records show that there is a high incidence of y). In any case, whether he is concerned with perils he is willing to cover or perils he wants to exclude, the insurer needs a clear rule about the causal connection. The rule of law[1] which seems to meet his needs is that the loss must be proximately caused by the peril covered. If he makes a close examination of the decisions of the courts, however, he will find that the law is far from clear on the point.

Insurance law starts from an important and helpful premise. The entire exercise is one of contract construction; so, only perils or excepted causes actually mentioned in the policy are considered as possible causes. An important corollary is that, unless the contract

---

[1] The leading case is *Leyland Shipping Co. Ltd* v. *Norwich Union Fire Ins. Sy. Ltd.* [1918] AC 350. See further, Clarke, *Law of Insurance Contracts*, ch. 25.

very clearly states otherwise, the insured's own negligence, whether in the events leading up to loss or in his attempts to contain it, is not considered to be a relevant cause, and thus, unless the contract is clearly to the contrary (139 ff. above), does not prevent cover. If a cause mentioned in the policy occurs, when is it the proximate cause?

The answer given by one school of thought is an analytical answer in the form of (tentative) rules. First, if the kind of loss that has occurred was the *inevitable* result of a cause, whether a peril insured or an excepted cause, that cause is the proximate cause. Further, in the case of a peril, the insurer is liable for the full extent of the loss, although its extent may not have been inevitable, as long as it was not too remote. The application of this first and basic rule leads to more rules.

The second rule is that, if an insured peril leads inevitably to an excepted cause, and this leads inevitably to the loss, the loss is covered. If fire (covered) leads to an explosion (excepted) the effects of the explosion are covered. The third, however, is that, if an excepted cause leads inevitably to an insured peril and this leads inevitably to the loss, the loss is not covered. If under a fire policy an explosion (excepted) leads to fire, the fire damage is not covered. The fourth is that, if an insured peril operates concurrently (independently or interdependently) with an excepted peril, and together they lead inevitably to the loss, the loss is not covered. If the combined effect of a design defect in machinery on trial (excepted) and careless operation of the machinery by the insured owner (covered) is fire, the fire is not covered. Finally, as all these 'rules' are, strictly speaking, rules of interpretation of the contract, they may be changed by the contract so long as the change is clear: courts are not well disposed to changes that make the claimant's position even more difficult than it is.

In contrast, the answer given by another school of thought, led in the recent past by Lord Denning, is to dismiss intellectual abstraction, rigidity, and technicality. This school insists that causation is all a matter of common sense. Common sense, of course, defies instruction. Relatively speaking, it is easy to apply and hard to challenge, but also hard to predict in its effect. Whether common sense can be distinguished from the instinctive discretion of the judge and reduced to predictable principles is doubtful. In most cases, the proximate cause is clear enough. On the margins, however, the decisions can be reconciled only with the help of some phantasmically fine lines. For example, the Accidental Insurance Co. covered people against accidental death, unless caused by epileptic fits or by disease. When Mr Winspear had a fit while crossing a small river and was drowned, the claim against the company failed.[2] But when Mr Lawrence had a fit while standing on a station platform, fell under a passing train, and was killed the claim against the company succeeded.[3] It is hard to see how common sense would have predicted these decisions, although it might have been done, albeit with difficulty, with the aid of the fine lines of the 'analytical' rules. The ideas of insurance law about causation are not those of ordinary people. Some people tend to attribute events to things closest in space and time. Others select events or features that are out of the ordinary; this has some resonance with the law of tort but, as we have seen, little with insurance law, which is concerned only with construction of the insurance contract and the causes mentioned in it. The rules of insurance law can be hard to draw around future cases, as well as hard to explain to present clients, with the kind of confidence needed to go to court.

Marginal questions of causation are always difficult but, for all that, they can never be ignored or smothered by talk of common sense; that is fair neither to insurers, who must assess risk, nor in the end to the insured, who needs to know where he stands. The common-sense school of thought was once condemned by a cynic from the Chancery Division of the High Court as the last refuge of the intellectually idle. That goes too far. Nonetheless, the common sense school of 'thought' does not go far enough. The 'analytical' rules of the first school are better than no rules at all.

Common Perils

The loss insured must have been caused by an event, a 'peril', covered by the contract of insurance. Although the law assumes that the insured has read his policy (114 above), it is clear that most people do not until they try to claim, and that some do not read it even then.

---

[2] *Winspear* v. *Accidental Ins. Co. Ltd* (1880) 6 QBD 42.
[3] *Lawrence* v. *Accidental Ins. Co. Ltd* (1881) 7 QBD 216.

If a claimant does read his policy, he may not know what it means. Even among insurers there is division, for example in 1994, there was controversy over whether modems and fax machines can be regarded as 'contents' under a domestic house policy. The meaning of most wording, however, is well settled—among insurers: their understanding of what the words mean may not be quite what the lay person would expect.

Fire

The person who takes fire insurance may think that he (and his insurer) will recognize a fire when they see one. The farmer who sees billowing smoke with intense heat from his grain silo might think he has a fire on his hands, and doubtless the fire brigade would agree—but his insurer might not. The world of insurance, which is built on a mixture of tradition and pragmatism, is one in which there can be smoke without fire and in which some 'fires' are not fires at all.

First, however great the smoke and heat, fire does not include slow conflagrations from spontaneous combustion in vegetable matter, such as grain, caused by too much moisture in the matter. This is explained by the courts' resort to the dictionary, where the definition of fire is ignition and this requires not only heat but visible light, with the result that some fires, like that of the farmer, are not covered; and by the concern of insurers with causes rather than effects. Yet, if the farmer's grain is damaged by the water hosed on the insured fire at the silo next door in a bid to stop it spreading, his damage is covered by 'fire'. This is explained by the pragmatic concern of insurers with the best interests of the parties: hesitation with the hosepipe is in the interest of neither.

Secondly, fire does not include conflagration caused by explosion. So, if live coals fall on the farmer's carpet, the damage is fire damage, but if his boiler explodes, the consequent conflagration of his carpet and perhaps everything else is not—unless, as is common, the cover is expressly extended to explosions of that kind. The reason for the distinction between fire and explosion lies not only with the concern of insurers with causes but with the way that insurers have classified risk in the past and compiled the records, which are essential for assessing risks in the future. The risk of explosion in industrial premises was and is such that, for statistical and other purposes, it has always been classified separately. This is an instance of a recurrent feature of cover, that it may be defined less by reference to language and the understanding of laymen than to the traditional classification of risks by insurers.

Personal Accidents

In law, an accident occurs to the insured himself when he sustains an injury that he neither intended or expected. More precisely, there is an accident, first, when the injury is the natural or probable result to the person of the insured of a fortuitous and unexpected occurrence in the life of the insured, which is external to the person of the insured: 'for instance, where the assured is run over by a train, . . . or injured by a fall . . .; or . . . drinks poison by mistake, or is suffocated by the smoke of a house on fire; or by an escape of gas, or is drowned whilst bathing'.[4] Secondly, there is an accident when the injury is the fortuitous and unexpected result to the person of the insured of a cause that is a natural or probable occurrence in the life of the insured, which is external to the person of the insured:

for instance, where a person lifts a heavy burden in the ordinary course of business and injures his spine, or stoops down to pick up a marble and breaks a ligament in his knee, or scratches his leg while putting on a stocking, or ruptures himself while playing golf. In this case the element of accident manifests itself, not in the cause, but in its result.[5]

In law, illness or disease is not an accident. If a man swimming off Cap Gris Nez gets cramp and drowns, that is an accident. If a man at Cap Gris Nez cuts his foot on a rock, and dies from an infected wound, the cases suggest that that too is an accident. If, however, a man swimming off Cap Gris Nez is infected by untreated sewage and dies later in hospital, that is not accident; that is illness. But what of the man on the beach who takes too much sun and dies later in his hotel or in hospital? The Court of

---

[4] A. W. B. Welford, *The Law Relating to Accident Insurance* (2nd edn., London, 1932), 268 ff., quoted with approval in *De Souza* v. *Home & Overseas Ins. Co. Ltd* [1995] LRLR 453, 458–9 (CA).

[5] See Welford, n. 4 above.

Appeal[6] has told us firmly that that is not an accident but a case of disease. Why?

As our expectations of life and everything else rise, we feel more easily let down when life does not come up to scratch. The aches and pains we put up with in the past have become a condition, a medical condition, for which we expect treatment and cure. The man who, in 1900, might have died at sea, aged 40, and who might now reach the calmer but costlier waters of old age can be kept afloat. The life expectancy of a man in 1900 was 46; now it is 74. But, with the increase in the expectation of life has come an increase in cost. Medical treatment and medical insurance are big business and, to the insurer, medical insurance against illness and disease is something quite different from insurance against accidents; it is a risk of a different kind and a different magnitude. Indeed, a line must be drawn; however, it is drawn at a point that makes more sense to the insurer than to the insured. On one side of the line the man who drinks poison by mistake suffers an accident. On the other side of the line the man who drinks water contaminated by typhoid suffers illness. Nonetheless, the lay person might well echo the poet, Yeats, who spoke of 'the discourtesy of death'; it is lawyers rather than lay people who speak of death by natural causes.

All Risks

The words of cover, 'all risks', are ambiguous. To the insurer, the emphasis is on the second word, but the insured is likely to give more emphasis to the first. The insured will find, however, that he is not covered against each and every risk, but only those risks which, in the law's interpretation of the contract of insurance, are regarded as risks. All-risks insurance normally covers a risk but not a certainty.

In law, there is a certainty and not a risk, first, if loss is caused by the wilful misconduct of the insured; of course, the wilful misconduct of others, such as thieves, is a risk and is usually covered. Secondly, in the case of property insurance, there is a certainty and not a risk if loss is caused by ordinary wear and tear, depreciation, or 'inherent vice'. Inherent vice is deterioration in

---

[6] *De Souza* [1995] LRLR 453.

things as a result of natural processes in the things themselves, and in the ordinary course of events during the period of cover without the intervention of any fortuitous external accident. As one court put it: 'Foods rot; iron rusts; some wines simply do not travel well.'[7] Whether it is wear and tear or inherent vice, the significant feature is that the loss or damage was going to happen anyway. Another feature of wear and tear, but not of all cases of inherent vice, is that the loss or damage is something the insured should have expected from the start. In at least two respects, however, the law may not have been what the insured expected at all.

The first is that the insurability of the goods with reference to inherent vice is assessed afterwards with the hindsight wisdom of the court and, if necessary, of science. If, as the result of some internal and invisible defect, the goods were doomed from the start to damage or loss, that is not covered, whether the insured could or should have discovered this or not. Once again, the explanation appears to be that the exclusion of this risk from 'all' risks is what insurers intend; insurers then know where they stand, although the insured may not. 'The commercial purpose of the use of standard form policies (i.e, [*sic*] legal certainty as to the risk they cover) would be defeated if their construction varied from case to case according to the different circumstances.'[8] With these words, Lord Diplock rejected any reference to the actual knowledge of the particular insured. That was, in his view, one variable too many; but it is otherwise in other kinds of cover (Chapter 7 below), so why not here? Surely, if the number of insureds is large enough and the points of reference are in all cases the same, the insurers will have enough certainty to rate the risk. For the insureds the certainty that matters is that they have (or have not) cover and this they need to know at the beginning of their venture, and not months later when experts have had their say.

The second element of the unexpected concerns proof. One of the purposes of all-risks cover is to accommodate the insured who, for example, can prove that the goods have disappeared in distant parts but not how it happened. This purpose has been lost from sight, however, in some cases of 'wilful misconduct'. These are the cases in which there is a suspicion but not proof that the property

---

[7] *Perzy* v. *Intercargo Corp.*, 827 F Supp. 1365, 1370 (ND Ill., 1993).
[8] *Soya GmbH* v. *White* [1983] 1 Lloyd's Rep. 122, 125 (HL).

was deliberately destroyed or damaged by the insured. In these cases, there is a dilemma. If, as has been argued, wilful misconduct should be treated as an ordinary exception to cover, the insurer must prove the misconduct. If, however, wilful misconduct is seen as an obverse aspect of an essential feature of 'all risks' cover, then fortuity, and with it an absence of wilful misconduct, must be proved by the insured. The courts have resolved the issue and the dilemma by requiring that the evidence produced by the insured to establish cover does not *suggest* any misconduct.[9] Suggest to whom? Of course, to the court, and the more suspicious the court the more particularity it requires of the circumstances surrounding the loss and of possible causes. Some courts are more suspicious and more demanding than others. Even a wholly innocent insured may find it unduly hard to satisfy a suspicious insurer and, later, a suspicious court. So, in spite of the recognized purpose of all-risks insurance, uncertainty surrounding the circumstances of loss will always raise a degree of uncertainty about whether the insurer will pay.

Proving the Claim

In law, the claimant must prove the truth of his claim on the balance of probabilities. In practice, many claims, usually small claims, are paid without the required degree of proof. For example, the claimant may manage to convince the insurer that he lost his wallet on holiday, but to prove the amount of money in it at the time may be all but impossible. Nonetheless, the insurer may well pay the claim. Why?

According to one insurer, who sponsors cricket because of a connotation of fair play and honesty, the most important thing in the insurance business is trust. If the insurer pays an unproven claim, however, this may or may not be because he believes or trusts the claimant. Although insurers commonly invite the trust of the public (36 ff. above), it is a trust that is not often reciprocated. Suspicion of claimants among insurers and adjusters, their agents, seems to be a recognized occupational hazard. If the insurer pays an unproven claim, it may be because he trusts the broker, if there

---

[9] *British & Foreign Marine Ins. Co. Ltd* v. *Gaunt* [1921] 2 AC 41, 47, 52, and 58.

is one, handling the claim; or because the claim is small and to reject it would be at the cost of too large a loss of goodwill. Even routine investigation costs money; the cost may be out of proportion to what, if anything, may be saved. Bearing that in mind and also that claimants often have little notion of what is evidence of loss and what is not, one thoughtful innovation for small damage claims is this: the insurer sends the claimant a disposable camera capable of twenty-four shots and asks the claimant to use it on the damage and send it back.

Generally, as the sum claimed increases so does the insurer's distrust and the degree of proof that he requires of the claimant. Moreover, occasionally an insurer cracks the whip by fighting a small but suspicious claim, regardless of cost, *pour encourager les autres*. The distrustful insurer can do this because, whether the claim is large or small, the whip hand of the law and the tactical highground of litigation are his.

First, the insurer can defend the claim simply and 'cheaply' by doing nothing. The insurer can sit on his cheque book and wait for the claimant to prove his claim in full. In one instance a contents insurer demanded receipts for all 147 CDs claimed to be stolen. In another, a travel insurer, whose claimant had his wallet stolen fifteen minutes before boarding the coach to catch the plane back to England, insisted on the local police report required by the policy. In another, a disability claim arising out of psychiatric illness was rejected because the contract required diagnosis by a 'relevant registered medical specialist' but the claimant had been diagnosed by his general practitioner.

Secondly, for a more active defence, the insurer has various moves to test the strength of the claim or of the claimant's resolve. Against a fire claim, for example, the insurer may subpoena documents relating to the claimant's financial affairs. Against any claim, he may apply for security against the cost of proceedings. In Australia the Ombudsman found, on the part of claims investigators, 'a seductive show of concern for the insured, painting a frightening picture of litigation and costs, with no hope of success, in order to discourage the insured from pursuing the claim and persuading him to sign a release'.[10] Genn found something similar

---

[10] General Insurance Claims Review Panel, *Annual Report 1993* (Canberra, 1994), 12.

in England. She has spoken of the self-serving circularity of the arguments by insurers who, defending personal injury cases, assert the advantages for plaintiffs of settling their claims out of court. The plaintiff is advised to accept a discounted offer because he has been spared the stress of litigation—stress which the insurer deliberately exacerbates by use of legal procedure. This the insurer does, she contends, because it induces the plaintiff to settle cheaply.[11]

Thirdly, as well as money, the insurer has time on his side. Often the claimant has neither. In 1994 a conference on policy wording disputes was advertised to enable insurers and their lawyers to 'rigorously scrutinise all claims'. This led to an outcry in a wide range of newspapers. Understandably, insurers dislike this kind of press. When a particular claimant issued a press release with allegations of this kind, the insurer sought and obtained an injunction to stop him issuing further press statements of his version of his claim. However, newspaper stories do not run for ever; the insurer who is minded to block a claim has time on his side and is well placed to do so. In the United States, if the insurer is slow to pay without just cause, he is liable to pay large sums of punitive damages for 'bad faith'; but there is little or no legal sanction against the slow insurer in England: 209 ff. below.

Finally, the insurer has the advantage of experience and expertise. In the past the insurers' practice was to have claims investigated by their own claims inspectors or, if the claim was large or difficult, by loss adjusters.

Loss Adjusters

Loss adjusters are self-employed specialists in the handling and investigation of claims and, formally, are independent of the insurers that employ them. Adjusters say that they 'take care' of the claimant. Indeed, the industry view is that the availability of independent third parties to negotiate and settle claims is one of the great strengths which has been displayed by the UK insurance market; and that without loss adjusters it would be only the very

---

[11] H. Genn, *Hard Bargaining* (Oxford, 1987), 123.

largest companies that could afford to retain such expertise on their own staff. This traditional and rather rosy image of the adjuster is one which the insurance industry would like customers to share. But the independence and objectivity of the adjuster are open to question on at least two points.

First, it is doubtful whether the adjuster comes to a claim with an open mind. A letter from an insurance broker published in the same journal a few months later spoke of the 'never-ending tale of the impartiality of loss adjusters' and asked why, in reality, 'every loss adjuster starts from the point that every insurance claim is either fraudulent or at best grossly inflated?'[12] Indeed, one firm of adjusters advertised in a leading journal for insurers like this:

Missed A Trick? We won't. Getting to the bottom of a dubious claim isn't a job for amateurs. Professional experience, dogged determination and hard graft are what you need to question suspects, extract statements and build a body of evidence. Staffed by Ex-CID officers from all over the UK, our unit is an expert force. Unleash our detection skills and lateral thinking to crack your next case.[13]

Secondly, why, when the adjuster's investigation is complete, is the report drawn up by the 'independent' adjuster available to the insurer but not to the claimant? The answer is that, in reality and in law, the adjuster is the agent of the insurer; and according to the Chartered Institute of Loss Adjusters, it has been difficult for the profession to avoid the criticism that 'they only exist to beat the claim down'.[14] That is still the perception of many claimants, who view the adjuster with resentment and distrust.

To face the adjuster, seen as the champion of the insurer in this adversarial arena, the claimant today finds a champion of his own in the insurance assessor. In 1994, for an example, an assessor led a campaign in the money section of the *Daily Mirror* to 'take on' insurers, urging readers to 'stake a claim and rake in the benefits'. He too, projected an image of aggression ready for conflict. This new branch of the industry is unregulated and the standard of performance, it seems, variable.

[12] *Post Magazine*, 5 Jan. 1995, 10.
[13] *Post Magazine*, 7 July 1994, 7.
[14] *Post Magazine*, 28 Oct. 1993, 17.

The Reality of Fraud

Insurers believe, no doubt correctly, that they are paying out more than they have to. This belief has been encouraged by loss adjusters, who talk to them of 'leakage', including above all fraud, and of the need to 'audit' leakage—with the help of adjusters. Fraud, they say, is 'a national sport', in which insurers are 'fair game'. The fear of fraud and other 'leakage' is also fanned by the promoters of conferences, attendance at which will, said one, 'help you minimise your claims exposure by using law effectively' because, it is 'estimated that 35 per cent of claims received are invalid, either in whole or in part'. Is fraud really the big business they would have us believe?

Agreement is found in the industry that most fraud occurs under travel, motor, household, commercial contents and fire insurance. For example, 10–15 per cent of travel claims are believed by insurers to be fraudulent, at an estimated cost to insurers of £50 million a year. Research at Leicester University, published in 1994, indicated that at least 10 per cent of home-insurance claims could be described as fraudulent, whereas a survey by the Association of British Insurers (ABI) put them at 5.7 per cent of claims by number. As for fire, damage to property in the United Kingdom amounts to about £1.5 billion a year. The Arson Prevention Bureau has estimated that around 50 per cent of the cost of fire claims is due to arson; but that, of those actually convicted of arson, only about 6 per cent are fire insurance claimants. The main motive for arson is not fraud but revenge, and more than one third of the cases were 'accounted for' by mental illness, drugs, or alcohol. As for other lines, at the end of 1994, the ABI published the 'largest ever' survey of insurance fraud, which showed that the percentage of claims reckoned to be fraudulent was 5 per cent overall; and that fraud added on average nearly 4 per cent to the cost of insurance.

In addition to the fraud of claimants is that of third parties who spot an 'insurance job'. Garages stretch repairs to cars and private hospitals have reportedly charged as much as a pound to administer an aspirin. Hospitals abroad, for example in the United States, are said to have charged as much as 50 per cent more to the sick holiday visitor than to local residents for the same treatment.

In a survey of social attitudes in England, 3,000 people were asked about an exaggerated burglary claim. Only 6 per cent thought that there was nothing wrong in exaggeration, and the rest thought it wrong in varying degrees. Of course, that people think it wrong does not mean that they will not do it. Even so, the case against the public, that fraud is as endemic as the adjusters would have us believe, is not proven.

The Importance of Fraud

Whether or not fraud is really widespread, what is clear and what really counts is that insurers believe that fraud is widespread, and often approach claims in a spirit of suspicion. In view of the position of strength from which he considers a claim (164 ff. above), the insurer's perception of the claimant and his claim is crucial to the outcome.

The legal framework for claims assumes good faith and trust—on both sides. Society is reluctant to believe that claimants are fraudulent, and the law makes it hard for the insurer to prove that they are, but it also assumes the good faith of the insurer, with the result that, if he wants to, it is easy for him to drag his feet over payment. In the early 1990s one measure of commercial 'success' applied by insurers was the reduction of 'leakage', especially perceived fraud. The handling of claims to reduce fraud tended to seem complex, slow, and hostile.[15]

Matters were made worse because, in a climate of distrust, judgments about the 'stance' to be taken on the claim were often made at an early stage, and more on instinct than information. Many investigators of claims believed that they did not need proof of fraud as they have a 'nose' for it. Do they? One reason for the importance attached to oral evidence in the courts of common law is the belief that the experienced observer can indeed tell from the demeanour of witnesses whether or not they are telling the truth. Studies suggest, however, that this assumption is questionable.[16] Is there reason to think that insurance investigators, many of whom are former policemen, are better

---

[15] M. Clarke, 'Insurance Fraud' (1989) 29 *Brit. J of Criminology* 1–20, 4.
[16] W. A. Wagenaar *et al.*, *Anchored Narratives* (Hemel Hempstead, 1993), 188 ff.

judges of human nature and honesty than the courts? If not, the negative stance taken by the suspicious claims department is in the interest of neither the insurer nor the insured. It is not in the interest of the insured because it results in settlement that is slow, and perhaps for less than he should get. It is not in the interest of the insurer because it is not clear that the suspicious insurer really saves money. By stopping leakage in one place the insurer may spring a leak elsewhere. The money saved in the claims department may well be lost in the marketing department seeking new customers to replace those that have left in disgust at the way their claims were handled.

This may be why, most recently, there are signs that many insurers are having second thoughts about service. One leading insurer has published a 'customer service charter', and a central feature is speedy payment. This is the model found in Japan, where insurers measure the success of the claims department by the amount of goodwill generated with the public, by courtesy and speed of settlement.[17] It was also found in England in the more distant past and, hopefully, we are now seeing a welcome revival of the old ethos of service.

The Meaning of Fraud

The duty of good faith between insurer and insured is sometimes specified as the foundation, although not the only foundation, of the rule that a fraudulent claim by the insured defeats the claim and terminates the contract of insurance. This will surprise nobody; on the contrary, the point of claim is where one might expect the law to make the greatest demands of the honesty and good faith of the insured. What is surprising, however, is that the same rule of good faith, which demands so much of his memory for the purpose of disclosure when he makes the contract (83 ff. above), actually demands so little of his scruples when he makes a claim. Inflated claims and economy of truth are overlooked.

If the claim includes a statement which the claimant knows to be false, that is fraud; but if a false statement is made inadvertently or

---

[17] J. Itoh, 'The Challenge to the Future', *Geneva Papers on Risk and Insurance*, 72 (1994), 334–56.

carelessly it is not. Between these points there is the statement made recklessly, not caring whether it is true or false: that too is fraudulent. In contrast to common law fraud, however, an insurance claim is not regarded by insurance law as fraudulent unless it is wilfully false in a substantial respect.

Substantial Falsehood

The falsehood must be more than trivial; it must be material, i.e. 'substantial'. So, if a falsehood affects neither the readiness of the insurer to pay nor the amount, it is not material. If, for example, a claimant presents false evidence to bolster a valid claim, that is dishonest but not substantial: he is not seeking to get from the insurer money to which he knows that he is not entitled. Another reason suggested by American courts, which tend to be more hostile to insurers than those in the United Kingdom, is that to 'hold otherwise would encourage an insurer, after the loss, to continually attempt to question its insured in the hope of obtaining misstatements'.[18]

Wishful Thinking

Fraud requires a state of mind, but it is one which is hard to prove. Moreover, in view of the serious nature of an allegation of fraud, claimants are given the considerable benefit of quite small shreds of doubt. Wishful thinking may be foolish, but in law it is not fraudulent.

Accounts of accidents, for example, are notoriously unreliable, and no less so when they come from the persons most affected. Most people tend to believe that the cause of an event was what they would like to think it was or was one consistent with some preconceived idea of what the cause ought to be or to be likely to be.[19] If an event is charged with emotion, as is likely when the claimant insured is a victim, this affects the claimant's recall. Moreover, most people forget a great deal about events in the first

[18] *Longobardi* v. *Chubb Ins. Co.*, 560 A 2d 68, 83 (NJ, 1989).
[19] See, e.g., R. Nisbett and L. Ross, *Human Inference: Strategies and Shortcomings of Social Judgment* (Englewood Cliffs, NJ, 1980), 205 ff.; and Wagenaar, n. 16 above, 151–3.

few hours after they occur; this may well be marginal detail of little importance, but it may lead to manifestly inaccurate accounts later which make the less experienced investigator suspicious—unjustifiably perhaps, as the substance of the story and of the claim may still be true.

Wishful thinking is no less widespread where money is concerned. So insurance law overlooks the over-valuation of cherished possessions in contents claims. Over-valuation is scarcely discouraged by the practice, less prevalent today than in the past, whereby the insurer accepts the value put on lost jewellery by a jeweller who was chosen by the claimant and may reasonably hope for replacement business. Once upon a time, claims exaggerated in amount were regarded as fraudulent, but by 1937 we find no less a pillar of rectitude than Goddard J saying that 'mere' exaggeration 'is not conclusive evidence of fraud, for a man might honestly have an exaggerated idea of the value' of his goods.[20] The claim may be fanciful, but it is not for that reason fraudulent.

Exaggeration

On the one hand, in some instances such as claims for personal injuries where the real extent of loss will not be clear for some time, it is in the interest of everybody that the initial estimate should be pessimistic and err on the high side so that adequate money can be reserved. On the other hand, a culture has developed in which a degree of calculated untruth and exaggeration is regarded not as cheating but as bargaining. Some insurers see this as supporting their cynicism about society. But if, indeed, it is an aspect of the endemic evil of fraud, it is one which has been partly sown by the insurers themselves: many claimants feel that they have to inflate their claims because they will be beaten down by the insurer. Be that as it may, a line has to be drawn. In practice, a line has been drawn between knowingly claiming too much for things that have been lost, which is bargaining or 'mere' exaggeration, and knowingly claiming for things that have not been lost at all, which is fraud. Even so, there are problems about the practice.

First, although it has attractions as a rough but workable line in

---

[20] *London Assurance Co.* v. *Clare* (1937) 57 Ll.L Rep. 254.

most cases, in some, such as the stamp collection with thousands of items, it may be a very difficult line to draw. Secondly, arguably, the line of insurance practice does not match up to the law. Both law and practice agree that the person who claims for the loss of things that he or she knows are not lost commits fraud. But if, as seems to be the law, any claim made with intent to recover more than the claimant is entitled to is fraudulent, the exaggeration, which insurance practice does not regard as fraudulent, may be fraudulent in law. If a person takes a bargaining position by deliberately exaggerating the loss, hoping that to keep goodwill and cut costs the insurer will not dispute the claim, that, surely, is fraud.

If, indeed , people do not see or do not want to see this kind of claim as fraudulent, it may be undesirable to enforce law that is so far out of line with the *mores* of the time. This is the kind of conclusion that commentators have drawn from the consequences of the prohibition of the sale of alcohol in the United States in the first part of this century, and of the reluctance of English juries to convict reckless motorists when the offence charged was 'manslaughter': in each case the law was out of line, did not work and damaged the moral fabric of society. However, no unassailable empirical research in England shows that exaggerated insurance claims are of this kind. When convictions have been obtained, sentencing has been severe, but to prove fraud is difficult: 174 below. This may be why a recent case of exaggeration was so hastily summarized in the insurance press as confirming that a degree of deliberate exaggeration is acceptable in law, although the court said nothing of the kind. What the leading judgment said was that, of course, 'some people put forward inflated claims', especially house contents claims, 'for the purpose of negotiation, knowing that they will be cut down by an adjuster', but that in an insurance claim the court 'would not condone *falsehood of any kind*'.[21] Recent opinion polls suggest that most people would agree. The honest majority have begun to see a connection between increases in premiums and the rise in fraud. What the courts will not condone, however, the insurers may have to accommodate nonetheless because, apart from cases in which the

---

[21] *Orakpo* v. *Barclays Insurance Services* [1995] LRLR 443, 450, *per* Staughton LJ (emphasis added). See further Clarke, n. 1 above, 27–2.

degree of exaggeration speaks for itself, the fraud in the claimant's mind is hard to prove.

Proof of Fraud

Proof of fraud is hard. The imputation and the consequences are serious for the claimant. So the burden of proof on the insurer, although not the burden 'beyond reasonable doubt' of the prosecutor of crime, is somewhere on a descending scale between that and the 'balance of probability' required in ordinary civil cases. The precise point on the scale varies from case to case. If the allegation of fraud is that the insured fired his own property, that is serious and the burden is close to that of the prosecutor in a criminal case on the same facts, involving a high degree of probability. The more serious the allegation the higher the degree of probability to be established.

Understandably, insurers are reluctant to take on this task. The Consumers' Association has urged insurers not to absorb the cost of fraud and spread it, but to fight it.[22] But insurers are slow to spend the time and money required. Moreover, they are mindful of their own image with the public and of the perception of people in the past that insurers are there to pay them and not to police them. So, they grit their teeth and pay, or, if they do bare their teeth and refuse, it is usually on some ground other than fraud: 181 ff. below.

The Effect of Fraud

A fraudulent claim is a breach of the duty of good faith. Clearly, the claim itself is not one the insurer has to pay. Moreover, if a single claim is honest in part and fraudulent in part, the entire claim fails, the honest with the dishonest. As a point of public policy against fraud, fraud in any part of the claim corrupts the rest of the claim. Less clear is the effect of the fraud on the rest of the cover—on the insurance contract as a whole.

If the duty of good faith is broken by non-disclosure at the time of contracting, that breach entitles the insurer to avoid the contract altogether: 80 above. If the duty is broken by a

---

[22] *Which?*, Sept. 1993.

fraudulent claim, the consequence is the same. There is force in the view, however, that sometimes the consequence is out of all proportion to the breach. Moreover, if fraud is to be strictly defined and strictly censured, there may be a temptation for the claims inspector to scour large claims for small sins with which to end the contract although, as we have seen, this kind of crusade is in the best interests of neither claimant or insurer.

In other kinds of contract, discharge does not occur unless the relevant event, breach, or impossibility is objectively serious and substantial. However, an exception has always been made in general contract law for contracts which can only work properly if trust and confidence are maintained, such as contracts for personal services. Insurance, surely, is not unlike these. So, on balance, the current rule of insurance law, that *any* fraud in making the claim goes to the root of the contract and entitles the insurer to be discharged, can be justified. Fraud of any kind or dimension puts a new but darker light on the moral hazard and entitles the insurer to reconsider his position.

So, if a claim is fraudulent, the contract of insurance can be terminated at the option of the insurer. For the future, the effect is to terminate the insurer's primary duty to pay the current claim, but any secondary duties, such as a duty to arbitrate or settle an earlier honest claim, remain. For the past, if honest claim A is followed by fraudulent claim B, the contract may end but claim A remains enforceable; and the insurer cannot recover insurance money paid in respect of earlier loss, or even payments on account of present loss made prior to the fraud.

A problem arises when the insurance has been contracted by more than one person, and one is in breach of the duty of good faith but the others are not. The fraudster cannot sustain a claim, but what of the others? In the case of composite cover, a fraudulent claim by one insured does not affect an honest claim by the others.[23] In the case of joint cover, however, the traditional view has been that their interests are inseparably connected, so that loss or gain necessarily affects them all, and that, therefore, the fraud of one contaminates the whole insurance and bars a claim by the others. The partnership claim is polluted by the fraud

---

[23] On this distinction see *General Accident Fire & Life Assurance Corp. Ltd* v. *Midland Bank Ltd* [1940] 2 KB 318, 417 (CA).

of one partner. The wife's fire claim is defeated by the arson of her estranged husband, even though she was the intended victim of the fire and the defeat of her claim is victory of a kind for him. As with the claim by one single person, which is part honest and part dishonest, the traditional view was formed from the high ground of policy and principle, leads to some hard cases, and has been abandoned by courts in the United States and in Canada.[24] There the rule has become that the success of a claim by the innocent joint insured depends on the construction of the contract. No English court would argue with that, but, free of the constraints of policy and principle, courts over there have found more freedom to do what is thought fair and reasonable in the particular case.

Countering Fraud

Image Problems

The insurance industry agrees that its public image is geared very largely to the public perception of claims settlement. The industry is divided, however, on the best approach to take to fraud. In the past, insurers have tended to believe that to allege fraud by one insured goes down badly with the rest, even the honest majority; and that, if one insurer took a tough line, brokers would steer clients to another insurer who would not. Indeed, in 1994, the claims manager of a leading company warned a conference of loss adjusters of the harm done to the industry by claims handlers who, as he put it, 'look for a spine to shiver down' every time they pick up a claims file.[25] However, the spread of both insurance and consumerism to a wider section of society has made claimants more aggressive, and some, at least, deliberately play on the insurers' sensitivity about bad publicity.

Recent surveys, including a Gallup poll commissioned by the Association of British Insurers (ABI) in the same year, indicate that nearly 90 per cent of the public realized that a fraud on the insurer was a fraud on the honest majority of insured, and supported measures against it. That was why, in recent years, some insurers took a harder line on claims, but they found that

---

[24] e.g. *Scott* v. *Wawanesa Mut. Ins. Co.* (1989) 59 DLR (4th) 600 (Sup. Ct. of Can.).   [25] *Post Magazine*, 5 May 1994, 6.

indeed their image suffered. The *Today* newspaper in March 1994 reported a conference on resisting claims by reference to the 'small print' under the headline 'Twisters', and the *Sunday Times* also picked up the story with the 'Scandal of the insurance companies that love to say "No" ', speaking of 'crooks in bowler hats' who were 'in danger of taking over from the banks as the scourge of British society'.

The insurance industry responded to the newspapers with talk of a conspiracy between journalists and loss assessors who, it said, had a vested interest in reinforcing the misguided prejudices of policyholders and claimants towards insurers. However, it is interesting that it did not deny that the prejudices were there; indeed, an industry journal, in a leading article, admitted that behind 'the sensational headlines there is an underlying and widespread public concern that honest policyholders are not being dealt with fairly'.[26] Since then, however, some insurers, at least, have continued to pursue a compromise, much as before. They settle small claims with little investigation because of the cost, and fight large claims in the hope of finding grounds for denial, or exhausting the plaintiff and reducing the settlement.[27] They are more likely to pay £500 for the elderly Fiesta than £5 million for vintage Ferraris. As a means of fighting fraud this is said to be inefficient and counter-productive. First, some fraudsters have got a sense of the figure at which a small claim becomes a large claim and keep their claims below that amount. Secondly it leads to more fraud, because claimants inflate claims in the expectation that the insurers will dispute them.

Most important is that the manner in which insurers have sought to counter fraud has fostered a general atmosphere of distrust and created conditions which reinforce the distrust. A claimant who believes that he is being manipulated or outdone is a hostile claimant. That is not to suggest that fraud is caused by revenge; but it has been suggested that the main motive (greed) is backed by the sort of specious self-justification which says 'they weren't honest with me, why should I be honest with them?' Or, as one writer put it, 'the insurance companies are screwing their

---

[26] *Post Magazine*, 7 Apr. 1994, 7.
[27] J. Radcliffe, 'The Role of Central Databases to Counter Insurance Fraud' (1994) 84 *BILA Jo.* 42–8, 44.

customers therefore I shall screw them'.[28] Recent study of claims settlement shows that claimants become irrational and persist with claims that make no economic sense, in certain situations.[29] One is when they feel that they are being manœuvred by others and that, in effect, they have been left out of the settlement process. Another, the one most in point here, is when they feel, rightly or not, that they are 'losing the match', and in danger of getting significantly less than they are 'entitled' to. 'I paid £100 for my mobile phone so that is what I should get'—even though prices have dropped. Like fear about the safety of certain food products, the reaction may be quite unjustified, but what counts in the insurance market is that it is there.

Moreover, if, as he sees it, one claim is beaten down, the claimant is resentful and more likely to exaggerate the next time. The Treaty of Versailles which ended the First World War was one of the causes of the Second. Rubbing noses in dust is no way to make peace or to maintain friendship for a future relationship based on good faith. In other words, the language of social psychology, when people find themselves in an inequitable relationship, they become distressed and, by one means or another, attempt to eliminate their distress by eliminating the inequity. Be that as it may, it seems that in too many cases the distrust between insurers and insured is now mutual, and is impeding the equitable and efficient settlement of claims.

Better Information

Widespread agreement exists that to combat crime, whether fraud or anything else, there must be efficient detection. Detection requires information. Current measures include registers of stolen property. For example, an estimated forty to fifty yachts disappear every day in the EU. A central European register of stolen yachts has been set up by the Marine Intelligence Exchange (MIX), a mutual association of loss adjusters formed to disseminate information about marine theft, run by a loss adjuster in the United Kingdom. Another is MIAFTR, the Motor Insurance Anti-Fraud and Theft Register, a central UK record of stolen cars

---

[28] See M. Gill (ed.), *Crime at Work* (Leicester, 1994).
[29] R. Korobkin and C. Guthrie, 'Psychological Barriers to Litigation Settlement', 93 *Mich. L Rev.* 107–67 (1994).

In 1994, the recovery rate for cars was about 30 per cent but, although larger and more conspicuous, it was only 5 to 8 per cent for contractors' plant. Since November 1994 there has been a register for that too.

All this helps at the point of claim, but loss registers are but a catalogue of the horses that have bolted. More attention is now being paid to information at an earlier stage, in particular information about the 'stable'. The key to underwriting profitability, whether it be private or commercial, is often the moral and other standards of the insured. Fearing that interrogation of the proposer puts people off and is no way to sell insurance, the tactic has been one of oblique inquiry. For example, Equifax Europe is a database that allows insurers to determine an individual's financial status and personal lifestyle classification, the assumption being that there is an established connection between 'financial stress' and extravagant spending, on the one hand, and fraudulent or inflated claims on the other.

A further but related tactic is mainly aimed at the recovery of stolen property, but it is also connected to moral hazard. For example, one offer of cover has a discount on highly valuable goods, such as fine arts and antiques, on condition that they are registered with photographs. For more mundane property such as televisions, videorecorders, computers, fishing tackle, bicycles, and caravans, selected items can be tagged with a barcode and a postcode and registered on a central database, the National Property Register. The idea is not only that the register aids recovery of property lost, but that the sort of person who is willing to take time and trouble to comply is a better risk.

In addition to property registers insurers now have a validation service, which values property accurately. This is aimed at the exaggerated claim but also reduces the cost of handling claims: it replaces the former practice of meeting a claim for consumer durables, for example, by ringing around the local shops and making guesses. One validation service has a database of over 50,000 items, including 1,800 models of television sets. For a fee, the insurer can access the database on-screen and check the figures submitted by the claimant or, if the claimant is vague about the model or item lost, work out what it was. Then the same validation service can be used to replace the item from a network of chosen retailers.

The new practice ensures business for the retailers and is a guarantee of sorts that the retailers are sound. If, nonetheless, the replacement is defective, the claimant has rights against the insurer in the insurer's role as supplier, but does he have an enforceable contract with the retailer? Some sort of guarantee may be offered, expressly or impliedly, by the retailer, but what (consideration) does the retailer get in return from the insured? The retailer was chosen not by the insured but by the insurer. What does the retailer get from the insured? The answer lies in the fact that, if the practice is to work for the benefit of all concerned including the retailer, it is one in which it takes not two, but three, to tango. The consideration lies in the insured's co-operation in the commercial triangle, without which the retailer cannot get the payment he wants from the insurer; 48 above.

For the insurer, however, the best protection against fraud (because it is extensive and does not need the co-operation of the insured) is the Claims and Underwriting Exchange (CUE). This is a database, started in November 1994 by the ABI to check statements made in claims with what the claimant said in his proposal. CUE also records claims so that past claims can be scanned for any patterns that arouse or justify suspicion. Indeed in 1996 it was reported that most (90 per cent) of the insurers using it did so not at the time of underwriting but at the point of claim. Once the public is aware of it, a deterrent effect on doubtful claims is likely. Some sensitivity has been shown, as there have already been protests in, for example, the *Sunday Times* about 'black lists of black sheep'. Although nothing in law requires it, industry announcements are that data will not be entered unless and until policy-holders consent; and that if claimants are concerned about the content of their entries, they can write to the company set up to operate CUE and request copies. This possibility is not mentioned to the insured, however, and perhaps it should be. Moreover, as regards consent, so far the practice of some insurers seems to be simply to tell the insured that the data entry is being done and infer his consent from his silence.

Reinstatement

If, instead of paying cash, the insurer can insist on replacement or reinstatement of property, fraud is less of a temptation to the insured. For buildings, the insurer has a right of reinstatement under the Fires Prevention (Metropolis) Act of 1774: he can insist on reinstatement of buildings on mere suspicion, without proof, of arson, but, in practice, few insurers insist on reinstatement and few insured are aware that they may. A right of this kind is now found as an express term of contents cover, however, and, it seems, insurers are enforcing it.

A related measure is to ensure that the repairer or supplier of property is chosen by the insurer rather than the insured. This can cut the cost to the insurer in two ways. First, if the things or services are required often enough, the insurer can arrange a discount with the supplier thus 'paying', let us say, an insurance indemnity of £500 with something that only cost him £400. Secondly, as regards repairs, in the past insurers felt at the mercy of the conspiratorial wink by the claimant to the repairer, such as a garage, that said 'insurance job'. Evidently, insurers choose repairers who, they believe, do not do this. Further, some insurers monitor the repairers or even run their own repair centres. Indeed, in some cases, a video camera in the garage of an approved repairer enables the insurer's own engineers to monitor the extent of damage and the progress, nature, and quality of repairs. If the work is not done properly, the insurer may be liable to the insured: 193–4 below.

Technical Defences

If convinced that a claim is suspect but unable to meet the difficult task of proving fraud, the insurer may block the claim on other more 'technical' grounds; and, in England and abroad, the public has been made aware of this. In Germany, strikingly, the common insurance market has been presented as an open door through which the German consumer is threatened by Celts and Angles with cut-price insurance—cheap, it is said, because under English law insurers who do not want to pay do not have to pay.[30] This picture cannot be lightly dismissed. Although it is contrary to the tradition of English law that one party should have a large measure of discretion about whether to perform his contract or not, an

---

[30] H. E. Gumbel, 'Neue Vertriebswege und das Beispiel des britischen Versicherungsmaklers' [1992] VersR 1293–336, 1301.

English judge with considerable experience in the field has described English law as 'probably the most favourable to insurers of any in the world'.[31] The two most tried and trying of the technical defences available to the distrustful insurer concern notice and disclosure.

Notice

As we have seen (129 above), one type of insurance 'condition' is that which confers no direct benefit on the insurer but is mainly designed to make the rest of the contract work. Prominent among these are 'procedural' conditions such as that requiring notice of loss, usually notice to the insurer via his local agent. A term like this will be implied as a matter of common sense as well as common law but, in any event, it is common for the contract to contain an express term about notice of loss. These terms pose problems of construction.

Reasonable Notice

If the term requires something like 'immediate' notice or 'notice as soon as possible', these words are construed not literally but sensibly, in favour of the claimant, as meaning 'reasonable' notice. This is in line with the Statement of General Insurance Practice, clause 29a, which prescribes notice 'as soon as reasonably possible'. Whether notice is reasonable or not depends on striking a balance between the interests of the parties.

On one side the claimant needs time to discover that the loss has occurred, that there may be cover, and what to do about it. In *Verelst*,[32] for example, the insured knew she had life cover, but she did not tell anyone else. Having died, she was not in a position to notify the insurer, and nor was anyone else, so it was a year before her family discovered the policy and gave notice. In spite of the delay, the notice was held reasonable. On the other side, the insurer wants notice as soon as possible. His concerns are to test the claim before the evidence disappears, to mitigate the extent of

---

[31] J. Mance, 'Insurance Brokers Negligence' (1993) 82 *BILA Jo.* 32–53, 40.
[32] *Verelst's Administratrix* v. *Motor Union Ins. Co.* [1925] 2 KB 137. See Clarke, n. 1 above, 26–2.

loss, and, if the claim is very large, to make appropriate financial arrangements. Notice is reasonable or not according to the comparative weight of these considerations. In *Verelst* the effect of late notice on the insurer was slight, but the effect of non-payment on the family would have been serious.

Seven Days' Notice

If the term requires notice within a specified period, for example seven days from the loss, the court's hands are tied: it cannot construe seven days as eight days or more. In *Evans*,[33] disablement cover required notice of any disabling event within ten days and, although the insured had been seriously ill in hospital throughout the notice period, notice later was held to be too late. This was an early Canadian case, but English courts are unlikely to decide differently today, unless the insured is a consumer and a case can be made against such a term under the Unfair Terms in Consumer Contracts Regulations: 235 below. In other cases, it is still likely to be the English court's perception of its role to apply contracts as they are written; it is for the parties to write the contract, not the court. Contrast, for example, Swiss law, which provides (Versicherungsvertragsgesetz, Article 38) that late notice has no adverse effect on the claim unless the claimant was at fault or the insurer can prove that the delay in notice was fraudulent, and only in the latter case of fraud does the claim fail altogether.

Swiss law appears to be concerned with judging the conduct of the claimant rather than responding to the concerns of the insurer. In other countries a rule is found that is more flexible than the English rule and perhaps more balanced than the Swiss. In these countries the argument runs that terms like this should be construed in the light of their purpose; and that, therefore, late notice should not defeat the claim as long it causes the insurer no prejudice. The argument is supported by considerations of fairness and such a rule is found, for example, in Australia (Insurance Contracts Act, section 54), Belgium (Act of 1992, section 19 ff.), France (Code d'assurance, Article L113–2 al.4) and Germany (Versicherungsvertragsgesetz 6). In the United States, there appears to be no legislation on the point, but the courts have addressed it nonetheless and are divided; for late notice to defeat

---

[33] *Evans* v. *Railway Passengers* (1912) 3 DLR 61.

the claim, prejudice is required in California, for example, but not
in New York.

In England, however, the prejudice argument was rejected in
Pioneer.[34] Bingham J was not bound by precedent, but he thought
that a requirement of prejudice would not be in accord with
'general contractual principle'. Indeed, if, as in that case, notice in
time is expressed to be a 'condition precedent', words well known
to the law, the condition is strict and prejudice is irrelevant:
132 ff. above). If those words are not used, however, there is
ambiguity enough to give room for argument.

The more absurd the effect of a literal construction of words,
whatever they are, the harder the court will strive to find
ambiguity—even when the only evidence of ambiguity is the
absurdity itself—because the less reasonable the effect the less
likely it is that the parties intended it: 118 above. True, this kind
of argument was rejected in *Pioneer*, but the decision is not a
binding precedent and, anyway, the case was one in which there
was some prejudice to the insurer; it is hard to believe that the
argument will not be better received by a court today. In practice,
however, that may never arise because insurers relax the notice
requirement. They are likely to insist on its terms only when they
have reasons other than prejudice to refuse payment, such as
suspicion of fraud, and such cases rarely get as far as a hearing in
court. The practice is sensible, perhaps, but, it being a matter of
discretion, once again we find a needless source of uncertainty in
the practice of insurance.

Non-Disclosure

Usually, non-disclosure is not discovered until a claim is made
and, for example, the claim form is checked against the original
proposal. Checking has been greatly facilitated by modern
methods of storing and retrieving data. If the insurer decides to
raise a defence of non-disclosure, it may be as a provisional tactic
to test the good faith of the claim: a formal letter is sent, which
refers to the non-disclosure and refuses payment. If no more is
heard of the claim, that is that. If the claimant protests, some

---

[34] *Pioneer Concrete (UK) Ltd* v. *Nat. Employers Mut. Gen. Ins. Assn. Ltd* [1985]
2 All ER 395.

insurers see protest as suspicious, a sign of guilt, and maintain refusal; but others see it as a sign that the claim is genuine, reconsider, and negotiate.[35] In any event, it is clear that, in the past, insurers have used the defence to refuse payment when they suspected fraud but could not or did not want to prove it. Indeed, in 1992 the advice given to insurers by the Arson Prevention Bureau, in a booklet entitled *Fraudulent Arson*, was that where 'confirmatory evidence is not available or may not be available without incurring substantial expense always bear in mind other defences', such as non-disclosure and misrepresentation. This possibility is undoubtedly beneficial to insurers but not at all to the insured. It gives insurers what Lord Templeman in *Pan Atlantic* called, '*carte blanche* to the avoidance of insurance contracts on vague grounds of non-disclosure supported by vague evidence'.[36] It is most damaging to the certainty of cover that every honest insured is entitled to seek from his insurance.

People also feel that the dice are loaded and the game less than fair. People no longer take their losses on the chin, and those who have employed a broker may well recover from the broker, who has failed to warn them of what the law of disclosure required, what they have failed to recover from their fire insurer. In such cases, the chicken has come home to roost, but in a different sector of the insurance market. There is some satisfaction in the irony of this, but it is also wasteful.

Education

Finally, an obvious measure against fraud is to 'educate' people about fraud. As for insurers, the Arson Prevention Bureau offers them advice on dealing with claims believed to be fraudulent. Recent falls in the cost of fire claims were attributed partly to the work of the Bureau. Further afield, the Insurance Fraud Bureau of Massachusetts has set up an Insurance Fraud Research Register. Its objects are to encourage the study of insurance fraud, and to identify available information on the subject. As for the public, the ABI has recognized the need to counter the perception that

---

[35] I. Cadogan and R. Lewis, 'The Scope and Operation of the Insurance Practice Statements' (1992) 2 *Ins. L & P* 107–111, 109.

[36] *Pan Atlantic Ins. Co. Ltd* v. *Pine Top Ins. Co. Ltd* [1995] AC 501, 515.

insurance fraud is not really criminal, that it is a victimless crime like tax evasion or a sport like the smuggling described in Compton Mackenzie's *Whisky Galore*. The public is not a ready audience for such a message, and the ABI has to seize what opportunities it can to attract people's attention to the real social gravity of fraud.

Recoverable Loss

Under the rules about causation (157 ff. above) the insurance indemnity is restricted to loss which is effectively an inevitable result of the peril insured. The indemnity differs from damages in that the insurer does not pay 'consequential' loss—does not pay for types of loss suffered by the claimant which, although not inevitable, were consequences that the reasonable person would foresee (the tort rule) or contemplate (the contract rule). In *Theobald*,[37] for example, the claimant's accident insurance covered medical expenses but not his (very foreseeable) loss of earnings: if the railway had been sued, whether for negligence or breach of contract, its liability would have extended to both. As in tort, however, the object of indemnity under insurance contracts is to restore the fortunes of the insured as if the insured loss had not occurred—with the following reservations.

The amount of the insurance indemnity is a sum less than the actual loss suffered by the claimant insured, not only in cases of consequential loss like *Theobald*, but also if (a) he cannot prove the amount of his loss, or (b) his loss is greater in amount than the ceiling on recovery stated in the policy, or (c) he has agreed, reluctantly perhaps, to be his 'own insurer' for part of the loss. A commonplace example of (c) is the 'excess' in motor insurance. Both (b) and (c) remind us that it is mainly the contract of insurance that determines the loss assumed and distributed by the insurer, and that the contract is likely to indicate a sum less than the insured's actual loss. What a contract of indemnity cannot do, however, is to promise him more than that: there is a substratum of public policy (23 above) that the insured should not recover a sum manifestly greater than his actual loss. Evidently, in

---

[37] *Theobald* v. *Railway Passengers Assurance* (1854) 10 Ex. 45.

particular cases importance attaches to the measure of actual loss.

The Measure of Loss

If the claimant has been deprived of property, for example his car has been stolen, the measure of his loss is the cost of replacing it. If the car is recovered soon but damaged, and if he had been planning to sell it, his loss is the difference between its market value before and after the damage. If he was not planning to sell it but to use it, his loss is the cost of making it usable—the cost of repair.

When the cost of repair is high, it may be cheaper to abandon what remains of the car and for the insurer to pay the cost of purchasing a similar car. This is the rule of marine insurance law, the rule of 'constructive total loss'. It is not the rule for other branches of insurance, although a contract term to that effect may be inserted and, if so, will be enforced. In any event, it is sometimes the sensible course to take.

In *Dominion Mosaics*,[38] the claimant's business premises were severely damaged by fire. The normal measure of indemnity would have been the cost of rebuilding but, if the claimant company had waited for that, it would have lost a lot of business; so, the company took the quicker course of purchasing alternative premises, and recovered the purchase cost. In that case the action was against the wrongdoer responsible for the fire, but the recovery would have been the same against his fire insurer. In *Dominion Mosaics*, as it turned out, the cost of the alternative purchase was less than the cost of rebuilding. If, however, the cost of alternative premises had been greater than the cost of rebuilding, the award might well have been the same against a wrongdoer, but would it have been the same against the insurer?

One argument against recovery is that, when the cost of the alternative factory is higher than that of rebuilding the original factory, the insurer is paying more than he has to. The force of this argument depends on what he has to pay, which turns on the

---

[38] *Dominion Mosaics & Tile Co. Ltd* v. *Trafalgar Trucking Co. Ltd* [1990] 2 All ER 246 (CA).

contract and on what exactly is insured. If it is the loss to the insured, then the insured may well reply that the indemnity is the sum that puts him, the claimant, in as near as can be the position he would have been in if the loss had not occurred; and that this is the sum that restores him as soon after the damage as possible, even if that is more costly for the insurer. If, however, as is more likely, what is insured is not the loss to the insured but the loss of the property, the insurer surely has force in the argument that the measure of loss insured is the cost of repairing the actual property (later) and not that of buying a similar but different property (sooner).

A further argument is that, if the insurer paid the (higher) cost of the alternative factory, in effect, fire cover would have been extended to business interruption cover which, *ex hypothesi*, was not the risk insured. The logic of a contention like this is equally sound, although perhaps less palatable, in the mouth of a medical insurer who declines to pay for costly medical treatment which would shorten the time that the insured was unable to work. The flaw in the argument, however, is the assumption that fire or any other kind of insurance of tangible property does not and should not have the effect of paying, quite incidentally, the cost of preventing loss of business as opposed to paying for the loss itself. This is the incidental effect of many kinds of insurance indemnity, about which there is no dispute, such as the payment for the stolen van which also prevents (further) loss to the van owner's business.

Problem: The Cost of Cutting Losses

The Insured

Insurers sometimes talk as if the insured has a duty to cut or mitigate loss. In law, the insured has no such duty unless the contract imposes one in very clear terms: 139 ff. above. On the contrary, insurance law starts from the assumption that one of the usual purposes of insurance is to cover the insured against his own negligence; and, in this, no clear line has been or can be drawn between negligence leading up to loss and negligence in mitigating it once some loss has occurred. If the insured does mitigate loss, all well and good, but, even then, the position is not without problems in law.

Suppose that a house, 'Casa Roma', is damaged by fire and that the insured brings in engineers, who prevent the collapse of part of the original building, thus reducing the insurer's liability to pay in due course the cost of repairing it. Most people would expect the insurer to be liable to pay the engineers' bill but, in law, this is far from clear.

Against liability is the argument that the loss insured was loss to the building and not the bill, which is consequential loss to the insured's pocket, and hence (188 above) not covered. Moreover, argument by analogy with tort indicates a clear though controversial line between physical damage, such as damage to a building, for which a wrongdoing builder may be liable, and the cost of preventing the development of physical damage, for which the builder is not liable: the cost of prevention is 'pure economic loss', which is a different kind of damage and for which, in general, there is no liability in tort.

Tort, replies the insured, is irrelevant. What counts is the construction of the contract. Strictly speaking, that is correct, but the reason for the distinction between physical damage and 'pure economic loss' is not confined to tort. It stems from the fear that liability may be boundless and crippling and, for the insurer therefore, hard to rate. As a matter of contract, an insurer with such concerns on his mind may indeed intend to exclude the costs of prevention; the insurer, who wants to control the degree of risk assumed, may well be wary of extravagant expense authorized by a distraught insured to save his cherished possessions. The insurer does not want the insured to fiddle while 'Casa Roma' burns, but nor does he want the insured to hire men who put out oil fires in Kuwait.

What the insured will have had in mind is likely to be different. First, indeed he does not want to stand idly by while 'Casa Roma' burns, not only because that is prodigal but also because he may well be fond of it and want to save it from the flames. Secondly, he may remember that one of the heroes of recent television advertisements is the insurer, the insurer who comes to the rescue not just with money but with help to prevent future or further loss. From this the insured infers that, if a stitch in time saves nine, the insurer will be only too happy to pay for it. Indeed, he may recall that a part of the service offered by some insurers is emergency work, and he may not see why the insurer should be prepared to pay for that but not for the local plumber who comes more quickly and perhaps costs less. Thirdly, as the fire is normally covered even though it was caused by the insured's negligence or *aggravated* by his (negligent) response once it has started (158 above and 216 ff. below), the insured might find it odd if he were not covered for the cost of trying to *mitigate* the extent of the loss, especially if he was successful. Both common sense and common interest suggest to the insured that he should 'do something', and that, provided perhaps that he does not do something patently silly, the cost of his action should at least be shared with the insurer.

Clearly, this is an issue between insurer and insured. Some countries have rules that require the insured to do something. For example, German law (VVG, Articles 62 and 63) imposes a duty to mitigate loss and also stipulates that expenses, which the insured was justified in regarding as 'necessary under the circumstances', shall be paid by the insurer. A similar rule is found in Switzerland: VVG, Article 70. Further afield, a similar rule is found in Israel as regards 'reasonable expenses': Insurance Contract Law 5741–1981, section 61; and in the United States the current trend of the cases is in that direction. Expenses 'necessarily incurred in the course of mitigating damages are recoverable by an insured'.[39] In England, however, it is not at all clear that common sense is confirmed by common law. If the contract says that the cost is covered, indeed, it is covered: but what if the contact is silent?

In fire insurance, the damage done by pouring water and taking other measures to prevent fire damage is covered, provided that the risk of fire (or more fire) damage is imminent. These measures, however, can be seen as part of the traditional definition of fire cover, rather than as a distinct head of insured loss, or the application of a general rule about prevention. Moreover, arguably, the cover is limited to indemnity for physical damage inflicted to stop fire and does not extend to expense which, as a head of loss, looks like something quite different. If, however, the fire rule is an application of a more general principle, as has been suggested, what may that be?

One possibility lies in causation and the view that the measure of

---

[39] *Curtis O. Griess & Sons* v. *Farm Bureau Ins. Co.*, 528 NW 2d 329, 334 (Neb., 1995).

prevention is 'proximately caused' by the peril insured. This explanation carries some conviction when the measures are required by contract or they occur automatically (e.g. fire sprinklers) or, being measures decided by the insured himself in the face of the peril, the decision itself is not regarded as a relevant cause: 158 above.

Another possibility is that the cost is, after all, insured loss—not loss covered expressly but loss covered by implication. In one case,[40] a standard term of the cargo insurance obliged the insured to minimize loss but said nothing about who bore the expense. The insured started proceedings against the carrier responsible for the loss and recovered the cost of these proceedings from the cargo insurer on the basis of an implied term necessary to give the contract business efficacy. If and when the insurers paid for the damaged cargo, they would be subrogated to the rights of the insured against the carrier and would be entitled to take over the insured's proceedings against the carrier; and after payment, certainly, the insurers would bear the cost of the litigation. Unless the insurers were also responsible for the costs incurred earlier, they would have an incentive to delay payment of the indemnity. 'Business efficacy', i.e. commercial common sense, required an implied term that removed any such incentive. It is this commercial common sense that suggests the answer. When, as is the current trend in household cover, the insurer specifies a 'helpline' to the assistance of a repairer, plumber, or other handy superman chosen by the insurer, the insured must comply. Otherwise, an appropriate implied term is that the insured shall recover costs of prevention, perhaps only those reasonably and not foolishly incurred; and not only in cargo insurance but in other branches of insurance too.

The Insurer

Salvage

Salvage activity by insurers and others has a long history. A Dutch ordinance of 1769 prohibited the populace from prowling on beaches at night or during storms, with axes, hammers, and saws.

---

[40] *The Mammoth Pine* [1986] 3 All ER 767 (PC). But cf. *Lancashire Water Services Ltd* v. *Sun Alliance* [1997] CLC 213 (CA). See Clarke, above n. 1, 28–85.

The London Fire Brigade, formed in 1861 after the catastrophic Tooley Street warehouse fire, was partly financed by the fire offices. These offices also formed the London Salvage Corps to conserve property threatened by fire. More recently, when theft of cars in the United Kingdom reached epidemic levels, one measure to assist recovery and, incidentally, detection was the installation of a chip that enabled a stolen vehicle to be rapidly located. Another chip the size of a grain of rice is available for a range of property from bicycles to jewels. Such measures have been actively supported by insurers.

The legal doctrine of salvage applies only to marine insurance, but the non-marine insurer too may want to pick up any pieces and save what he can. The insurer has a right to the pieces as a matter of 'equity', whereas the insured does not. On the contrary, if the insured gets enough insurance money to buy something new, he must give up what is left of the old, lest, contrary to the basic principle of indemnity, he ends up better off than if the loss had not occurred. In practice, the insurer may let him have the thing back, but only if he pays for it.

If what is left is a poisoned chalice that nobody wants, what then? Is the insurer obliged to take it? If the lorry is leaking toxic chemicals, whose responsibility has it become? In early cases some judges indicated that ownership of abandoned insured property vested automatically in the insurers. But the law, as restated in the Marine Insurance Act, section 63(1) was that the insurer was 'entitled' to the property. One judge thought that section 63(1) meant that the property belonged to nobody, but the balance of opinion now is that, if the insurer does not take the property, it and the responsibility for it remains that of the insured.[41]

Advice to Mitigate Loss

Some insurers have anticipated the situation by pressing their insured to work out a plan for contingent action after the insured event, for example, a business continuity plan for the aftermath of a bomb or a fire. In other cases, there is little doubt that insurers give advice and assume some degree of responsibility after loss has occurred. Indeed, to distinguish their cover from cheap direct

[41] R. Goff and G. H. Jones, *The Law of Restitution* (4th edn., London, 1993), 615.

insurance, some speak of 'assistance insurance', of providing 'immediate help to remedy the immediate problem, even to save life'. To the extent that the insurer has assumed responsibility for the situation, he owes the insured a duty of care actionable, if not in contract, in tort: 144 ff. above.

Disincentives and Discounts: The Insurer as Supplier

In the main, the insurer pays (insurance) money to the insured; but sometimes, as we have seen (181 above), the insurer is entitled to have the thing repaired or rebuilt, or to see that the thing lost is replaced. The main purpose of this is to deter the insured who wants to convert his VCR into cash for something else. But reinstatement also affects honest claimants, the majority, many of whom find it frustrating. First, the belief is still widespread that claimants have a 'right' to cash. Secondly, more to the point, a feature of a consumer society is that upwards of 70 per cent of the items claimed are no longer manufactured at all or in quite the same form. Replacement with an equivalent item requires thought and consultation and, therefore, cost. Many claimants have a very particular and more informed idea than their insurer about what kind of replacement, if any, is equivalent and meets their needs. Such claimants resent being given no say in the matter—not least because, in the campaign against 'leakage', some insurers have arranged discounts with certain suppliers and, inevitably, this limits the range of replacements available. Moreover, the arrangement faces the claimant with a supplier who has an interest in insisting that chalk can be replaced by cheese, because the supplier happens to sell cheese. Worse, some insurers have used the threat of unwanted replacement to ensure a discounted cash settlement. The insurer's right to insist on a particular supplier or repairer is open to abuse and therefore it has been prohibited, for example, in Mississippi: Mississippi Code Annotated, section 83–11–501. Not so in England. What insurers gain in cutting costs they appear to be losing in goodwill.

Moreover, the insurer may lose more than goodwill. The insurer, if he insists on replacement or repair, whether from his 'own' supplier or not, has assumed the role of supplier under the insurance contract and is liable for the quality of the goods or services provided. First, in the case of repair, he guarantees, collaterally and implicitly, that the chosen repairer is competent. Secondly, although it seems that the insurer is not liable as one who 'agrees to carry out a service' under section 12 of the Supply of Goods and Services Act 1982, common law states that, when the insurer decides that the insured property should be repaired, the contract of insurance becomes a contract 'for reinstatement' and that the insurer is obliged not just to appoint a competent contractor to do the work but to assume responsibility for the quality of the work itself. More than that, common law regards it as a contract to complete the work, however difficult or expensive it becomes, within a reasonable time. Indeed, one motor insurer has been offering a three-year guarantee on repairs carried out by repairers appointed and remunerated directly by the company. Further, by analogy, if the insurer replaces old goods with new he has the responsibility of a seller under the Sale of Goods Act 1979, and of a supplier under Part 1 of the Consumer Protection Act 1987.

Compromise and Settlement of Claims

When an insurer 'settles a claim', that usually refers to the process whereby the insurer considers and pays an insurance claim. Distinguish that from the settlement of a disputed insurance claim, whereby the insurer and the claimant, who cannot agree about what is payable under the contract of insurance, make a new contract of compromise to settle the amount payable. The distinction matters because, if the insurer later thinks he paid too much by mistake, he will find it harder to get money back in the second case than in the first. Equally, if the claimant thinks later that he agreed to take too little, he may well find it harder to get more in the second case of compromise than if he had accepted the insurer's first offer. Settlements, which we refer to here in the second sense of the contractual compromise of claims, are subject to a principle of public policy, the principle of finality.

Unfair Settlement

The concerns of society to avoid litigation and strife as well as to see that its citizens are fairly compensated are not always compatible. To avoid strife, society encourages the settlement of disputes and is slow to set aside a settlement—as long as it is fair. Fair settlement is promoted by the rule of good-faith disclosure. The claimant must be open and frank about his loss. The insurer, at the very least, must explain the terms of the settlement proposed.

Generally, the interests of all concerned are in finality. The insurer, however, wanting to close the file and minimize the cost of handling the claim, may pay too much. The claimant, worn out by a process that took longer than expected and, perhaps, being in urgent need of the insurance money, may accept too little. In some few but ill-defined circumstances the settlement may be set aside. Although few of the cases decided so far have concerned insurance, these circumstances have been much litigated recently in connection with other kinds of contract, and this has had an unsettling effect on the settlement of insurance claims.

Undue Influence

The general law allows agreements to be set aside if one party has undue influence over the other. If a claimant has come to rely on the insurer for guidance and advice, not just on the meaning of the terms of settlement but upon the substance, the wisdom of it, the settlement may be set aside. The corollary is that the settlement stands, if the claimant has agreed the settlement freely: that usually means that he has taken informed advice from someone else about the settlement. With all this in mind, the insurer is well advised to keep the claimant at arm's length. But even that counsel of caution may not be enough, if a liability insurer is (or should be) aware that a third party, such as the claimant's employer, is wielding influence on the claimant to agree a settlement: then too the insurer may have to see that the claimant is advised to seek independent advice lest the settlement be set aside later.[42]

Duress

The general law also allows agreements to be set aside, if they are the result of economic duress by one party on the other. Duress,

---

[42] *Barclays Bank plc* v. *O'Brien* [1994] 1 AC 180.

however, is more than just pressure. Many a claimant may settle under the pressure of his need for the money, but the settlement will be set aside only if the pressure comes from the insurer, it is strong enough to suggest absence of true consent, and it is in some significant sense 'illegitimate'. What is 'illegitimate' is a matter of some debate.

On the one hand, it would not be illegitimate for an insurer to indicate that, unless the claimant stopped being so 'unreasonable', the insurance would not be renewed; or that, unless the claimant accepted the insurer's final offer, it would be withdrawn and the claimant would be left to his remedy at law. On the other hand, it has been argued that the well-known case of *D & C Builders Ltd* v. *Rees*[43] is really an instance of economic duress, and, as such, authority for something like this: if the insurer, aware of the claimant's urgent need of money, 'beats him down' and offers a relatively low amount, a settlement for that amount may later be set aside and the question of the amount payable reopened. A further and more difficult contention is that a settlement may be set aside if the claimant has settled for too little on account of his own ignorance.

The Power of Information

In general, it is 'unconscionable', it has been argued, for one party consciously to take advantage of the other's ignorance or lack of advice to close a contract on terms unfair to the latter; and that terms are unfair if one party is 'sold short'.[44] Although not an argument with much appeal in an ethos of enterprise and bargain hunting, it deserves serious consideration within the confines of a contract of settlement between parties in a relationship of good faith. The implication of the argument is that the contract will be set aside unless the terms are fair or, at the very least, the insurer has done something to save the claimant from his own ignorance; and that, possibly, the insurer is obliged to see that the claimant is sufficiently informed and, to some extent therefore, to help him with his claim.

The rule of general contract law for settlement of a disputed

---

[43] [1966] 2 QB 617 (CA). See also 150–1 above.
[44] H. Beale. 'Inequality of Bargaining Power' (1986) 6 *OJLS* 123–36, 126.

claim is that the claim must be *bona fide* or 'honest'. The focus of that rule has been on the openness and 'honesty' of the claimant. General contract law does not provide much guidance about insurance claims except perhaps this: a settlement may be *bona fide* and honest, even though agreed between parties without knowledge of all the facts. Indeed, there is force in the argument that one of the objects of settlement is to avoid the time and expense involved in the production and assessment of all the accounts, documents, and other evidence required to decide whether the claim would succeed in a court of law. 'Honesty' does not require disclosure of all information which, regardless of trouble and expense, might have been obtained. Clearly, however, the 'dishonesty' that vitiates a contract of settlement, including the settlment of insurance claims, embraces a wider range of misconduct than common law fraud.

Insurance law requires good faith that continues until the insured's claim has been definitively rejected by the insurer. Good faith takes the form of a requirement that one must disclose to the other information needed to make a decision: 96 above. As long as the two are in dispute but are still seeking a settlement, the duty continues and insurance law requires disclosure. For his part, the claimant must 'lay his cards on the table' and make available to the insurer all the information he has at his disposal in support of his claim. Moreover, the duties of good faith and of disclosure being mutual, for his part too, the insurer must lay his cards on the table, the weak suit as well as the strong. If, as must surely soon be, insurance law is coloured by the more general patina of good faith that is currently being developed in general contract law, leading to a spirit of co-operation that seeks to promote the purposes of insurance (233 below), some of the implications are as follows.

First, the insurer is not obliged to undertake a factual investigation to ensure that the claimant has not understated the amount claimed, although the insurer is obliged to make appropriate suggestions if some understatement is obvious. Secondly, however, insurers can and do check a claim against the cover and is required to point out any respects in which the merits of the claim have been understated. The American decision,[45] that the

---

[45] *Dercoli* v. *Pennsylvania Nat. Mut. Ins. Co.*, 554 A 2d 906, 909 (Pa., 1989).

claimant who was unaware of a change in the law in her favour should have been informed by the insurer, may well be followed here: some recent decisions point in this direction.[46] Thirdly, the English court is also likely to adopt the spirit of the American decision,[47] that the insurer was obliged to advise a claimant about the existence of arbitration for claims of that kind. The reasoning was that, in general, when an insured submits or discusses a claim with the insurer, the insurer is relied on for information about the insured's rights under the policy. Arbitration is not a step favoured by claimants in England, but the spirit of the case does suggest, at the very least, that the insurer may be required to ensure that the claimant is aware of the possibility of a complaint to the Insurance Ombudsman: 201 below.

Enforcement in the Courts

If the insurer does not pay, the claimant can bring court proceedings to enforce the contract: 209 ff. below. Equally obviously, the claimant, rich or poor, does not want to have to do this. Those poor enough to be entitled to legal aid are not among those most likely to have both insurance and the stamina for the journey to justice through the courts. If, however, such a claimant comes forward, he does so in the confidence that, even if he loses the case, he is unlikely to have to pay the insurer's costs. The balance of power has shifted by means of the legal aid rules, but the shift is not so much against the insurer as a shift in the direction of the claimant to a point of just equilibrium. Still, in many instances that point has not been reached if, as has been suggested, some solicitors acting for claimants are so inexperienced in that kind of work that they are no match for those regularly employed by insurers as 'habitual' defendants; but the truth of this suggestion is hard to assess.

As it is seen by some insurers, legal aid encourages the unscrupulous pursuit of flimsy claims in the expectation that the insurer will make a 'nuisance payment' rather than incur a larger

---

[46] See *Scally* v. *Southern Health and Social Services Board* [1992] 1 AC 294; but cf. *Reid* v. *Rush & Tompkins Group plc* [1990] 1 WLR 212.

[47] *Davis* v. *Blue Cross*, 158 Cal. Rptr. 828, 835 (Cal., 1979).

sum in defending the claim. Indeed, it seems that the insurer is more likely to grit his teeth and settle a claim backed by legal aid than one which is not. A more general view is that the granting of aid suggests that the claimant has a case and that the insurer should think twice before going to court. With the advent of contingency fees, a similar pause for thought may be imposed on the claimant's solicitor, as his chances of payment will also depend on the outcome of the case. At the same time, American experience of contingency fees suggests that the insurer is more likely to test the nerve of the claimant and to refuse a settlement until all have reached the door of the court.

As claimants see the situation, they are likely to think twice or more before going to any court: 3 ff. above. Litigation takes time and trouble and, whether or not it also takes money directly, it always costs money in lost time. Moreover, it is an unequal contest. For example, unless the amount claimed brings the case within the jurisdiction of the High Court in London, in theory at least the insurer can insist on being sued in his local court which may be far off from middle England in deepest Dorset. The insurer has easy access to experts, one of the many advantages enjoyed by the 'habitual' litigator. The insurer knows all this when considering a claim; any settlement he chooses to offer is made from a position of strength.

Whether the claimant is legally represented or not, uncertainty about the outcome of litigation provides the conditions in which delay and cost pressures push parties towards settlement rather than trial. In one respect, of course, this is desirable. But uncertainty, delay, and cost pressures can also be consciously manufactured or exacerbated by the strategies of defendants, who are themselves relatively insulated from the effects of these pressures. The claimant is not in a good position to counter strategies of this kind.

Arbitration

Legal aid is not available for arbitration. If the insurance contract requires the claimant to go to arbitration before going to court or any other place, the claimant, who may have been granted legal aid to go to court but who is disadvantaged by being unable to afford legal representation in the arbitration, must submit to arbitration first. If the claimant goes to court nonetheless, the insurer can have the proceedings stayed. The court's discretion, however, allows it to refuse the stay if it would result in a 'denial of justice', in particular, if the claimant's poverty is the consequence of the defendant's breach of contract. So, if the claim is that the fire insurer has not paid on the claimant's only business premises, the stay will be refused. A stay might also be refused, if the insurer were to make tactical use of the general rule in a way unfairly prejudicial to the claimant. An example is that of the insurer who did not exercise his option for arbitration until the insured had incurred expense preparing an action in the courts.

In Switzerland, in contrast, the position is clear and straight-forward: arbitration clauses in insurance contracts are not allowed by the law. In England, however, the arbitration of insurance disputes is referred to with evident approval in the Statement of General Insurance Practice; but in actual practice, arbitration is not a hazard to which consumers are often exposed, as most insurers will take any dispute through whatever in-house procedures that are in place and then to the Insurance Ombuds-man: 201 ff. below.

According to the Ackner Report,[48] in common with other ombudsmen, the procedure of the Insurance Ombudsman may have the following advantages over arbitration. It is more accessible, cheaper, and quicker; one reason for this is that most, if not all, of the requisite information has been gathered during the prior attempt at conciliation. It is less formal, and thus, if any kind of hearing is needed, more 'user friendly'. The Insurance Ombudsman is not bound by the strict black letter of the law and can sidestep what the Ackner Report (paragraph 78) called well-recognized defects in insurance law. The Insurance Ombudsman has produced annual reports which set standards for the industry. The Ombudsman is in a better position than an arbitrator to develop a relationship with the industry and with the media, as well as a consistent line on regular issues in his sphere of adjudication. To the claimant, some of these advantages make the Insurance Ombudsman a forum more attractive than the court.

---

[48] Lord Ackner, *Report on a Unified Complaints Procedure* (Personal Investment Authority, London, 1993), para. 66.

The Insurance Ombudsman

Occasionally, dissatisfied claimants band together, for example those with subsidence claims brought together through the columns of a newspaper, for mutual assistance and encouragement in the unequal struggle against the insurers concerned. Most claimants, however, are lone claimants and need help. Informal dispute-resolution for insurance disputes has been developed in a number of countries. One is Australia, where there is the General Insurance Claims Review Panel (ICRP) and a distinct but parallel institution for life insurance. For disputes in the United Kingdom, there is the Insurance Ombudsman for most general business and, for long-term investment products such as life insurance, there is the ombudsman of the Personal Investment Authority (PIA). A generic picture of ombudsmen emerged from the first UK Ombudsman Conference in 1991. The essential features are independence from those under investigation and a scheme that is 'effective, fair and publicly accountable'.

Independence

One or two complainants, usually when they discovered that the Insurance Ombudsman had rejected their claim and was funded not by the government but insurers, have questioned his independence. The budget of the Insurance Ombudsman is controlled by a Board, which is appointed by insurers and, as the Ackner Report (paragraph 76) reminds us, 'he who pays the piper almost invariably calls the tune'. This perception of any tribunal is clearly important and must be countered, so, the Ackner Report (paragraph 77) laid down criteria of independence.

First, the jurisdiction, the powers, and the method of appointment, and, we might add, the existence of the ombudsman should be matters of public knowledge. In the case of the Insurance Ombudsman, this information is available to those who research the public documents of the Insurance Ombudsman Bureau, an unlimited company not having share capital. Secondly, the people who appoint ombudsmen should be independent. Appointment of ombudsmen should be either for a specified period (renewable) or until a specified retirement age; in any event, appointment should be for a sufficient period not to undermine the independence of the ombudsman, and not subject to premature termination other than by an independent body and, then, only for incapacity or misconduct or other good cause. The Insurance Ombudsman is appointed for a finite period of seven years made up of an initial term of three years, renewable for a further four. He has a Deputy Ombudsman who has comparable terms of service. The Ombudsman appoints the rest of the staff of the Insurance Ombudsman Bureau, many of whom are qualified lawyers. Thirdly, an ombudsman should have power to decide whether a complaint is within his jurisdiction. The Insurance Ombudsman has the power to reach a decision, but not one that is without more (arbitration or resort to the courts) binding on insurers. Fourthly, the ombudsman should be required to report to an independent body, which should also be responsible for safeguarding his independence. In the case of the Insurance Ombudsman, that body is the Council of the Insurance Ombudsman Bureau. Fifthly, the organization should be sufficiently staffed and funded to enable effective and expeditious investigation and resolution of complaints. In the case of the Insurance Ombudsman, funding is the responsibility of the Board but, in view of its impact on independence, funding is also a major concern of the Council. Finally, on all of these matters, the independent body should be one that is independent of those subject to investigation by the ombudsman—but not so as to exclude minority representation by such people on the appointing body, provided that decision is by majority decision. In the case of the Insurance Ombudsman, the body, the Council, meets this standard.

Subject to this, however, there is one question of both difficulty and importance, that the Ackner Report does not address: who should appoint the appointers? In the case of the Insurance Ombudsman Bureau, a minority of Bureau Council members is appointed by the Board of the Bureau, and thus by the representatives of insurers. The majority are appointed by the Council itself, and there is thus a line of succession from the original members and the outside interests represented at that time, such as consumer groups. Although the names of members and their affiliations are published, there is no really convincing answer to the criticism that in practice they are answerable only to themselves.

The Public Perception

How does the public come to know about the Insurance Ombudsman and the nature and scope of the service offered? Clearly, many people do not. Equally clearly, most who do hear about the Insurance Ombudsman do so from newspapers and broadcasts. Under the Insurance Ombudsman scheme insurers are obliged to mention the scheme in the insurance contract, and most do. What would be better would be an obligation to mention it to the claimant at the time that a claim is disputed. Arguably, insurers are obliged to do this under the general law (198 above) but mostly insurers do not. When the Insurance Ombudsman finds that a complainant has incurred solicitors' fees, which could reasonably have been avoided if the member had told him about the Bureau, the Ombudsman has required the member to pay up to 50 per cent of the fees. Compliance also addresses an information problem of another kind that arises in England from the proliferation of ombudsmen. A survey reported in the *Financial Times* in June 1995 found that for someone with a complaint about an insurance policy or an investment product, there were no fewer than eleven 'ombudsmen', from whom the complainant could not simply choose but among whom the correct choice had to be made. In practice, the 'wrong' ombudsman refers a complainant to the 'right' one, but best practice, surely, would be for insurers to tell the complainant in the first place.

Be that as it may, public awareness of the Insurance Ombudsman has increased, and with it, it seems, the number of complaints. The increase in the number of complaints dealt with between 1988 and 1992 was 265 per cent; that between 1992 and 1993 a further 46 per cent. Since then the number has fallen back as certain cases have been transferred to the PIA. Although in most cases the insurer's decision is confirmed by the Ombudsman (66 per cent in 1994 and 59 per cent in 1995) and most insurers belong to the Bureau, the number of insurers that belong has declined slightly. The pattern of complaints, however, should be kept in perspective: they are but a tiny percentage of claims made on the insurers that belong to the Bureau. Moreover, although the overall increase in cases might be seen as an increase in dissatisfaction with insurers, it is probably a reflection of consumerism and of public awareness of and confidence in the Insurance Ombudsman. This in turn has increased public confidence in insurance and in the insurance industry. As the Ackner Report (paragraph 66(5)) pointed out, 'the better the service which is provided to the public, the more use is made of it'.

Role

As stated in the Terms of Reference, the role of the Insurance Ombudsman is to act as counsellor or conciliator, to facilitate the satisfaction, settlement, or withdrawal of the complaint, and, failing that, to act as investigator and adjudicator in order to determine the complaint. As amplified in announcements to press and public, the role is 'to resolve disputes between members and consumers in an independent, impartial, cost-effective, efficient, informal and fair way'. The Ombudsman is very conscious of the importance of the public perception of how cases are handled: 207–9 below. The role of the PIA is similar and complementary for long-term business, including term life insurance, permanent health insurance, and cover for long-term care, but a line must be drawn. The Ombudsman is empowered by his terms of reference to investigate any complaint to see whether it is within his jurisdiction; if insurers disagree with his conclusion, i.e. he thinks he has jurisdiction but the insurer in question does not, the matter goes to arbitration.

Jurisdiction

Members Only

The complaint must be one against a member of the Bureau. For the Bureau this means (most) insurers, whereas for the PIA this means both insurers and intermediaries, thus offering the complainant the advantage of 'one-stop shopping'. The public often does not appreciate the difference between makers and retailers of insurance (45 above), this limit on the jurisdiction of the Insurance Ombudsman is unfortunate and is now being reconsidered. A limit on both Ombudsman and PIA is that a complainant can complain only about his own insurer and not someone else's. Thus the victim of tort cannot complain about the wrongdoer's liability insurer, from whom payment is overdue; and the employee, who has group health or life cover arranged by his employer cannot automatically complain about that. Moreover, now that the EC Third Insurance Directive[49] extends the range of insurers that can carry on business in England, there is a need to bring into the net insurers who do so but are not based there.

Private Lines

The policy in issue must be one that the complainant took out as an individual in a private capacity. This distinguishes the jurisdiction of the Insurance Ombudsman in England from, for example, that of the Banking Ombudsman and the Australian ICRP, which includes small commercial claims—a remit that some would like to see in England but which the Board and the Council of the Bureau have ruled out, even in the case of sole traders—unless a particular insurer agrees to the extension. Compare also Denmark, where the corresponding service is for consumers, except complaints about motor insurance, but there is a parallel body for commercial complainants.

Another corollary of the limit to private policyholders is that, in theory at least, group policies are excluded, if taken out by organizations such as banks, building societies, or employers, unless the latter contract as agent for the individuals concerned. These have to be resolved from case to case, a process which creates uncertainty in an important area of consumer cover. There is much to be said for the Ombudsman's recommendation[50] that, when a group policy is contracted, the parties should also agree whether the Insurance Ombudsman is to have jurisdiction.

Subject Matter

The jurisdiction of the Insurance Ombudsman is limited by the terms of reference to a 'complaint (including a dispute or claim) referred to him in connection with or arising out of a policy', provided also that it concerns 'a claim under the policy or the marketing or administration, but not the underwriting of the policy', the latter being normally within the insurer's discretion.

---

[49] [1992] OJ L360/1.
[50] The Insurance Ombudsman Bureau, *Annual Report 1994* (London, 1995), 18.

Moreover, marketing (procedural unfairness) is within the Ombudsman's jurisdiction only if the marketing was by a member of the Bureau rather than some other seller of insurance such as an independent financial adviser. Further, if the Ombudsman considers that court proceedings or arbitration would be more appropriate for a particular complaint, the Insurance Ombudsman is not actually forbidden to take such a complaint but may decline to deal with it. The PIA is in a similar position under the Pension Schemes Act 1993 sections 146 and 148.

Local Remedies

Another condition of reference to both the Ombudsman and the PIA, which is something of an obstacle, is the 'exhaustion of local remedies'. The complainant, keen perhaps to get to the Insurance Ombudsman, must first 'exhaust' the insurer's complaints procedure. Specifically, the matter must have been considered by a senior officer of the insurer, and only when his offer or observations have not been accepted by the complainant is the latter free to go to the Ombudsman. That the insurer should have a chance to be just or to be generous, and to be seen to be so, is fair enough. Consideration first by the insurer's claims department and then by a senior officer, however, can take time and create uncertainty for the complainant. How does he know how far his claim has got? What can he do if he receives no response at all? The PIA has power to consider a complaint if the member has failed to respond adequately within two months of the member having notice of the complaint. Other schemes such as those in Australia and Denmark have a default rule of some kind, which limits the time for which the matter is held up in house with the insurer. The Insurance Ombudsman in England does not. The best that he can do, if apprised of delay, is to exhort the insurer complete the procedure.

Imputations of Fraud

In many instances, the reluctance of an insurer to pay comes from the conviction that the claim is fraudulent. If the Australian ICRP finds, not that the claim is indeed fraudulent, but that the insurer has reasonable grounds for the belief, it must decline to take the case. Although not obliged to take a line like that, in practice the

Insurance Ombudsman does so: if the evidence against the claimant is sufficient to raise an issue of fraud, the Insurance Ombudsman exercises discretion not to take the case further: the Bureau is not the appropriate forum in which to resolve questions of fraud.

Awards

Adjudication may lead to monetary awards or such recommendations as the Ombudsman thinks fit. Although recommendations may exceed the limit, the upper limit for awards by the Insurance Ombudsman is £100,000. In contrast, the PIA's limit is £50,000, but the limit may be exceeded with the consent of the member concerned. The PIA has a specific power to make an award for distress and inconvenience (limited to £750), whereas the Insurance Ombudsman has not but does it anyway. The PIA must make awards in writing and give reasons. In practice, the Insurance Ombudsman does this too in thoughtfully drafted letters to complainants. Although the recommendations are not, the awards of the Ombudsman, like those of the PIA, are binding on members. Awards are not, however, binding on the complainant, who, if dissatisfied, can still go to court, though in practice rarely does so.

Law and Market Practice: Justice Certain and Justice Seen

When adjudicating complaints, both Insurance Ombudsman and PIA must have regard not only to the contract and to the law but also to the codes of insurance practice and to 'general principles of good insurance, investment or marketing practice'. If they are inconsistent with rules of law and are more favourable to the insured, these principles are to prevail.

In the early days of the Insurance Ombudsman Bureau good market practice was equated with actual practice. More recently, it has been interpreted as what good practice ought to be, whether it actually is or not. This has allowed the Ombudsman flexibility to sidestep sharp edges of the law such as the law of non-disclosure, but has led inevitably to differences of view between the Ombudsman and some insurers. It led also to unfavourable comment in the Ackner Report (paragraph 93).

First, Lord Ackner said that the 'price of self-regulation involving, *inter alia*, the obligation to provide consumers with a free complaints service which, while binding on the industry is not binding on the complainant, and remedies more extensive than those obtainable by litigation, is surely a high enough price to pay'. To the complainant, however, this might well seem lofty and patronizing. The legal system was (and perhaps still is) largely inaccessible to small claimants, who deserve better. Moreover, the setting up of the Bureau was less a magnanimous gesture by a public-spirited industry than a defensive move to forestall public hostility and associated interference by Parliament. As the Ackner Report pointed out (paragraph 55), the industry's standing in the eyes of the public is greatly affected by the extent to which it can get proper redress for its complaints. The Insurance Ombudsman has improved the image of the insurance industry with the public at large—insurers may have paid a price but they have got something for their money.

Secondly, said Lord Ackner, to 'super-add to this, the hostage to fortune of uncertain and therefore unpredictable liability, which may result from the Ombudsman acting as the embodiment of the conscience of the industry, a wholly subjective perception subject to no appellate process, is in my judgment, asking too much'. This, however, betrays the thinking of the Commercial Court, which the Insurance Ombudsman is not and does not purport to be. Although he is obliged to have regard to his previous decisions, neither the Ombudsman nor the PIA is bound by previous decisions. This does not make them more unpredictable than, for example, those tribunals of other countries that have no rules of binding precedent. The Ombudsman publishes a selection of its decisions every year in its annual report. Further, the Ombudsman has followed a recommendation of the National Consumer Council and published a digest of decisions in conjunction with the Chartered Institute of Insurers. Thus, more consistency and predictability is achieved than is possible, for comparison, among arbitrators, each of whom is entirely his own master and whose mission may differ from case to case. This is important because, as has been powerfully demonstrated in the United States, adjudication is more than the settlement of particular disputes. It is also a form of 'social ordering' which in some degree enters 'into the litigants' future relations and into the future relations of other parties who see themselves as possible litigants before the same tribunal'.[51] The Insurance Ombudsman faces the challenge of any tribunal, to balance justice in the particular with certainty in general. The case that the Insurance Ombudsman will fail in this challenge has yet to be made out.

Thirdly, the Ackner Report (paragraph 94) continued:

Quite apart from the unreasonableness of the Ombudsman being entitled to sit under his own individual palm tree and there administer his own particular brand of justice, it is in the interest of both the members of the industry and consumers that insurance against liability can be and is in fact obtained. If liability is or becomes unpredictable, insurance cover will be unobtainable.

Out of context, the last statement is true. It is true, for example, that many insurers have refused to cover toxic waste liability in the United States. Uncertain law makes for uncertain underwriting. But that is another world. The percentage of cases that goes to the Insurance Ombudsman is small and the percentage of those decided against insurers on 'palm tree' principles, if that is indeed what they are, much smaller still. The Ombudsman has endeavoured to ensure that its conception of what is fair and reasonable is consistent and well known, notably by the publication of the digest of cases. As far as most things can be, his justice is certain and seen, both before and after in the event of a complaint.

Compensation for Late Payment

As we have seen, insurers sell their services as rescue services which 'take the drama out of the crisis'. One advertisement for professional indemnity cover shows the insurer as a rescue helicopter pulling the sinking professional from a sea of liability. In many instances, the image of urgency and speed is justified in practice. At Lloyd's, for example, many major hull losses have been paid within ten days and any outstanding liability issues sorted out later. Out in the High Street, however, is a business culture of non-payment or, at least, slow payment. In 1994 a

---

[51] L. L. Fuller, 'The Forms and Limits of Adjudication', 92 *Harv. L Rev.* 353–409, 357 (1978).

leader in the *Financial Times* concluded that business in the United Kingdom has one of the worst records in Europe for late payment, and a survey by a leading credit insurer showed that only 2 per cent of UK invoices were paid on time. This culture seems to have rubbed off on some insurers.

In the United States, if the insurer drags his feet over payment without justification, that is said to be bad faith and the insurer may be liable to the claimant for large sums of 'punitive' damages. In the United Kingdom, with a few reservations, it can be said that the insurer can delay payment indefinitely and with impunity.

Lost Business

One reservation concerns contingency (non-indemnity) insurance. The claimant's action against the insurer is seen as an action for debt. Although section 35A(1) of the Supreme Court Act 1981 gives the court a discretion to award interest against debtors who pay late, two gaps are left. First, the court has no power to award interest, if the debtor pays late but before proceedings for recovery have been begun; and, secondly, interest does not compensate special damage over and beyond loss of the normal use of the money.

In general contract law, the second gap is filled by the common law rule of remoteness of damage and the second limb of *Hadley* v. *Baxendale*.[52] It appears that this rule also applies to contingency (non-indemnity) insurance contracts. In the case of indemnity insurance, however, the law is unclear. The claimant might well expect a similar rule to apply. If the owner of a heavily mortgaged business property suffers a substantial fire loss, the owner may be unable to meet the mortgage payments, and may be in jeopardy of losing the property and becoming a bankrupt. A major reason why a person in business buys fire insurance is to guard against such eventualities. That person may reasonably expect that if a fire occurs, the insurance money will be promptly available for protection from those eventualities. After all, if someone's roof is damaged by fire and the insurer elects to have it repaired but the work is done badly, the insurer is liable for consequent rain damage to contents; so, if the insurer elects to pay him the money

---

[52] (1854) 9 Ex. 341.

for repair instead but pays late, the claimant may reasonably expect the insurer to be liable for the rain damage. So does the Insurance Ombudsman. However, in England decisions conflict, and the most recent is against him.[53] In contrast, in California,[54] for example, damages of this kind are recoverable against the insurer, as they are in Australia and New Zealand.[55] Moreover, under 10 California Code of Regulations (CCR) Section 2695.1 ff., which govern insurance claims procedure, the Insurance Commissioner has power to fine an insurer who pays late. In France, there is also a remedy but a different one again: the insurer pays interest at a rate that rises with the passage of time.[56]

Distress

In the general law of England, damages for distress are now recoverable for breach of a contractual undertaking, the object of which was to secure peace of mind or freedom from distress. As we have seen (3 above), peace of mind is one of the objects of most consumer and many commercial insurance contracts. Research shows that, for some people, losing property causes as much distress as losing a friend. The corollary in many cases must be that distress is a likely consequence if the insurer delays payment and, unless the delay is justifiable, the insurer should be liable in damages. Although no insurance decision of this kind has been reported from the courts, the Insurance Ombudsman has won praise from the press for awards of that kind. Moreover, in his Report (paragraph 96) Lord Ackner appears to have assumed that this was a correct application of rules of general contract law. With respect, in principle he is surely correct.

Insolvency

Between 1844 and 1883 no fewer than 519 new insurance

---

[53] *Sprung* v. *Royal Ins. Co.* [1997] CLC 70 (CA); cf. *Grant* v. *Co-operative Ins.* (1983) 134 NLJ 81.

[54] *Reichert* v. *General Ins. Co.*, 428 P 2d 860, 864 (1967).

[55] See K. C. T. Sutton, *Insurance Law in Australia and New Zealand* (2nd edn., Sydney, 1991), para. 15.67.

[56] Y. Lambert-Faivre, *Droit des Assurances* (9th edn., Paris, 1995) no. 271.

companies were formed, but 471 failed or were wound up, and this became a matter of concern to government. *Laissez-faire* ended first for life companies. The idea of floating a company to receive large sums now (premium) against the mere possibility of payment on policies at sometime in the future was most attractive, sometimes to the wrong people. So, intervention began in the first half of the nineteenth century and became marked with the Life Assurance Companies Act 1870, which required life companies to submit accounts, actuarial valuations of their businesses, and a substantial deposit. Society has an interest in the solvency of its insurers.

Society has an interest because of the importance of insurance, and because of the size of the insurance industry's investment in other industries: the importance of the insurance industry 'as the guardian of the country's nest-egg' was described in March 1994 by the *Sunday Times*, a severe critic of insurers, as 'awesome'. The business of insurance, however, to which society is increasingly committed, has become increasingly difficult. The number and cost of natural catastrophes—usually defined by insurers as those costing over five million dollars—has been rising. Man, too, has got 'better' at causing damage. In 1993 the cost of the damage inflicted by the IRA bomb in the City of London was about 740 million dollars and that of the bomb at the World Trade Centre in New York about 510 million dollars. Only one major insurer has failed in the last few years; but banks have failed, and there is no obvious reason for thinking that insurers will not, or that the DTI can watch insurers better than bankers. When the ABI suggested that the market should provide cover against the long-term risk of insurers' insolvency, the response of the insurers themselves did not inspire confidence: quotations were hard to obtain and those that were given were high. What is being done?

Watchdogs

The solvency of insurers is monitored by the DTI. Insurers must be licensed to commence business. After that, the Secretary of State has wide powers of intervention under sections 38 to 52 of the Insurance Companies Act 1982. But the staff allocated by the DTI to the task of assessment is small and, it has been said, under-qualified.[57] A more rigorous assessment of insurers has been demanded of intermediaries (52 above) seeking cover for clients but, if an assessment raises doubts about an insurer, can the intermediary really be expected to raise the alarm rather than lower his sights and look elsewhere? And, anyway, can the intermediary or anyone else be sure of the assessment?

Under the Acts, the financial health of insurance companies is measured by their solvency margin, which is monitored by the DTI and which purports to ensure that the volume of business underwritten is not excessive in relation to the insurer's capital base. The measurement is made, however, on the assumption that there is a close relation between premium income and the degree of risk to which the insurer is exposed, an assumption that dates from the days of tariffs and standard rates. Today, rates are not standard. So, when insurers try to push into new areas they often undercut rivals with the result that the risk profile of one insurer is quite different from that of another insurer, although their premium income may be the same. Of course, each company must submit accounts. But accounts do no more than present a picture of a company—a picture of a time that is past and a picture painted by the company managers and auditors, some of whom may be more inclined to the school of Monet than Canaletto. By the time the alarm has been raised, the company may have collapsed.

The Policyholders Protection Act 1975 (PPA)

If the insurer is insolvent, the PPA offers protection in respect of UK policies. These are policies under which the performance by the insurer of any of his obligations would, at any time, constitute the carrying on by the insurer of insurance business of any class in the United Kingdom. The Act, in the view of the courts but not, it seems, the intention behind the Act, extends this protection to private policyholders not only in the United Kingdom but also those without any connection with the United Kingdom, other than the policy itself.[58] This may not be a bad thing in the long

---

[57] See R. Lewis, 'The Regulation of Insurers and the Long Term Security of Structured Settlements' [1994] *IJIL* 75–96, 78 ff.

[58] *Scher* v. *Policyholders Protection Board (Nos. 1 and 2)* [1993] 3 All ER 384, [1993] 4 All ER 840 [1994] 2 All ER 37 (HL).

term. The British insurance industry's net income from abroad is large and the PPA protection underlines to the overseas market the security inherent in buying from an authorized UK insurer. Be that as it may, payment is from a fund built up from a levy on premiums and, whereas between 1975 and 1990 the levy was £1.5 million, in 1993 alone the levy was £80 million. The interpretation put on the Act by the courts will multiply that, and the Act of 1975 was amended by the Policyholders Protection Act of 1997, which limits protection, broadly speaking, to policies issued and risks situated in the UK and EEA states.

7

Insurance and Society

The Role of Insurance

The main issues in this Chapter are whether insurance should be left entirely to the insurers and insurance law to the lawyers. We start from the position that people should be free to contract insurance, like other services, as they wish, and that insurers should be free to write what terms they please. We ask whether, when, and how that freedom is or should be restrained.

The main role of insurance in society is to spread risk and, if the risk materializes, to spread the resulting loss. Thus, the few who need it can be compensated from the contributions paid by the many who do not need it but who, as people who are risk-averse, need the reassurance that, if they were the ones in need, they too would be compensated; so that, in the words of an Act of 1601, there 'followeth not the undoing of any man, but the loss lighteth easily upon many than on few'. Incidental to this role but, increasingly, an important ancillary role of insurance in itself is the management of risk and the prevention of loss: see 136 ff. above.

When insurance carries out these functions effectively, the consequences are, first, to encourage activity and enterprise that might not otherwise have occurred. Insurance has been called the 'hand-maiden of industry'. A second consequence is the reduction of loss, damage, and stress in society to more acceptable levels. But life without any risk at all would be simply dull. Surely the American was right who said that without risk much of 'what makes life challenging, complex, and satisfying would be missing. The right to take risks is very much part of our political tradition and social compact. Indeed, the availability of a rich variety of risky endeavours is part of what is special about our culture.'[1]

There are those in England who would ban walkers from Helvellyn in winter—but not many. Nor are there many who

---

[1] K. S. Abraham, *Distributing Risk* (New Haven, Conn., 1986), 2.

would suggest that the walker should walk there without any insurance, of one kind or another. If he thinks about it, he can meet the concern of society and the concerns of his family by cover on his life, his limbs, and perhaps liability. But sometimes, not perhaps on Helvellyn but back at home, the comfort of insurance cover may make him careless. This is the main instance of what insurers call 'moral hazard'.

Moral Hazard

From time to time anxiety surfaces that insurance encourages behaviour that is, in some sense, objectionable or anti-social. Top of the list in the past was the concern that life insurance would encourage death—that the beneficiaries of a life policy would be tempted to hasten the event. The concern was reflected in the Life Assurance Act 1774. Today a more subtle form of the temptation, on which the statute is silent, faces the family in a position to have a life-support system switched off before the next premium is due. Today, however, as every reader of detective fiction knows, the prime beneficiary is the prime suspect, and it is a very cool or very foolish beneficiary who kills the life assured. Today, the most common concern about the insidious effect of insurance is more mundane: that insurance makes people more careless.

Carelessness

From early days one of the stated purposes of insurance was to provide cover against human frailty, and, therefore, to cover human negligence; fire insurance that does not cover fires started by carelessness is of little use. Indeed, psychology tells us that everyone makes mistakes, and that mistakes are a normal and necessary part of the human cognitive function. If possible, the response of society should be to correct rather than punish, whether by loss of liberty or loss of insurance cover. Society expects the insurer to play a parental role. On the one hand, both effective loss prevention and accurate underwriting are better promoted not by 'punishing' people for mistakes—that just encourages them to suppress information or blame others—but by seeking a climate of openness the better to assess the extent of the risk. The parent picks up the careless child and comforts it. On the other hand, the parent may punish the child that is careless too often. So, the more claims made, the more it costs the claimant in premiums or the higher the excess.

Today, however, the strong arm of technology has strengthened the hand of human beings and made matters worse. On the one hand, it has increased people's potential for inflicting damage, and with it the need for compensation. On the other hand, it has given people a sense of power over events so that what was once accepted with resignation as an act of God is now seen with anger as the actionable act of others. Before dialysis machines, people with kidney failure simply died. Now some do not die but, if they do, the search is on for failure, some human 'failure' to check through inadvertence which can be characterized as negligent. On the roads, 'accidents' cost the United Kingdom about £12 billion a year. The 'case for wearing seat belts is so strong', said Lord Denning,[2] 'that I do not think the law can admit forgetfulness as an excuse. If it were, everyone would say: "Oh, I forgot".' Negligence as inadvertence or forgetfulness is inevitable. Insurance to cover all concerned against the consequences of negligence has never been more necessary.

Negligence may be 'strategically intentional'. It is intentional when the cost of precautions against it is relatively high and a deliberate decision is taken not to buy the precaution, to take the risk of negligence and to buy insurance. A current example is the decision of the railways not to install an advanced and expensive system (ATP) against driver error.

Negligence may also be 'stubbornly intentional'. There are still people like the man who answered his call of nature in a dangerous place because it was the only place where he could be sure that he would not be seen; or the man who went back into the burning building to save his dog. Whether or not our courts would find, as did courts in the United States, that he was negligent, the very least he might reasonably expect would be to be covered by his insurance. We may not tolerate rashness or non-conformity in people as much as we did once, but at least we allow them to insure against it.

Somewhere between stubborn negligence and strategic

---

[2] *Froom* v. *Butcher* [1975] 3 All ER 520, 527.

negligence comes the casual negligence of the insured who has relaxed his guard. Indeed, the relaxation may be something of which the insured is more or less aware. With 'the passing of time the insured have increasingly come to look on the premium as a payment that gives rights. People took less care and personal responsibility made way for the shifting of responsibility onto society as a whole. Higher claims led to higher premiums, thus reinforcing this behaviour'.[3] This is the observation of a Dutch sociologist; however, a similar view can be taken of attitudes in England. Concern may be more or less justified according to context. As regards liability insurance, for example, there is little ground for this concern, but it remains a concern for the property insurer. This is what concerns insurers most as 'moral hazard'.

As regards extreme cases of moral hazard, the law helps the insurer with the rules requiring insurable interest (20 ff. above), and rules against wilful misconduct but not rules against more casual carelessness. Recently, some insurers were so concerned to cut claims and costs that they sought to exclude loss caused by negligence altogether. From the perspective of history the tail in the claims department was wagging the underwriting dog. In Switzerland (LCA Article 14.4.), the code effectively prevents insurers from excluding ordinary negligence. English law does not go quite that far, but the courts have reacted with great reluctance to construe cover as excluding negligence: 139 ff. above.

Now, no less than in the past it is a central purpose of insurance to cover the consequences of what others see as negligence. So, what general tort law sees as negligence and, therefore, actionable, insurance law sees either as not negligence but 'inadvertence' (property insurance) or as insurable negligence and also actionable—by the insured against the insurer.

Wilful Misconduct and Intentional Loss

In *Tinsley* v. *Milligan*, Nicholls LJ spoke of a 'public conscience test', whereby the court weighed the adverse consequences of granting relief against the adverse consequences of refusing relief.

---

[3] C. J. M. Schuyt, 'The Paradox of Welfare and Insurance' *Geneva Papers* 77 (1995), 430–8.

He admitted that this called for a value judgement.[4] The test was rejected in the House of Lords by Lord Goff,[5] without apparent awareness that a test of this kind has long been applied in insurance cases throughout the common law world.

Construction and Public Policy

The wilful or deliberate damage done by persons other than the insured, such as malicious damage by neighbours, is insurable; but, generally, loss or damage which is inflicted deliberately by the insured himself is not. That may be a rule of law, as in Germany (Versicherungsvertragsgesetz, Article 61) or as in common law countries, either a rule of public policy or a canon of construction applied by the courts.

Obviously, society has an interest in discouraging me from deliberately damaging the gnomes in my neighbour's garden. Equally obviously, the right to destroy my own property is a basic incident of ownership and, otherwise, I would be overwhelmed by my own rubbish; so, I can throw away my own gnomes—as long as I do not throw them into the street or into my neighbour's garden. My insurer's interest in me and my gnomes is different. For him what counts is that, if I have 'nothing to lose' by dumping my gnomes, loss depends on my whim, and to allow whims to affect risk makes it unpredictable and hard to rate. So there is a rule against the insurability of deliberate loss. As it is based mainly on the intention of the insurer, however, there can be exceptions.

First, life insurance can cover suicide. If it does, however, usually it covers not suicide straight away but suicide after, let us say, one year: the chance, at the time of contract, of suicide a year later is small and thus insurable. Secondly, insurance is available against the consequences of events that the insured has always wanted to bring about, indeed, events that he strives and drives daily to bring about, but of which, again, the chances are sufficiently small for the insurer to take the risk. So, the golfer, who succeeds in 'holing in one' and must then observe the potentially ruinous custom of buying drinks for everyone in the clubhouse, can cover the cost by insurance. So can the manu-facturer of golf clubs who offers a large prize—a kind of

---

[4] [1992] Ch 310, 320 (CA).   [5] [1994] 1 AL 340, 358–9.

contingency insurance called 'prize indemnity'. Although premiums for golfers have risen on the suspicion of collusion with caddies, and one golf course has installed CCTV cameras to monitor 'claims', in most such cases, the insurer has no concern about moral hazard.

Construction: Complication and Confusion in the Courts

Away from the golf course, insurance contracts commonly seek to rule out cover for anything like deliberate loss. In the case of liability insurance, for example, cover extends to liability for 'accidental' loss (death, injury, or damage to property); or, to the same effect, liability (generally) with an exclusion of liability for loss which is 'either intended or expected' or which is 'intended or expected from the standpoint of the insured'. Loss must be more than just foreseeable for the exclusion to apply. Equally, it is only when the loss is probable that it is not accidental but to be 'expected' and the loss is not insured. Few cases on these clauses have been reported from the English courts. What the draftsmen had in mind is clear enough. What courts in the common law world, notably in the United States, have made of the words is anything but.

A survey of cases[6] shows three markedly different interpretations of the exclusion of what is intended or expected. First, an objective interpretation, sometimes called the 'objective tort standard', is that the insured is taken to have intended the natural and probable consequences of his intentional acts. Secondly, a purely subjective interpretation is based on what, on the evidence available, the insured seems to have intended in fact. Between these two interpretations is a third, 'semi-subjective' interpretation: the loss is not insured either if the evidence is that the insured actually did intend the loss or, although actual intention is unclear, intent can be inferred because the loss was practically or substantially certain to follow from his (intentional) act or omission.

To complicate the picture further, each of these three interpretations comes in two versions—according to whether the perceived

[6] M. A. Clarke, 'Insurance of Wilful Misconduct: The Court as Keeper of the Public Conscience' (1996) 7 *Ins. LJ* 173–96.

intention is to inflict *any* loss or, the narrower version, to inflict loss of the kind or to the extent that actually occurred. A court might require, for example, not only purely subjective intent to injure but also intent to inflict the more or less precise injury that occurred. Most courts, however, do not see punching people in the face as an exact science, and that kind of limit is usually found only when the court wants to rule against the exclusion and in favour of cover.

Attempts to relate the cases to more general concepts must be made with caution. Although, for example, the objective test has been referred to as the 'tort standard', it would be facile to suggest that the less stringent tests of accident, notably the subjective test, resemble a 'criminal law standard'. Sometimes principles of criminal law are overtly applied, but, in other cases, courts have been careful to distinguish them. Equally, inability to distinguish right and wrong, which may be a defence to a criminal charge, does not make something an accident; for an accident the decisive element is not moral awareness but intention or capacity for effective choice of action, so that, for example, an attempted suicide may be accidental. Cross-reference to concepts of criminal law is made, but is not consistent.

Public Policy

One explanation of this diversity of interpretation is that courts' construction of the contract is randomly affected by elements of public policy. The court may or may not mention the public policy in mind. When it does, the emphasis depends on the decision that the court wants to reach. The court that wants to enforce cover usually stresses the importance of compensation. The court against cover stresses the seriousness of the act of the insured and the importance of discouraging that kind of behaviour.

Moreover, the impact of these policy factors depends also on the kind of cover in question, and, when there is express reference to them, it should not be taken entirely at face value. In practice the weight given to compensation in liability cases is rather different from that in personal accident (PA) cases. In a PA case the urge to compensate the main victim, the insured himself, or his dependent, is less strong than in the liability insurance case, where the victim is a third party. Again, the apparent importance attached to deterrence, especially in liability insurance cases, should not be taken too seriously. The idea that wrongdoers who do wrong in spite of the possibility of other sanctions such as imprisonment will be deterred by the thought of losing insurance cover is not overwhelmingly convincing. In practice, however, deterrence is often associated with retribution. Some courts refuse cover explicitly in order to punish the insured, and others see deterrence as an objective ancillary or related to punishment. Even when deterrence alone is mentioned, there is some suggestion that deterrence is really a proxy for punishment and retribution directed at wrongs which the judges find most objectionable. Finally, deterrence, whatever it means, and compensation are not the only values that affect the decision.

First, courts have clearly been influenced by the form of harm. On the one hand, courts in liability cases show no sympathy for the insured guilty of sexual offences, and in effect, therefore, remarkably little practical sympathy for victims. On the other hand, even in sex cases, courts are more likely to enforce cover if it is not the offender's own insurance but his employer's—in respect of the alleged vicarious liability of the employer or, more likely, the negligence of the latter in the employment or supervision of the offender—especially if the court can be persuaded that the offence is 'inextricably intertwined' with professional activity, such as medical treatment or psychotherapy. One ancillary factor in these decisions appears to be that, for professionals (but why not others?) there are other uninsurable deterrents, such as loss of reputation in the community and loss of livelihood.

Secondly, courts have been influenced by the means of harm—the weapon. In liability insurance cases, courts are most reluctant to indemnify the insured who used a gun, even when the gun was used in self-defence. In contrast, when guns have not been involved, although deliberate injury in self-defence is not likely to be held to be an accident, an instinctive reflex reaction, such that the insured did not have the time to form the intent required for the exclusion, may well be an accident. By the same token, however, the insured is not likely to be covered when he, in a deliberate and calculated way, seeks to take the law into his own hands.

Between the reflex and the Rambo response is brawling, about which courts have been more ambivalent. On the one hand, even on the purely subjective approach, neither a one-sided beating nor a man hitting a woman in the face is likely to be seen by the courts as accidental. On the other hand, brawling on the sports field is more likely to be covered. So is violence on the roads. Even in cases of utter recklessness on the roads, people still speak of motor 'accidents' and, on the whole, courts dealing with insurance in the past have seen events in a similar way. It is in the absence of anything that can be described as direct physical violence that courts recoil least and are most likely to enforce insurance. An important example is cover for liability for 'calculated' pollution.[7]

The same inclination to enforce cover is shown to the 'passive' insured who poisons himself. Even so, there are 'drugs and drugs'. Most likely to be covered by insurance are accidents with drugs that might have been obtained from a doctor on prescription, such as sleeping pills. Indeed, a line of this kind is drawn by some insurance contracts, which exclude injury or death by drug use unless used on the advice of a licensed medical practitioner. Again, courts in the past have been less hostile to alcohol than to other 'street' drugs. As recently as 1990, a federal court in the United States declined to apply an exclusion (of death occurring 'during the commission of a crime') because, although the insured was drunk and driving fast when his car hit a tree, the court considered that people would not regard that as a crime. Moreover, it may be significant that, both in England and in Canada, courts which have applied the subjective test, the one most favourable to the insured, have done so in cases in which the insured was drunk.[8] In contrast, a generation of judges, for whom coke was something that came in a can from the corner shop, has been less than sympathetic to users of illegal drugs, hard or soft, when things go wrong.

Finally, courts are more likely to favour insurability, if what the insured was doing at the time of the 'accident' is considered useful, such as keeping the peace, than if it was foolish, such as Russian roulette. So, the death of a person demonstrating his 'nerve' to his

[7] M. A. Clarke, 'Liability Insurance on Pollution Damage: Market Meltdown or Grist to the Mill' [1994] *JBL* 545–65, 553.

[8] Canada: *Mutual of Omaha* v. *Stats* (1978) 87 DLR (3d) 169 (Sup. Ct.); England: *Beller* v. *Hayden* [1978] QB 694; but cf. *Dhak* v. *INA (UK) Ltd* [1996] 1 Lloyd's Rep. 632 (CA).

companions by walking a parapet thirteen floors up after drinking vodka will not be an accident but, clearly, if he is trying to rescue a person trapped in the building, the assessment is different.

Property Insurance: Commercial Practice

The question whether a leg is broken accidentally or not is usually answered by the law in the same way, whether the leg is that of the insured himself or that of his Chippendale chair. Usually it is only when the injury or damage is intended or probable that it is not accidental but to be 'expected', and the loss is not insured.

The exception concerns the insurance of goods in transit: all-risks (AR) transit insurance does not normally cover loss due to ordinary wear and tear or to inherent vice. Inherent vice in goods refers to some defect in the goods, which was present at the time cover commenced and which materializes during the period of cover; it may be food that has gone off or metalwork that has rusted. The most common explanation of the absence of cover, both for inherent vice and for ordinary wear and tear, is that, in the particular case, the deterioration was going to happen anyway; and that AR insurance covers risks but not certainties.

The result is a notion of 'accident' that is narrower and an exclusion that is wider than those encountered in liability and PA insurance. The event is always objectively assessed, and it is assessed not with the knowledge of the insured at the time of contract but, in England at least, with that of the court with the benefit of hindsight. If it proves later, perhaps after an examination of the goods that could not possibly have been made earlier, that all along the goods suffered from a deeply latent and inherent defect, the loss is not covered. The insured, to whom the defect came as an unpleasant surprise, may well feel the same about the law.

First, in everyday language and experience, taking risks concerns something about to happen with an outcome yet to be resolved. So, he may think, an insurance risk too should be assessed before the risk has been run. At that point in time, it may appear that the weather will be favourable, that the goods are in good condition and that, even if he knew the true state of the goods, the inherent vice would not develop while cover lasted; or that the defect would be dealt with in time to arrest its progress or to prevent loss. If loss is not certain at that time, he may think, the loss is not a certainty but a risk.

Secondly, the insured may ask also why life and health insurance contracts are different. True, they sometimes exclude the effects of pre-existing conditions, but that is not universal and not a rule of law. If he contracts life insurance, for example, in ignorance of a fatal condition, he is likely to be covered nonetheless. The farmer's life insurance covers a latent defect in his liver, so why does his transit insurance not cover the similar defect in his meat? The answer given by the law is that, if the meat were covered, in effect the insurer would be guaranteeing the quality of meat when shipped, and that this is not a liability under the policy that the insurer has assumed. But, then the farmer might ask, if, as they do, insurers will guarantee the fitness of refrigerators, why not also the fitness of the contents when shipped?

Indeed, although English courts talk of 'risk but not certainty' as if these defects are inherently uninsurable, that is not the case. They can be insured, for example, in French law and, moreover, in English law too, provided that the contract makes that clear.[9] The insurability of latent defects in buildings is confirmed by the willingness of French insurers to offer such insurance. English insurers do too, although in England it is described not as all-risks insurance but as something else.

The real explanation of the AR exclusion probably lies, not in the realm of law or ideas, but in the unwillingness of insurers to assume that kind of risk on account of moral hazard. The conjecture is that, as a result of past experience in this context, the real concern, as with the kindred exclusion of wear and tear, is that people might be tempted to dump defective goods on insurers, and so, this being hard to prove, they protected themselves by ruling out cover of loss which, as it appeared later, was always going to occur, and which just might have been one which was anticipated all along by the consignor.

Analogies

In the construction of insurance contracts by the courts we find what psychologists call 'heuristic' patterns of analysis, i.e. cautious

---

[9] *Soya GmbH* v. *White* [1983] 1 Lloyd's Rep. 122, 126 (HL).

use of analogy with more general legal concepts such as the 'tort' standard. In particular, a court may rephrase the issue in terms of categories with which it is more familiar. The outcome for insurance contracts is that, in general, what lawyers understand as negligence is covered, but that, in many instances, recklessness is not. By rephrasing the issue, however, the courts have also altered the answer. Whereas the question whether an injury is to be expected, although hardly one of scientific precision, is 'purely' one of probability or likelihood, the question whether the insured is reckless is more subjective and more relative. In its latter form, the question gives the court licence to refer not only to 'pure' probability but, like the court seised of an action in tort, to consider the social impact, the usefulness or otherwise of the person's conduct. The result is that, as we have seen, the fireman who falls from a parapet suffers an accident but the exhibitionist does not, although the probability of falling may be the same in each case. Again, the heatstroke suffered by the stoker of a steamship is an accident, but the heatstroke suffered by the holidaymaker on the beach is not. This form of enquiry, although appropriate to an action in tort which concerns the liability of the actor and affects the duties of the community at large, is rather less appropriate to an insurance claim, which is concerned with the liability of the insurer and the construction of a particular contract.

In conclusion, whereas it is clear that courts *do* weigh up what the court perceives as the social factors involved, it is not clear that they *should* do so. First, it is questionable whether the court has adequate information (242 ff. below). Secondly, even if the court does have enough information, the weighing process is necessarily imprecise and a source of uncertainty.

Controlling Contract Terms

Contracting insurance, it is said, does not meet the optimal standards of economic efficiency (whatever that is) because the applicant lacks the information needed to bargain efficiently. It is argued that, in the case of consumer insurance, the cost of obtaining and evaluating information about the terms of the insurance contract will tend to direct competitive forces away from this exercise and towards broad price–quantity comparisons. The result may be 'harsh-term-low-price policies, whereas many consumers, in the absence of information and transaction costs, may have preferred an easier-term-higher price combination'.[10] In other words, the consumer takes one look (if that) at the small print, his eyes glaze over, and he goes for what appears to be adequate cover at the lowest premium.

Of all the important transactions made by the consumer, insurance stands out as the one clear of outside control and, as the industry sees it, free from regulatory 'interference'. The hazards of employment are regulated largely by statute. If the consumer buys a car or borrows money, the terms are controlled by statute. If he buys a house the terms are standardized to similar effect. For other hazards of life not covered by social security, which is regulated by statute, he can or must buy insurance by contract. Until very recently, however, when he bought insurance, there was no such control at all: 236–7 below. In the 1990s the perception that the industry could be trusted to regulate itself has been doubted as never before. This kind of perception points to some kind of regulation or control of policy terms.

Validation

In some countries in the past and others still today, insurers cannot use terms unless they have received prior approval by a state supervisory agency of some kind. The advantage for the public is that, just as the buyer of licensed drugs can have some confidence that the right drug will do some good, it can have confidence that the insurance will provide some cover. However, licensing has some disadvantages too.[11]

The first is the cost of having all terms examined by both the insurer's draftsman and the agency. Secondly, the expertise of the agency can never be comprehensive, so its scrutiny will be slow, incomplete, or both. Thirdly, the draftsman will tailor the terms of

---

[10] V. P. Goldberg, 'Institutional Change and the Quasi-invisible Hand', 17 *J Law. & Econ.* 461–96, 483 (1974); cf. M. J. Trebilcock, 'The Doctrine of Inequality of Bargaining Power: Post-Benthamite Economics in the House of Lords' (1976) 26 *U Toronto LJ* 359–85, 375.

[11] See P.-O. Bjuggren *et al.*, 'Should a Regulatory Body Control Insurance Policies Ex Ante or Is Ex Post Control More Effective?', *Geneva Papers* No 70 (Jan. 1994), 37–45.

the insurance to the perceived views of the agency, and this discourages innovation. Fourthly, if the agency is sensitive to the first two drawbacks, it is likely to be restrictive of unfamiliar insurance terms, so this too inhibits innovation. Finally, the cost and trouble of getting new terms approved discourages insurers from tailoring contract terms to the needs of minority groups of customers. In Europe, the current view is that the disadvantages outweigh the advantages to a degree that is anti-competitive, so state validation is not a viable option.

Construction

Insurance contracts are a prime context of a tradition of construing contract terms in a way that makes them less unfair. For example, as the effect of a breach of warranty is so serious for the insured, the courts construe strongly both against the argument that a term is a warranty at all (131 ff. above) and, if it is, that it is a warranty continuing throughout the insurance period or that it has been broken by the insured (139 ff. above).

One example is the construction that the insured warrants belief rather than truth. Although something is true or not regardless of what the insured believes, warranties are construed not absolutely, but in relation to the honest belief and intention of the insured.[12] So, if the insured promises that 'the vehicle *will* not be driven by any person under 25', a future which he can control, courts have limited the undertaking to a statement of what he intends at the time. Again, if the insured states that he is in good health, that refers not to his actual state of health but to what he honestly and reasonably believes at the time of contract. Moreover, health is relative to expectations of time and circumstance. When an insurer complained that the proposer had not disclosed venereal disease, Lord Mansfield retorted that with such common complaints, 'if such objections were admitted, there would be no end of insurance litigation'.[13] Not so today no doubt, however, health is nonetheless relative to what is expected of the body concerned. In London, for example, the porter who opens taxi doors at the

---

[12] See Clarke, *Law of Insurance Contracts*, 20–5.
[13] *Smith* v. *Mather* (1778) reported in J. A. Park, *A System of the Law of Marine Insurances* (6th edn., London 1809), 482.

Savoy Hotel may not be fit to work as a porter humping carcasses in the early hours of a winter's morning in the meat market at Smithfield.

A second example is that, although it has been strongly argued by insurers that the safety practice of the insured at the time of the contract is of little value to the insurer without a promise that it will continue (lest the insured respond to cover by relaxing his guard) the courts have rejected the argument. Even as a promise confined to the present, it still has value to the insurer as an indication of the sort of person the insured is (then) and is likely to remain (thereafter during the insurance period); so it has been construed as being limited in application to the state of affairs at the time of contract.

Thirdly, a clause requiring precautions or reasonable care during the period of cover conflicts with the supposition that it is a normal and proper purpose of insurance to cover people against their own negligence. In the recent past, the conflict has been resolved by restrictive construction of the clause. In most instances, the court scales down what is required of the insured so that he is covered, unless he has been more than negligent—grossly negligent or reckless: 139 ff. above. Note, however, that the court must be able to justify its decision as a matter of construction of the policy. If the contract specifies precautions clearly, the insured must comply. For example, some travel policies exclude theft of personal possessions from unattended motor vehicles, unless stolen from a locked boot in a vehicle in which all doors and windows have been secured. Although in some cases the boot was not large enough for the possessions of a family on tour, such clauses, being clearly drawn, have been applied.

Although the attitude of the courts is clear, the decisions they will reach are not; at least, they are not so clear that the insured can always be advised with confidence about the effect of every clause in his insurance contract. The courts' duel with the draftsman in years past has left scars and jagged edges. This is what Americans have called the 'juridical risk'. Courts have made it difficult for insurers to tailor premiums closely to narrowly defined risks. 'Insurers capable of making estimates of the probability of natural occurrences are far less able to determine the inclinations of individual judges. Thus, companies must over-estimate premiums to reflect not only the primary risk, but also the secondary risk that courts will extend coverage beyond a policy's intended scope.'[14] The cost of the court's construction in favour of one claimant must be paid for by the rest of the pool. Risk spreading of a kind, perhaps, but is it efficient? To preserve his clause from narrow construction by the courts the insurer must write it into the description of risk covered or spell out the consequences of breach in unequivocal terms.

As a general and central means of controlling insurance contract terms, the tradition is not satisfactory, because it is of only marginal assistance to most consumers. They know that going to court is expensive and that success cannot be guaranteed. Insurers know this too, so they have little incentive to remove unenforceable terms from their contracts. More satisfactory might be institutional intervention of the kind envisaged by the EC Directive (below), whereby bodies representing consumers might have clauses declared unfair on their behalf and to which we now turn.

The EC Directive

The EC Directive on unfair terms in consumer contracts (Council Directive 93/13/EEC of 5 April 1993 [1993] OJ L95/29) was implemented in the United Kingdom by the Unfair Terms in Consumer Contracts Regulations 1994 (SI 1994 No 3159). Unlike the Unfair Contract Terms Act of 1977, which does not apply to terms in insurance contracts, the EC regime does apply to some terms in insurance contracts within the scope of the regime.

The court must first ask whether one party is a consumer. If neither is a consumer, the regime does not apply to the contract. If, however, one is a consumer, the next question is whether the contract was individually negotiated. If it was individually negotiated, the regime does not apply. If, as is likely, it was not individually negotiated, the regime applies.

The first main thrust of the regime is that, unless a term is 'plain and intelligible', it will be 'given the interpretation most favourable to the consumer': regulation 6. The second thrust of the regime is addressed to a term, which is not a core term (see 234

---

[14] D. S. Miller, 'Insurance as Contract: The Argument for Abandoning the Ambiguity Doctrine', 88 *Col. L Rev.* 1849, 1862 (1988).

below), the effect of which is to create a 'significant imbalance' 'contrary to the requirement of good faith': regulation 4(1). Such a term is to be regarded as unfair and, although other terms of the contract remain in force, that term 'shall not be binding on the consumer': regulation 5(1).

Plain and Intelligible

The regime requires terms to be plain and intelligible—but to whom? At common law, if words are not plain to the lawyer, they are ambiguous and are construed against the insurer. The result is that *any* reasonable interpretation advanced by the insured will prevail; but, for the insurer's view to prevail, it must be the *only* reasonable interpretation. If, however, the test is whether it is plain to the lawyer, the regime rule may not go much further than previous common law; and, apparently, the new rule refers to what is plain to the consumer. Whether insurance contracts can ever be drafted in language plain and intelligible to the man in the public house is doubtful: 121 ff. above. Be that as it may, many if not most insurers have reacted to the regime by reviewing their current contracts. Subject to the pitfalls of plain English, this is likely to be beneficial, because, at least, insurers have been compelled to take a new look at some old clauses.

Unfairness

A term is not binding on a consumer if it is unfair. A term is unfair if, 'contrary to the requirement of good faith', it 'causes a significant imbalance in the parties' rights and obligations arising under the contract, to the detriment of the consumer': regulation 4(1). If parties agree a one-sided or unbalanced contract, that is their business and the court has no right to intervene, unless there is also something contrary to good faith. So the key concept is good faith.

Good Faith

The good faith requirement has been criticized as too vague, as one that allows judges to exercise discretion without intellectual rigour.[15] Certainly, for the English judge it is something new. Although some of the phrases used in the regime will remind him of the Unfair Contract Terms Act 1977, it is now agreed that 'unreasonable' under the Act is not the same as 'unfair' under the EC regime. Nor can good faith be equated with 'honesty', as it is understood in English law. But what is it?

Good Faith as an Exception

A famous answer starts from a discourse on ducks.

A real 'duck' differs from the simple 'duck' only in that it is used to exclude various ways of not being a real duck—but a dummy, a toy, a picture, a decoy etc. [The] attempt to find a characteristic common to all things that are or could be called 'real' is doomed to failure; the function of 'real' is not to contribute positively to the characterization of anything, but to exclude possible ways of being not real.

The ducks were those of J. L. Austen. They were borrowed and refloated in the United States as a common law image of good faith.[16]

The American idea is that, although 'good faith' is not usually mentioned, common law has already got a useful combination of rules against bad faith. These rules can be gathered and presented as a team doctrine of good faith, by way of exception. In other words, a term will be fair and enforceable unless, under one of these rules, there is bad faith. In England, the rules include those of estoppel, non-disclosure and misrepresentation, together with fiduciary duties. The English lawyer cannot comfortably say what good faith is, but can say with some confidence (and perhaps clarity) what it is not. This argument has the added attraction that it respects the English tradition of law reform by incremental movement and progress, a tradition which prefers the pragmatic and particular to sweeping generality. The difficulty about adopting the American approach to the good faith of the EC regime is that the Directive gives illustrations of unfair terms that would not be condemned by current English rules of law. A broader, more positive, and perhaps more dynamic concept must be sought.

---

[15] D. Yates, 'Two Concepts of Good Faith' (1995) 8 *JCL* 145–53, 145.

[16] J. L. Austen, *Sense and Sensibilia* (Oxford, 1962), 70–1; borrowed by R. S. Summers, 'The General Duty of Good Faith—Its Recognition and Conceptualization', 67 *Cornell L Rev.* 810–40 (1982).

Synthesis

Although based on German law, the good faith in the regime is not so similar that we can simply import German law. Good faith is also a general and established concept in EC law and in other countries, such as France. Inevitably good faith means slightly different things in different places, so we must look to the attempts made to synthesize the different versions in language that the common lawyer can understand.

According to one, good faith stands for the principle *pacta sunt servanda* and, in particular, a notion that requires the court to look to the spirit or true intent of transactions and the duty to fulfil expectations engendered by one's promise. Another, which is not at all at odds with the first and which seems to be the most promising, speaks of an 'ethic of co-operation'.[17]

An Ethic of Co-operation

The ethic of co-operation as a version of good faith has attractions. First, it is authentically international in so far as it can be traced in commercial arbitrations at that level. Secondly, it is European in so far as a similar version of good faith can be seen in France. Thirdly, it is anything but alien to the common law. A version of the idea of co-operation was a vehicle for the successful launch of good faith in the United States. Moreover, a limited version of that same idea is already part of English common law, where it has been found in two forms. The first is negative—less a positive duty of co-operation than a duty not to obstruct. The second is more positive: if 'both parties have agreed that something shall be done, which cannot effectually be done unless both parties concur in doing it, the construction of the contract is that each agrees to do all that is necessary to be done on his part for the carrying out of that thing, though there be no express words to that effect'.[18]

If the ethic of co-operation is to fulfil the 'reasonable expectations' of the parties to the contract of insurance and to 'achieve the goals' of insurance, those expectations and goals have to be

---

[17] R. Brownsword, 'Two Concepts of Good Faith' (1994) 7 *JCL* 197–243.
[18] *Mackay* v. *Dick* (1881) 6 App. Cas. 251, 263, *per* Lord Blackburn; cf. *Southern Foundries Ltd* v. *Shirlaw* [1940] AC 701, 717.

identified. For argument's sake, let us say that the main purpose of insurance is both to minimize financial loss to the insured and to maximize financial gain to the insurer: by spreading it when it occurs, as well as reducing it by measures taken both before and after its occurrence. If so, what might the parties expect of insurance carried out in an ethic of co-operation?

First, of course, there is the established requirement of 'good faith as disclosure'—mostly that of the insured whenever the insurer has to make a decision: 80 ff. and 168 ff. above. Secondly, insurers should, as many now do, offer not only cover but also advice to reduce risk and promote the prevention of loss. Thirdly, when the scope of cover is in issue, cover should be extended to the very limits of reasonable interpretation; the essentially negative and confrontational rule of construction *contra proferentem*, which is justified on the premise of the pursuit of self-interest on the part of the insurer, becomes a more positive rule in favour of cover. Finally, when claims are settled, co-operation demands speed rather than sloth because the insured needs the money so much more than the insurer.

In contrast, the slow, close scrutiny of claims is essentially non-co-operative and subtractive, and should cease. At the same time, the ethic of co-operation does not require the insurer to sacrifice the interests of his shareholders. The short-term financial gains from a hard view of claims have been at the expense of longer-term interests which, it has been argued (176 ff. above), are better promoted by longer-term relationships. Usually it costs less to indulge an existing customer and keep him than to save in the short term by savaging his claim—but then lose the customer and have to spend more than the money thus saved to attract another customer in place of the first.

Terms Affected

The rule against terms causing imbalance does not apply to 'core' provisions. They can be attacked as unintelligible, but not as being unfair. Core provisions are terms about the scope of cover: 'terms which clearly define or circumscribe the insured risk and the insurer's liability': regulation 3(2). These are not only terms defining insured perils and terms about duration, such as a cancellation clause, but conditions and warranties: 129 ff. above.

Clearly, the exclusion of core terms is important. What are left, for the thrust against imbalance, are mainly terms about claims, remedies, and associated issues of procedure. Schedule 3 of the Regulations contains, according to regulation 4(4), 'an indicative and non-exhaustive list of the terms which *may* be regarded as unfair'.

In a particular case, the eye runs down the list in search of a category for the case in hand. For example, category (i) indicates terms with which the consumer 'had no real opportunity of becoming acquainted before the conclusion of the contract'. English common law expects a certain amount of energy and enterprise on the part of the insurance applicant to seek out the terms. He is bound by the insurer's standard terms for standard risks on the basis of constructive knowledge: 75 above. Hence, it seems, the applicant may have notice under the common law rule, and yet have had no 'real opportunity of becoming acquainted' with them as required by the regime. The anodyne summaries of cover offered by some outlets, e.g. travel agencies selling travel insurance, will not suffice. Moreover, 'acquaintance' interlocks with the requirement of intelligibility. The more complex the terms the less intelligible they become and the harder it will be for the insurer to establish that the consumer had a real opportunity of becoming acquainted with the terms.

Another example is category (n), terms making the insurer's commitments 'subject to compliance with a particular formality'. This includes a term requiring notice of loss. At common law such terms have been rigidly applied, even to the claimant in hospital and in no position to give notice: 183 above. Under the regime he would not be bound. Only 'reasonable notice' could be required by the insurer. Again, the contents insurer, who demanded receipts for all 147 CDs claimed to be stolen, could do so with confidence under the common law but not under the regime.

Enforcement

Evidently, it is open to the insured consumer to plead unfairness before a court. Past experience, however, is that those who use unfair terms are not going to tell the consumer about his rights under the regime. If he does find out, they will insist that 'nobody has complained before' and that their terms are fair, thus raising a prospect of litigation that is likely to deter all but the most determined consumer.

With this in view, Article 7 of the Directive provides that Member States shall ensure that 'adequate and effective means exist to prevent the continued use of unfair terms'. What are envisaged are measures to prevent sellers and suppliers ignoring particular decisions against particular terms or bluffing it out with the consumer. Measures may include measures of criminal law but, in addition, Article 7 provides that the means of prevention shall include provisions whereby consumers' organizations may start actions in court for decision on whether contractual terms drawn up for general use are unfair.

To implement Article 7 English law has regulation 8. It is the duty of the Director General of Fair Trading to consider any complaint, whether from an individual consumer or from an organization, that a term is unfair. If he thinks a term unfair, he *may* bring proceedings for an injunction. This falls short of the facility for individuals or organizations to initiate proceedings, which the Directive requires. The Director must consider all complaints, as long as they are not frivolous or vexatious, but is not obliged to take them to court and, for that reason, the adequacy of regulation 8 is likely to be challenged in the courts.

Self-regulation: Codes

In 1976 it was said with sincerity and conviction that, although a heavy responsibility rested with the intermediary to see that the buyer gets the type of life insurance best suited to his needs, it 'can be claimed with confidence that there are very few life insurance salesman in this country who fail to discharge this responsibility' and that the proposer 'can safely entrust his insurance to the representative of whatever company approaches him'.[19] By 1993, however, the extensive misselling of personal pensions had become a matter of national concern, because it appeared that many people had been 'advised' to change their pension arrangements contrary to best advice. In March 1994 the *Financial Times* concluded that by the 'personal pensions fiasco' public confidence

---

[19] H. Cockerell, *Insurance* (London, 1976), 193.

in the life insurance companies and banks had been 'severely shaken'. In 1997 many victims of bad advice were still awaiting compensation.

Back in the 1970s, moves to regulate the industry, including the proposal to extend the operation of the Unfair Contract Terms Act 1977 to insurers, were countered with promises of self-regulation. Self-regulation by the industry took the form of various Statements of Insurance Practice (codes) for private lines. Their efficacy is a matter of dispute. One objection to the codes is that, although the practices as stated are more favourable to the insured than the general law, they give considerable discretion to the insurer and, therefore, create considerable uncertainty in the mind of the insured about whether a claim will actually be paid. Another is that, although the industry claims that the codes work well, it has little evidence to support (or contradict) this claim. A small-scale survey published in 1992 suggested that, although responsibility for enforcement is shared by the Association of British Insurers (ABI) and the Department for Industry (DTI), neither body actively monitors practice and each body moves only if a member of the public complains.

Parliament

Clearly, insurers do not want more regulation, do not want what they call government 'interference'. Clearly, some people, politicians among them, think that insurers have been left alone too much and too long. The tradition of many other countries, the United States, France, and Germany among them, has been one of control: notably, standard terms for domestic fire insurance and premiums which have to be approved by a state authority. In contrast, much 'law' in England is made by the insurer's own standard form, so it is important that it be 'democratic', i.e. with the agreement of both parties, but in practice it is not.[20] In practice, it is a kind of commercial 'subsidiarity' for the twentieth century, but an imposition of rules nonetheless, a one-sided contract.

Against the possibility of 'undemocratic' abuse, the law has developed rules of interpretation which tend to favour the insured

[20] D. S. Slawson, 'Standard Form Contracts and Democratic Control of Lawmaking Power', 84 *Harv. LR* 529 at 530 (1971).

and, more recently, provided for judicial intervention against unfair terms: 117 and 228 ff. above. Some say that this has worked, but other that, for example, consumer insurance contracts represent the abyss of exploitation permitted by free markets.'[21] On the merits of this debate this book has little to say—except this: any regulation of insurance must have bounds and one of those must be some kind of definition of insurance.

All-embracing 'definitions' of insurance are usually too broad and too bland to be useful. We have an element of insurance in any measure against an adverse event of any kind if someone agrees to compensate us or to help us out: repair, maintenance, cure. The helper's promise is an assumption of risk. Clearly, Parliament does not wish to regulate all these contracts; it does not wish to monitor the solvency of every computer support firm. At what point, then, does the contract become one of insurance, and one that perhaps should be regulated as such? Although judges refer grandly to 'those who are generally accepted as being insurers', they have not stooped to particularity. In most cases, it is clear whether there is an insurer or not. Not surprisingly, however, there is a marginal penumbra of obscurity where traditional insurance products meet the ingenuity of innovative financial markets. There, at the cutting edge, a definition which is sufficiently definite to be useful is not apparent. The best we can say is that the 'generally accepted' archetype appears to have certain features, the prominence of any one of which depends on the case but all of which are usually necessary for there to be insurance.

One feature is that the insurer is in the business of insurance—business in the broadest sense. The insurer may be a charity and insurance may be just one part of its business, but it is insurance business nonetheless. This is a feature because only a 'business' of a certain scale and regularity is an activity which warrants regulation by statute.

A second feature is the insurer's promise to pay—to pay in money or in kind. We think first of money, but in many cases the insurer provides something other than money or something in addition to money: services that range from the reinstatement of

---

[21] H. Collins, 'Good Faith in European Contract Law' (1994) 14 *OJLS* 229–54, 242.

damaged buildings to the provision of a driver or a car while the insured needs one, or of bereavement counselling for a survivor on the death of the life insured. If the insured 'goes down' and breaks his leg, his accident insurer pays money, but his health insurer may provide (and pay for) medical treatment. If his computer 'goes down', his business insurer may provide computer back up so that the business can continue—a service that may be hard to distinguish from that of the company that maintains his computer under what is called a service contract.

A third feature is that the benefit is due only if a specified event occurs. At the time of contracting, it must be uncertain whether the specified event will occur, and, when it does occur, the event must be adverse to the insured. All this still does not sufficiently distinguish insurance, however, because it shares the feature of adversity with the (secondary) promise of any contractor to pay money (damages) on the occurrence of an adverse event for which the contractor is responsible (breach of contract—the primary promise). To distinguish the secondary promise of the contractor, to pay damages, the archetypical insurance promise must concern an adverse event outside the control of either party, something which neither has in any sense brought about.

Most insurance has these three features. If definition is still elusive and even, perhaps, undesirable, what then? If, for example in a sales dispute, courts want to know whether or not a commodity can be regarded as cattle feed, they usually ask the market. Would a businessman in that market describe it as cattle feed? Something of this is found in insurance but with one reservation. An element of distrust of financial markets has led to more caution and, indeed, to the very statutes to regulate their activity and their solvency—statutes which do not define insurance but leave the courts to grasp the nettle instead. So, while having respect for the market view of insurance, the court also asks itself about the purpose of the statute. Is this thing, this cattle feed or this contract, something which it was the purpose of Parliament to regulate under this statute? To the lawyer the shape of insurance depends on the issue in question and hence, as regards regulation, on the statute in question.

The conclusion must be that an easy two-dimensional cut-out concept of insurance is not to be found. The lawyer may well echo the economist, who said that the changing 'concept of insurance is not only a continuum' but also 'a many-sided prism'.[22] Once again, we find, the law of insurance is uncertain, but it is not apparent what can be done about it or, fortunately, that the ordinary insured person suffers as a result.

The Abuse of Insurance

Insurance can be used for unlawful ends. The main example in the past was insurance as a vehicle for gambling. Another paradigm, past and present, is the villain who makes money from murder by first insuring the life and then ending it, or from arson by first insuring the house and then burning it. Clearly, in such cases, the courts would not enforce the contracts. Although it might have responded with specific rules against murder, arson and so on, the law did so with the more general rule requiring insurable interest: 20 ff. above.

The requirement of insurable interest does not deal with the case in which insurance is not the primary means of villainy but ancillary, in that it covers the primary instrument of illegality—hull insurance on the smuggler's ship or simply property cover on the smuggled goods. Clearly, the law will not enforce 'all risks' (AR) cover on cocaine in transit but the outcome of other cases is less easy to predict. Lines have to be drawn in the shifting sands of public policy, and this cannot be done without some sense of direction. Questions arise. What is the role of the court? What is it trying to achieve?

The Role of the Court

A common assumption is that the court, in its decision whether to enforce a contract, should consider the effect of enforcement on society at large. For example, if the smuggler of beer from Boulogne crashes his van, the court may ask whether non-enforcement of his motor insurance is an appropriate form of social censure or retribution? An affirmative answer has attractions but, if the van did not belong to the smuggler or a passing

---

[22] R. Schmidt, 'Considerations on the Significance for Insurance Law of the Consequences of Economic Studies', *Geneva Papers* No. 74 (Jan. 1995), 74–83, 77.

postman was injured in the accident, the attraction of not enforcing the insurance is less obvious. When the van is his (and nobody is injured) what the court may well ask itself is whether enforcement of the insurance will encourage bad behaviour of this kind in future? The sooner he can pay to repair his van, the sooner he can get back on the road to Boulogne, but, even so, the influence of insurance is at its most marginal and the court is likely to enforce it: 221 ff. above. If, however, the question is turned around and becomes whether non-enforcement will discourage bad behaviour of this kind not only by the insured but by others who might use vehicles for breaking the law, non-enforcement by the court is more likely.

One objection to all this is that social engineering, whether aimed at retribution or deterrence, is the role of the criminal court in criminal proceedings and not that of the civil court in a civil case like this. Generally, the civil courts do not set out to punish people, because litigation in the civil courts lacks the evidential and procedural safeguards developed for the protection of offenders by the law of criminal procedure. In a Consultation Paper (no 132, 'Aggravated Exemplary and Restitutionary Damages' (London, 1993), paragraph 5.32), however, the Law Commission has questioned whether that really matters when the liberty of the subject is not at risk. Be that as it may, the main objection to social engineering by the court is different: that retribution is pointless and that, generally, non-enforcement as deterrence simply does not work.

To take examples from actual cases (243 below), can it really be supposed that a cheated husband, inflamed by jealousy and a glass or two of wine, but advised that he may lose his liability cover, will be deterred from assaulting the other man? Or that a bank robber who is undeterred by the prospect of ten years in prison for inflicting injury will, on similar advice, be deterred from endangering the policeman, who is clinging to the get-away car?

If deterrence is to be a factor at all, it cannot be a primary objective of the court's decision but just one of several strands of public policy to be considered. When deciding whether to enforce a contract, the enforcement of which may have socially undesirable effects, the court, it has been said, must weigh the gravity of the anti-social act and the extent to which it will be encouraged by enforcement against the social harm which will be caused if the contract is not enforced. This test, which requires the court to make a value judgement about public policy, has been applied not only in insurance cases but also other cases, and called the 'public conscience test': 248 ff. below.

On one side of the scales the court puts factors for non-enforcement: the encouragement/deterrence factor and also the gravity of the bad behaviour. For example, murder matters more than most other kinds of mischief. On the other side, for enforcement, first, there is sanctity of contract. Society can function only if promises are kept: a central but sometimes forgotten principle of public policy is that, in general, insurance contracts, like other contracts, should be enforced. Secondly, there are the consequences that non-enforcement may have for third parties. In cases of liability insurance, for example, the court will consider carefully the need to compensate victims which, in many cases, will not be fully achieved unless the insurance is enforced.

The Problem of Information

In 1824 Burrough J, in words that have been his memorial, said that public policy is a very unruly horse and that you never know where it will carry you.[23] What he meant perhaps is that public policy is a horse that the judges have not been trained to ride. In 1971 another judge, Lord Denning MR, said that, with a good man in the saddle, it is a horse that can be kept in control; it can leap the fences put up by fictions and come down on the side of justice.[24] The trick, of course, is to ensure that the judge knows what he is doing.

As an instrument of public policy, the public conscience test has to be applied by judges—not according to their own views of public policy but according to precedent, unless, of course, they see no precedent. If indeed there is no precise precedent, in the past that was not perceived as a serious difficulty because, according to Lord Roche[25] in 1927, although 'their applications may be infinitely various from time to time and from place to

---

[23] *Richardson* v. *Mellish* (1824) 2 Bing. 229, 252.
[24] *Enderby Town FC* v. *FA* [1971] 1 Ch. 591, 606–7 (CA).
[25] As he then was: *James* v. *British General Ins. Co.* [1927] 2 KB 311, 322.

place', the principles of public policy are no more than 'a branch of the principles of ethics' and 'are themselves unchanging'. But can the judge today be so confident? Public policy is often obscured by a penumbra of uncertainty, which is beyond the reach of either precedent or the principles of ethics, and which may have as much to do with economics as with ethics. The principles of economics are not beyond dispute nor, like ethics, a matter with which judges can be expected to be familiar. How much does this matter?

Neither ethics or economics are necessary to know that murder is bad for people. Significantly, perhaps, many of the main precedents for the public conscience test concern motor insurance; in these cases, the problem was relatively simple, and in the end the compensation factor was dominant. The main case is *Gardner v. Moore*,[26] in which M had a row with G and deliberately drove his van at him. G survived, but was seriously injured. M was apprehended but was poor and, having been sent to prison, in no position to compensate G. So it is scarcely surprising that, although enforcement of the motor insurance relieved M of the burden of compensation, the House of Lords held that it should be enforced. In contrast, in *Gray v. Barr*,[27] the angry insured (unintentionally but recklessly) killed his wife's lover with a shotgun, but his liability insurance was not enforced. Crimes of violence, said the Court of Appeal, were one of the curses of the age and the public interest demanded that they should be deterred. Motor insurance, said the Court, was different. Perhaps, but on what evidence?

Why, for example, is the man who spreads his tormentor's brains over the stairs with a shotgun so much more of a threat to society, a curse of the age, than the man who spreads most of his victim over the pavement with a van? What evidence was there in *Gray* that death by shotgun was really more of a 'problem' in society than what we now call 'road rage'? Did the court believe and, if so, on what basis that deterrence worked better on angry husbands than on angry motorists? Or that widows in the one situation should be compensated more readily than those in the other? *Gray* gives no answers. Of what counsel said to the judges in *Gray* we know little; and of what the judges said to each other in private before giving judgment, as Lord Mustill has rightly

[26] [1984] AC 548.   [27] [1971] 2 QB 554 (CA).

reminded us,[28] we know next to nothing. We do know, however, from government records of the time, that for every homicidal shooting there were about twenty cases of death caused by reckless or dangerous driving. Is that something which the court knew or should have known?

Fleming has condemned *Gray* as a decision in 'the English judicial tradition' of being 'unequal to the heady challenge of "public policy" '.[29] The decision was unfair to the widow, but Fleming was unfair to the judges. The legal system is not well geared to getting information, such as government statistics, to the court. Judges have to decide cases. They have to do the best they can with the information that they have got. In the greater legal Europe, it is difficult enough, even with counsel before the court and CD-roms on the bench, to trawl current English law for precedent. If the court must go further, how far can it be expected to go? Comparative law? Economics? Psychology?

Consider again the insurance on a van hired to 'smuggle' beer from Boulogne into England for resale in Boozleton. One side says that smuggling beer is just a bit of clean fun and that non-enforcement of the insurance would be hard on the van owner, who may or may not have guessed what it would be used for. The other side says that smuggling is serious because it promotes a culture of lawlessness in otherwise respectable people; that cheap beer imports have serious effects on employment in the domestic brewing industry; and that petty crime associated with drink is a 'bit of a problem' in Boozleton. Is this really an issue best settled by a court of law?

The answer is 'sometimes' but that the response has been patchy. For example, disputes over restraint of trade have been resolved according to the 'interests of the parties'—but for the simple and sensible reason that the parties get an opportunity to participate in argument to the court about their own interests, and any differences are justiciable. In the result, the judgments carry conviction. Occasionally, however, restraint cases have been grounded on the interest of the public at large. Thus, in 1967, the House dealt with tied garages and spoke with the confidence and

[28] Lord Mustill, *What do Judges Do?* (Lecture to the Faculty of Law, Stockholm University, June 1995).
[29] J. G. Fleming, 'Insurance for the Criminal' (1971) 34 *MLR* 176–81, 176.

conviction that came, to a degree at least, from the coincidence of a recent report on the matter by the Monopolies Commission.[30] Later, however, in a case about restraints in the record industry the House did not have that advantage; it lacked the relevant data and, it has been plausibly argued, reached the wrong decision.[31] So in another restraint case requiring, as the judge put it, the balancing of a mass of conflicting economic, social, and other interests which a court of law might be ill-adapted to achieve, 'interests of the public at large would lack sufficiently specific formulation to be capable of judicial as contrasted with un-regulated personal decision and application'.[32] If that is so, can the judges be trained to ride horses of this kind? And should they be?

Gone is the golden age in which an ageing law professor did not read new cases but, nonetheless, could say grandly to his students, 'you will tell me about the cases and I shall tell you about the principles'. Detail can be tedious but, tedious or not, it cannot be ignored. We cannot, like Canute, order back the tide of information and bury Lexis in the sand. People expect judges to be wise—not only in the law but also in other matters, not only in the generalities but also in the detail. Outside every court lies the journalist who knows that he can sell copy by bashing the judges. Judges are not well placed to answer back, but can they at least get better information on which to reach their decisions?

In the United States, the justices of the Supreme Court have clerks to do research. There are moves to provide judges with legal assistants in Australia, Canada, and New Zealand, but not in England and not even in the House of Lords until very recently. There it has been for the insufficient reason that there was insufficient space, but there are more serious objections. First, of course, there is the inevitable objection of cost. Secondly, clerks on the American model are trained in law, and that may not be enough. With or without clerks, it has been doubted whether, to take an example germane to this book, American judges can tell which party to an insurance contract is better able to carry a risk.

---

[30] *Esso Petroleum Co. Ltd* v. *Harper's Garage (Stourport) Ltd* [1968] AC 269.

[31] Trebilcock, n. 10 above, concerning *Schroeder Music Publishing Co. Ltd* v. *Macaulay* [1974] 1 WLR 1308 (HL).

[32] Ungoed-Thomas J in *Texaco Ltd* v. *Mulberry Filling Station Ltd* [1972] 1 WLR 814, 827. More recently in this sense see Hoffman J in *Morgan Crucible Co. plc* v. *Hill Samuel & Co. Ltd* [1991] Ch. 295, 303.

Thirdly, it is fundamental to the English tradition that any opinion formed by the judge from his own research, or that of his assistants, would have to be subjected to the scrutiny and the argument of counsel.

The Role of Counsel

Sometimes the court states a principle in terms which conceal the fact that the process of deciding on liability begins with an answer which is largely intuitive, and reasons backwards from it. Thus one of the roles of counsel lies in what Sir Robert Megarry called 'the purifying ordeal of skilled argument on the specific facts of a contested case' as 'a safety measure against the peril of the judge who yields to preconceptions'.[33] Counsel has an essential role in the adversary system, said Lord Goff, 'in which opposing theories are propounded and debated by advocates on behalf of real clients in whose interests they act', which 'is more likely to reveal the strengths and weaknesses of conflicting arguments than the solitary ruminations of a scholar in the quietness of his study'.[34]

A second role of counsel is that of he is the voice of his client. A survey of public opinion conducted in England early in 1994 by BBC Radio 4 indicated that people believe that judges and magistrates are out of touch with the concerns of ordinary people. Even so, they go to court, and this is partly because they think that the judge will listen and reach a decision on the basis of argument—argument chosen and prepared by counsel, their counsel. The decision, any decision, is more acceptable to someone who has had his or her say than someone who has not. To the extent that the decision is influenced by considerations on which counsel has not been able to comment, whether the influence of bribes (not here an issue) or of the private research or the personal values of the judge, the litigant is excluded from the process of adjudication unless, of course, the research or values are exposed to rational comment by counsel.

At the same time, it follows from arguments of that kind that the court must support its statements with reasons and, when

---

[33] *Cordell* v. *Second Clanfield Properties* [1969] 2 Ch. 9, 16.
[34] 'The Search for Principle', Proceedings of the British Academy 1984. 169, 184–5.

appropriate, with references and statistics. Otherwise parties cannot be sure that their involvement in the decision has been real, or that the court has actually understood and taken into account their arguments. This brings attention back to the quality of the arguments and of the information on which the decision is based. A third role of counsel, it seems, is that of researcher, the source and channel of the information, legal and more. But, if so, where does he stop? Indeed, where does he start?

In the first century AD, Quintilian said to fellow advocates that they must 'not always burden the judge with all the arguments we have discovered, since by so doing we shall at once bore him and render him less inclined to believe us'.[35] In some ways some things do not change. Counsel can scarcely be blamed for not commissioning research on the economic implications of a case if there is little or no chance that it will be heeded by the court. So, if research is to come through counsel, in some measure, the initiative must come from the court. Indeed, in the report of Lord Woolf to the Lord Chancellor in 1996,[36] the recommendation is for more case management by the court. It is the court that will indicate what expert evidence should be brought. This brings our attention back again to the judge—not as researcher but as director of research.

Encouraged by the Lord Chancellor to cut the time and cost of days in court, judges will surely hesitate to commission research—research takes time and money and it is hard to predict how far it must go and how long it will take. Moreover, some observers have wondered whether counsel are the right people to do research of a kind for which some will have no taste and many will have no experience.[37] To that, of course, the answer is that research may be commissioned by counsel and does not have to be carried through by counsel. In the United States it is common for *amicus* briefs, some of high quality, to be put before the Supreme Court on the initiative not of the Court but of outside bodies concerned about the decision. They are welcomed by the Court not only for

---

[35] *Institutio Oratoria*, V, 12, 8.

[36] The Rt. Hon. Lord Woolf, 'Access to Justice' (London, 1996).

[37] P. Birks, 'Adjudication and Interpretation in the Common Law: A Century of Change' (1994) 14 *LS* 156–79, 170; B. S. Markesinis, 'A Matter of Style' (1994) 110 *LQR* 607–28, 622.

their content but also because of the prominent role of the Court
in the democracy of the country, and the associated feeling that
briefs allow the ordinary citizen to express his view to the court of
what the law should be. Why not in England? A prototype is
already in place. The Financial Law Panel (FLP), as one of its
'primary' terms of reference, is to be 'the central forum (working
closely, where appropriate, with existing associations and regulatory bodies) for consideration and practical resolution of legal
uncertainties and anomalies as they affect wholesale financial
markets and services in the UK'.[38] Perhaps we need something
like the FLP, but an institution that can, if required, work in
greater depth and on a larger scale that embraces not only law but
other disciplines.

If the right research is commissioned, it must still be put before
the court. As we have seen, the expert evidence must be available
for comment by counsel. Moreover, expert evidence in writing is
rarely intelligible by persons outside the 'knowledge', without the
opportunity to ask questions of the expert, without dialogue; it
must be distilled, focussed, and brought to bear on the case. All
this has to be done by lawyers, judges, or counsel or both. In the
United States the Supreme Court can cope with the volume of
information because the information is first vetted and filtered by
the clerks paid to assist members of the Court. The English judge
has none of this. English judges are mostly men and women who
have succeeded at the Bar and are, therefore, among the best of
those who show an astonishing ability to absorb new information
for the case in hand, to master any brief. If anyone can cope with
new information it must be the English judge. Even so, it seems
that the volume of information now is such that, whether or not
the *amicus* brief is allowed, the judge is faced with what society is
now calling 'information overload'. He faces problems of both
time and of training.

The Role of the Judge

Judges are trained to solve the immediate problem before the
court. They are not trained to see the distant scene, and most of

---

[38] Final Report, submitted to the Governor of the Bank of England, of the Legal
Risk Review Committee chaired by Lord Alexander, para. 1.1.

them are aware of their limitations. The duties of care in tort, for example, have been developed in recent years not by reference to broad principles or goals but 'incrementally' and with strict regard to 'traditional categories' of case. In *Tinsley* (205 above), a leading case on property and contract law, the public-conscience test was rejected by the House of Lords because it was imponderable and because it gave too much discretion to the judge—a degree of discretion, which the court did not have and probably did not want. Lest Homer should nod, it is, as Aristotle observed, best 'that everything should, as far as possible, be determined absolutely by the laws, and as little as possible left to the discretion of the judges'.[39] Most judges today prefer, it seems, to fall back on the technical black-letter rules in which they were trained, with which they feel comfortable, and into which public policy, economics, and the rest do not come. Is that due modesty or undue caution?

In 1625, Francis Bacon exclaimed that judges should be 'more learned than witty' and 'more advised than confident'.[40] Today, their wit is not an issue; but ours is an age of continuing education. Should something be done about their learning and, at the same time perhaps, even for their confidence? The Judicial Studies Board does excellent work, but is short of money and other resources; and judges are short of time. High Court judges are not obliged to attend sessions arranged by the Board and not many do. Lord Mansfield developed the law of marine insurance from his own knowledge of Continental practice and custom, much of it acquired by his own personal and professional contact with merchants and underwriters. Something of this tradition survives. In a jurisdiction where most judges once practised at the Bar, the feeling is that judges know what business people want, without having to ask. They have dealt with these people as clients and learned their ways. But, even if that is true of the mysteries of commerce and finance, the horse of public policy is not confined to the City, and a wider range of expertise may be required of the court.

Until judges are given the time and the incentive to learn, and the assistance to marshal the flow of information, the conclusion

---

[39] *The Rhetoric* (transl. Welldon) Bk. I, Ch. I.
[40] *Essays* (1625), LVI, 'Of judicature'.

must be that litigation will not be the best framework for research; the drawings for the social plan must be done somewhere else. Certain issues affecting public policy—those with the widest implications for the largest number of people—are often (but not always) those that take the case beyond the proper limits of adjudication. In such cases, it is not reasonable to expect either the parties or their counsel to undertake an investigation and to seek solutions, work best done in or for Parliament. Until that occurs, the cases will still come to the courts. The judges still have to decide them. What are they to do?

The Response of the Court

In *Tinsley* v. *Milligan* the House of Lords rejected the public-conscience test, which would have given discretion to judges in matters of public policy, in favour of an older and uncompromising principle of Lord Mansfield: 'No court will lend its aid to a man who founds his cause of action upon an immoral or an illegal act.'[41] This principle offers a more modest and more secure basis for refusing to enforce insurance contracts: that the court, conscious of the need to keep its hands clean, does not want to be seen to assist the claimant, through his insurance, to profit from his wrongdoing. Unlike the public-conscience test, this is a workable rule, which requires the court only to handle lawyers' law, to find the facts, and apply rules of deduction.

If the wrongdoing is murder, for example, the victim's life insurance has always been enforced except to the extent that the money goes to the murderer or, if he is executed, to his estate. Neither he nor his must profit from his wrong. This remains the rule. In *Davitt* v. *Titcumb*,[42] the defendant bought a house with a mortgage secured by life insurance on himself and his partner. When he murdered his partner, the insurance money on her life went to the innocent mortgagee. The house was then sold to pay off the small balance due to the mortgagee and other debts, leaving a considerable surplus. But for the murder, there would have been no insurance money and no surplus, to which, held the

---

[41] [1994] I AC 340, 360 ff. *per* Lord Goff, with reference to *Holman* v. *Johnson* (1773) I Cowp. 341, 343.
[42] [1990] Ch. 110.

court, the defendant was not entitled: he must not be enabled to profit from his wrong.

If the wrongdoing concerns property, theft, or smuggling for example, the principle is the same, although it is sometimes less easy to apply. In *Geismar*[43] insured jewellery, on which the duty payable had not been paid, was stolen. The insurance claim failed, not because enforcement would assist the claimant to obtain a profit—his profit had been made already when he brought back the jewellery without paying duty—but because the court would not assist him to keep it. As long as he had the jewellery, it might have been seized by the customs authority; but once it was transmuted into insurance money it was beyond its grasp. If, however, the claimant had sold the jewellery and used the money to buy jade, insurance on the jade would have been enforced. The lesson of *Geismar* is that the clean hands of the court may have to handle clean money that once was dirty; but the court cannot be expected actually to launder it.

If the wrongdoing is a tort, the enforceability of liability insurance, as we have seen, has been decided in the past on something like (but not called) the public conscience test. If, as is not yet clear, the rejection of that test in *Tinsley* extends to liability insurance, would the cases have to be decided differently? Probably not. The wrong (the crime) triggers the wrongdoer's liability and thus his insurance. If the court enforces the insurance, it does not thereby assist the insured to make a profit but it does reduce his loss. Although he is no better off than he was before his crime, he is still less badly off than he would have been after the crime because, to take a simple case like *Gardner* (243 above), the driver's liability to his victim has been discharged by the insurance. What counts is the role of the court, which is less one of assisting a wrongful design than of compensating a victim. Moreover, if the wrongdoer profits, it is not from the crime but from the insurance. Thus, it seems, Lord Mansfield's uncompromising principle has not been compromised. Conscience is clear and hands are clean.

Even so, in cases like that people might say that the effect of enforcing the insurance was that the wrongdoer 'got off lightly'. In a sense he did, but he did not 'get off' punishment; he went on to prison. The insurance paid his debt to the victim but not his debt to

---

[43] *Geismar* v. *Sun Alliance & London Ins. Ltd* [1978] 1 QB 386.

society. That is something that insurance cannot do. A distinction has been drawn between insurance of civil liability to the victim, which may be enforced, and insurance to cover the penalties of the criminal law, whether in money or in kind, which are not enforced.

The distinction is clear in principle, but in practice it may be difficult to draw. Between penalties and civil damages are exemplary damages. The Court of Appeal has held[44] recently that an award of damages made up both of compensation damages and exemplary damages can be covered by insurance. The court did not have to decide whether exemplary damages could be covered as a separate item of cover, and that is a question that remains open. Another unsettled question concerns 'mobility cover'. For many motorists the most serious consequence of a motoring conviction for 'drunk driving' is not the fine but disqualification. Currently this can be covered as just one part of 'mobility cover', which provides a driver or the cost of alternative transport in the event of the insured's loss of his own vehicle as a result not only of injury but also of disqualification. If the purpose of disqualification is simply to protect the public from a bad driver, the cover is inoffensive but if, as it is generally perceived, the purpose is to be part of the punishment, the cover is surely difficult to justify.

Insurance Law and Society

As we have just seen, the law is not well suited to be a negative instrument of public policy. It is more useful in a more positive role, to assist the social aims of insurance, and among the possibilities are fairness (256 ff. below) and economic efficiency.

Economic Efficiency

The meaning of 'economic efficiency' is a matter of debate, but it is sufficient here to say that it is achieved when people use resources in the way which is most valuable to them. It is often assumed, however, that people bargain with each other in a world of zero transaction costs, where there is no allocation of risks by law, so as to maximize the joint value of their resources. In these terms insurance is efficient at the lowest combined cost of

[44] *Lancashire CC* v. *Municipal Mutual Ins. Ltd* [1996] 3 All ER 545.

insurance and of loss prevention. The student in digs may well find that it is cheaper and thus more efficient to buy a good lock for the door of his study/bedroom than to pay for contents cover: if he pays £20 for a lock rather than £160 for the lowest level of cover available, that leaves him with £140 for beer or the replacement of anything which, in spite of the lock, may be stolen while he is at the pub. Meanwhile back at his home, his parents are seen as a 'better' risk by the insurer and are quoted lower premiums; so, in theory at least, they will not only buy insurance but spend money on locks and alarms until the cost of these precautions exceeds any discount on the premium quoted.

In both cases, insurance law can assist by seeing that, as far as possible, the parties have the information needed to make an efficient decision. This means, for example, that the insurer must have the information needed to rate the risks accurately and cheaply, and that the applicant understands the terms available—which, of course, usually he does not: 119 ff. above. In practice, perfectly informed parties contracting do not exist. For the student, who decides against buying insurance, the law can do little more. For the parents, who do buy insurance, the law can help by reducing transaction costs, notably by offering a good legal framework for contracting and for claims, and by enforcing the relevant contract terms.

When insurance is efficient, its function is to spread loss. This is not an immediate concern of the law, however, one problem concerns whether the law which allows subrogation actually impairs that function.

Subrogation

In insurance law, the function of subrogation is twofold.[45] The first is to preserve the principle of indemnity: 186 ff. above. If insurer U compensates insured A for the damage to his car by the careless driving of X, but then finds that A has also been compensated by X, the law of subrogation enables U to recover from A to the extent that A has been over-indemnified. The second function is to allow U, once he has compensated A for the damage to his car, to

---

[45] Generally, see Clarke, n. 12 above, ch. 31; and C. Mitchell, *The Law of Subrogation* (Oxford, 1994), 67 ff. and 174–5.

exercise any rights that A has against X, i.e. in that case, to claim in A's name against X in tort.

The first function of subrogation, to preserve the underlying principle of indemnity, could be achieved in other ways. For example, A might be required to claim as much as he could from X before he claimed from U. This alternative has been rejected because the burden of recovery, litigation perhaps, is one that U is usually better able to bear than A and is something that A wants to avoid—probably something which motivated him to insure in the first place.

The first function of subrogation could also be achieved by reducing the amount that A could get from X by the amount of the insurance money he could be expected to get from U. This alternative has also been rejected. The courts recoiled from the idea that the providence of victim A, in buying insurance, should relieve wrongdoer X of the burden of damages. Moreover, that would remove any incentive for U to proceed against X, and thus impair one aspect of the second function of subrogation, that people like X should be punished by being made to pay. Perceptions of punishment, however, usually premise that the punishment should match the 'crime'. So, inevitably it must seem a bit bizarre that a wrongdoer's liability varies according to whether victim A is rich or poor, whether his car is a Mercedes or a Mini; and no less bizarre, surely, if X's liability also depends on the chance of whether A is insured, so that he is let off the hook in the one case (more likely in prosperous communities) but not in the other.

As regards the second function of subrogation, to allow U to exercise any rights that A has against X, the loss has been moved in the direction of U and his pool, so, why redirect it to X and, if X's liability is insured with Y, to Y and his pool? To many people, this seems to be a costly and inefficient way of spreading loss. An entertaining illustration is Weir's discussion of a celebrated action in subrogation:

Shortly after Mr. Murphy's house in Brentwood settled, so did his insurance company. . . . Murphy was happy enough with the £35,000 it paid him, but [the company] went off to court (with which it is much more familiar than Mr Murphy) and claimed the whole of its payment from Brentwood District Council, allegedly at fault in passing plans for Mr. Murphy's house. The company won and the public paid. Now it hardly needs saying (any more) that a local authority does not normally have to pay companies which suffer merely pecuniary loss as a result of their carelessness as the [company] did in this case, and it is hard to imagine anybody less deserving than an insurer who profits from taking the risk that houses may collapse. . . . But our absurd law as to subrogation to tort claims means that in such cases the public must bail out our private insurers.[46]

True, to enforce the liability of X has the apparent attraction that wrongdoer X may get something of what he deserves, but is that a concern of the law of insurance?

One part of an affirmative answer is that subrogation allocates costs to the activity to which the damage is attributable, and through X to those who have benefited from the activity. However, if A is a motorist, A is in the same (or a connected) risk pool, and so it remains a costly and inefficient way of spreading loss. The other part of the answer is that subrogation is a tool of social engineering to implement a theory of deterrence. In theory, the cost of accidents is thus placed upon those who can avoid them most cheaply (X and his pool rather than A and his) and who will be spurred (mainly by higher liability premiums) to avoid them. This part of the answer is open to a number of objections.

One objection is that it is doubtful that X will be deterred. In particular, it is not all clear that he will respond to higher premiums by reducing the amount of dangerous activity (driving less) or pursue it with more care (drive better). Deterrence theory assumes that people behave 'rationally', whereas, arguably, motoring is an activity which, under the influence of powerful advertising, is motivated less by the light of reason than by much darker elements in human nature. Further, if A was damaged not by X's car but by X's product, producer X can simply pass the cost on to his consumers and thus perhaps back to A; in this situation, evidently, subrogation is wasteful, as well as insensitive to the needs of individuals.[47]

A further objection is that, even if X responds rationally, he

---

[46] Tony Weir, 'Government Liability' [1989] *PL* 40–63, 43, concerning *Murphy* v. *Brentwood DC* (1988) 13 Con. LR 96, later affirmed [1990] 2 All ER 269 (CA); appeal allowed [1991] 1 AC 378. See also R. Hasson, 'Subrogation in Insurance Law—A Critical Evaluation' (1985) 5 *OJLS* 416–38.

[47] See J. Stapleton, *Product Liability* (London, 1994), 73 ff., 150 ff., and 205 ff.

may well reason that, in practice, recourse in subrogation against him is not very likely, and has little effect on premiums, whether his own or those paid by others. As a deterrent, it seems that subrogation simply does not work[48] and, in conclusion, that the law does little service to society by allowing it.

Fairness

Most social institutions work better if the people affected perceive them as fair. The fairness of insurance depends in part on the law. One obvious way of promoting fairness between insured and insurer is by having rules of law designed to redress any imbalance of information or of bargaining power between them, both at the stage of contracting insurance and of settling claims. At first sight, the focus of these rules appears to be fairness between a particular insured and a particular insurer. But, unless some attention is paid to their effect on the rest of society, fairness may be at the expense of uncertainty, and thus cost to others in the future—especially in grey and value-ridden areas such as moral hazard.

Classification of Risk

Fairness between insured persons in general implies that there should be a fair distribution of risk. The problem here is that people do not agree entirely about fairness, whether it concerns insurance or other aspects of wealth; and, although there is a larger measure of agreement about *un*fairness, there is less agreement on what to do about it. The issue cannot be avoided, however, because insurers cannot insure risks without classifying them, and any classification must distribute risk. Classification, therefore, raises issues of fairness between the people affected.[49] It is not, however, an issue which is as important as instinct suggests. First, it is difficult to condemn a classification as unfair without being sure about the causes of the loss in question, and often we are not. A merely statistical correlation between loss and a certain risk 'factor' may be a good ground for insurance

---

[48] Abraham, n. 1 above, 154–5; R. Derham, *Subrogation in Insurance Law* (Sydney, 1985), 153.

[49] See further Abraham, n. 1 above, 19, 64, and 83 ff.; W. P. J. Wils, 'Insurance Classification in the E.C.' (1994) 14 *OJLS* 449, 456 ff.

classification without being sure ground for any judgement about fairness. For example, if there is a statistical correlation between smokers and road accidents, is it fair to charge smokers more for cover? Secondly, fairness may be too expensive. Insurers choose risk factors not for their fairness but according to how difficult and, therefore, how costly it is to get the relevant information and to administer the classification. Most people would agree that people who do not smoke should pay less for life and health insurance, but not many insurers offer a discount of this kind because it is difficult to check that the insured who tells the insurer that he does not smoke is telling the truth. Nor do many people demand discounts of this kind, once the administrative cost and associated effect on premiums is explained to them.

For the insurer, the best classification is one which enables him to sell insurance profitably. If, on the one hand, the insurer were able to assess each individual risk with complete accuracy and state a premium for it, he would put himself out of business—as an insurer; he would still be in business as an actuary and the applicant would pay for the assessment and then self-insure on that basis. Of course, complete accuracy is not possible for most risks, some applicants at least will run for cover in a pool of like risks and buy insurance. If, on the other hand, the insurer's pool is too large, i.e. his classification of the risk is perceived as being too broad, the effect in some cases is that the good risks pay for the bad risks to such an extent that, eventually, the former will react to perceived unfairness, leave the pool, and insure elsewhere ('unravelling'). If that happens, the insurer will be left with a disproportionate share of bad, i.e. unprofitable, risks ('adverse selection'), and will go out of (that kind of) business. The trick is to classify in a way that convinces the customer that he is in the 'right' pool; and this tends to more precise classification, smaller pools, and 'niche' marketing. The trend has been made possible by the power, speed, and, ultimately, cheapness of the computer. For example, one house contents insurer uses nineteen different rating factors, including exact geographical location down to groups of only fifteen houses.

A corollary of niche classification is that some people cannot find their niche, i.e. no insurer wants them at all or at a price they can afford. In some cases, along comes a specialist insurer and the bad risks are swept up into a niche of their own; but some are left out, and they, or someone for them, will call this 'unfair' and 'discriminatory'. Is it?

The primary dictionary meaning of 'discriminate' is 'different-iate' or 'distinguish'. A person who chooses to buy from one vineyard rather than another may be complimented as a discrimin-ating person; or, if his choice is criticized, it will not be because it is unfair but because it is ill-advised. Evidently, discrimination is not judged in the abstract but with reference to context. Nobody will think it unfair if an insurer (male) chooses to have sex with a woman rather than a man but, if he chooses to insure women but not men, that may be seen as unfair. In the context of insurance some degree of discrimination is inevitable—but is it acceptable?

Anti-discrimination law, which is concerned less with the blameworthiness of the discriminator than with a remedy for the perceived disadvantage to the 'victim', may say that it is never acceptable; this appears to be the position taken by the European Court of Justice (ECJ) to direct discrimination that infringes the Equal Treatment Directive.[50] The Sex Discrimination Act, how-ever, is more like international law, which allows the differential treatment of groups when exercised for the welfare of the community as a whole or when 'just and reasonable'. Insurance classification satisfies these standards, if it results in an acceptable distribution of risk.

The Distribution of Risk

Let us suppose that a fire insurer believes that fires are more likely to break out in the houses of first-generation immigrants from Arcadia than in those of other people living in the same area, and charges the Arcadians higher premiums. Will that be perceived as unfair?

One group in society may value freedom of contract so highly that it defends the 'right' of the insurer to load these people, as the insurer thinks fit, also pointing out that such underwriting practices promote fairness to the policyholder in not requiring him or her to bear in premiums the costs of insuring others in higher risk categories, and also the solvency of the insurer, which is in the

---

[50] See E. Ellis, 'The Definition of Discrimination in European Community Sex Equality Law' (1994) 19 *EL Rev.* 563–80.

interest of society at large. The law should not interfere with underwriters' commercial judgement. A second group, which values risk spreading, might argue that Arcadian immigrants are less likely than other groups to see the importance of adequate insurance and should be encouraged to insure by lower premiums. A third group might also argue for lower premiums, but for a different reason, namely, that Arcadians tend to be poorer than other groups and cheap insurance is a way of redistributing wealth. Studies suggest that it is not an effective method of redistribution,[51] nonetheless, the argument cannot be ignored. A fourth group might argue for higher premiums for Arcadians because they are less likely than other people to install solar heating, which is safer and greener and which the group wants to encourage. Finally, a fifth 'egalitarian' group might rule out consideration of all factors over which the applicant had no control, and thus rule out the (Arcadian) origin of the insured.

English practice currently takes the position of the first group, qualified, however, with some regard for the second and fifth positions. The interplay of the first and fifth positions can be seen in the operation of legislation against discrimination.

Unfair Discrimination

In the last century, at least one life office demanded an additional premium if the life insured was Irish. In England today, discrimination on the ground of nationality, whether it be Irish or Arcadian, is prohibited by Article 6 of the EC Treaty. So, for example, when German insurers tried to charge certain nationals more for motor cover, the Commission objected and, it is generally believed, the objection would have been sustained by the ECJ. Other instances of particular difficulty concern classification according to sex and, recently, certain aspects of the applicant's medical profile.

Sex Discrimination

The Sex Discrimination Act 1975 is infringed if a person is treated less favourably than persons of the opposite sex unless, as regards insurance, that treatment is based on 'actuarial or other data from

---

[51] Abraham, n. 1 above, 25; Wils, n. 49 above, 461.

a source on which it was reasonable to rely': see sections 1, 2, and 45. In *Pinder*[52] it was held that a self-employed female dentist could be lawfully charged health insurance premiums 50 per cent higher than self-employed male dentists, because the insurer had data suggesting that women in that position were more likely to be 'off sick'. In contrast, men are commonly charged more than women for motor cover, but this has yet to be challenged in the courts—by a man or a woman.

Perhaps this is because, in reality, the perceived evil is not discrimination by sex but discrimination by men against women. Hence the insurance exception has been attacked because, in the past, women were stereotyped as inferior and weak, and the retention of a series of exceptions in anti-discrimination legislation, which is ostensibly designed to eradicate such stereotypes, sends out competing messages. The protected class is said to be further stigmatized as inferior and weak by being singled out for protection.[53] Some critics go further and argue that all classifications encroach on the fundamental right of a person to be treated as an individual.

Arguments of this kind were adopted by the US Supreme Court[54] and may well have influenced the legislature in certain states (e.g. Pennsylvania and Ontario) to prohibit the rating of applicants on the basis of sex altogether. Such arguments were put to the ECJ in *Neath*.[55] Argument in that case started from the principle of equal pay for equal work in Article 119 of the EC Treaty and attacked a pension scheme, to which an employer contributed, under which contributions were higher for women than for men. The arguments were accepted by the Advocate General in his Opinion of 28 April 1993 but rejected by the Court. The Court ruled that inequality of employers' contribution schemes paid under funded defined-benefit schemes, justified as they were by actuarial tables that women lived longer than men, did not breach Article 119. The Court appears to have accepted the insurer's position, that it is in the nature of insurance that

---

[52] *Pinder* v. *The Friends Provident* (1985) 5 EOR (Equal Opportunities Reports) 31 (Westminster County Court). See also the Disability Discrimination Act 1996.
[53] M. Thornton, 'Sex Discrimination and Insurance' (1990) 3 *Ins. LJ* 12, 13. See also Wils, n. 49 above, 458–60.
[54] *City of Los Angeles* v. *Manhart*, 435 US 702 (1978).
[55] Case C–152/91 *Neath* v. *Hugh Steeper Ltd*; Wils, n. 49 above, 463 ff.

people must be seen less as individuals than as members of a class and that the data on sex classification speak for themselves. The terms of the judgment are narrow, however, and do not exclude altogether further assault on pension schemes under Article 119.

A further argument might be that data of that kind do not necessarily speak for themselves but may speak for something else: that the classification cannot be taken at face value and that there is an unacceptable hidden agenda. Just as insurance classification by colour has been shown in the United States to be really a cheap, convenient, and crude proxy or surrogate for other, usually cultural, risk factors, the same may be true of sex. Even if this is true, it may be, of course, that behind the classification lies another factor to which no objection can be taken; or it may not. If, for example, it emerged that a lower rate for women drivers under 25 is because they drive less, that is unlikely to satisfy those who believe that the lower mileage reflects other social disadvantages associated with sex: that women drive less because of lower economic status and because they are afraid to drive at night. Although critics see the avoidance of the historical stereotype as a social goal sufficiently important to require the more costly and less unfair search for the concealed cultural factors, it is clear that the investigation may be long and complex. Moreover, the more thorough the investigation and the more refined the classification, the more likely that any attempt to match applicants to the classification will infringe other values such as privacy. Finally, some women may be willing to put up with the discrimination. On the other hand, insistence in Montana on unisex rating for drivers between the ages of 17 and 23 led to a considerable drop in premium for men but an even more considerable rise in premium for women; some women at least preferred the 'discrimination' they had 'enjoyed' before unisex rating. Whether or not classification of this kind is justified is not our immediate concern, which is simply to demonstrate that issues of this kind tend not to be simple at all.

AIDS

The interplay of the first and second positions (258–9 above) is seen in acceptance by the insurance industry that it ought to cover certain groups that most insurers would prefer not to have on their books: 70 ff. above. An important instance is when the applicant has or is likely to have AIDS. For some years insurers asked whether applicants had had 'a negative HIV/AIDS test or counselling'. One objection to this question is that it is pointless, because, although a negative HIV test suggests that the subject is more likely to contract AIDS, it does not indicate a probability of AIDS; and that many of those likely to have received counselling were in certain professions, such as nursing, or were simply people who were concerned, and were by no means people more likely than others to contract AIDS. Another objection is that the question deters some people from having the test for fear that they will be unable to obtain (affordable) insurance or that the result will be leaked to third parties. A third objection, based on experience in the United States, is that insurers will be tempted to use the information in a way that discriminates unfairly against homosexual or bisexual men. For example, in 1985, an American reinsurer published an 'AIDS profile' in its 'underwriting guidelines'. This required underwriters to differentiate between 'single males without dependents that are engaged in occupations that do not require physical exertion' and named the occupations in mind: 'restaurant employees, antique dealers, interior decorators, consultants, florists and people in the jewelry or fashion business'.[56]

Finally, a broader objection of a different order is that ignorance of one's bodily condition, if not bliss, is a fundamental human right. The objection assumes the necessity of chance in life and a person's right not to know as an integral part of existential freedom, without which the human personality cannot fully develop. This kind of consideration has been recognized by the BMA. It has even been suggested that any infringement might be contrary to the constitution in some countries, such as Italy, or contrary to international conventions on human rights.[57] Of course, testing might be arranged in such a way that the subject was unaware of the result, but would such a procedure satisfy concerns about human dignity? In any event, in England, the Association of British Insurers (ABI) withdrew its previous support for that kind of question in 1994.

---

[56] B. Schatz, 'The Aids Insurance Crisis: Underwriting or Overreaching?' 100 *Harv. L Rev.* 1782–805, 1787 (1987).
[57] E. Deutsch and G. De Oliveria (eds.), *Genome Analysis: Legal Rules—Practical Application* (Coimbra 1994), 132–3.

Genetic Screening

On the one hand, insurers can and do require, for example, a general medical examination—without provoking public outrage. On the other hand, objections to testing are not confined to AIDS but are also raised with regard to genetic tests.

In December 1993, the Nuffield Council on Bioethics published a report, *Genetic Screening, Ethical Issues*, in which it supported the current practice of the insurance industry of not requiring any genetic testing. The Council also recommended a temporary moratorium on requiring disclosure of existing genetic data except, first, when there is a known family history of genetic disease that can be established by conventional questions about the applicant's family and, secondly, when the amount insured exceeds a certain figure (to be settled between the Government and the industry). The recommendation is based on practice in Holland and is not unlike that in Germany.[58] Elsewhere there is little accord. In New York, on the one hand, where insurers' use of tests for health insurance was condemned by the Superintendent of Insurance, his decision was challenged and the practice upheld by the court. Moreover, it has been suggested that a prohibition might infringe EC law as inhibiting the free provision of services unless justifiable in the public interest.[59] On the other hand, in Belgium the Insurance Act of 1992 (section 5) simply rules out the disclosure of all genetic data. In Norway, Law no. 56 of 5 August 1994 (Lov om medisinsk bruk av bioteknologi) provides that it shall be unlawful 'to request, possess or use information, concerning another person, obtained through genome analysis'. Exception is made for certain licensed health-care institutions and for physicians needing the information for diagnostic or curative purposes. Clearly, the prohibition is intended to apply to insurers. In England the Council's position is at odds with that of the insurance industry. In evidence to the House of Commons Science and Technology Committee in January 1995, a representative of the ABI stated that, if applicants have had genetic tests that indicated that they might be prone to disease, insurers expect this

[58] G. Wiese, *Genetische Analysen und Rechtsordnung* (Berlin, 1994), 77 ff. Further, see Y. Chiche, 'Genetics & Life and Health Insurance: International Aspects', *Geneva Papers* No 76 (July 1995), 274–78.

[59] Wils, n. 49 above, 467.

to be disclosed, and that, if insurers were banned from requiring this information, premiums would have to rise. This was confirmed by a statement in 1997; however, the ABI also announced that people will not be asked to take genetic tests when applying for life insurance. In response to a recommendation of the Committee, in June 1996 the government set up an advisory commission to report to minister on human genetic developments and to public its findings.

Until genetic tests have real predictive value, which currently they do not, except for a few relatively rare diseases such as Huntington's disease and cystic fibrosis, insurers may want tests but probably will not require them for fear of losing market share. Let us suppose, however, that science establishes a high probability that all those with the Arcadian gene will contract AIDS and that all insurers would like to test for the gene. If insurers are allowed to test, the Arcadian AIDS risks is likely to be carried not by private insurance, which might well be too expensive for most Arcadians, but by whatever social security is in place. If insurers are not allowed to test or underwrite on the basis of previous tests, insurers will have to raise premiums against the possibility that there are Arcadians in their pool, and the Arcadian AIDS risks will be carried by the pool. From the viewpoint of wealth distribution, it is not self-evident that the second solution is fairer than the first; indeed experience in the United States suggests secondary unfairness to the pool from adverse selection: people who suspect that they may be more than averagely at risk from AIDS are taking (more) insurance. Clauses that exclude pre-existing conditions are of limited use, not least because the latency period for AIDS is up to four years. In France, a more militant view has been advanced: to avoid unfairness to the pool and, we may add, to shareholders in insurance companies, the insurer has a duty to investigate genetic aspects at risk or, at least, will have such a duty once the predictive value of genetic testing has been established.[60] This thinking is reflected in the French code of conduct[61] that has been agreed with insurers there on the

[60] F. Ewald and J. P. Moreau, 'Génétique Médicale', (1994) 18 *Risques*, 111–20, 116.

[61] Convention sur l'assurabilité des personnes séropositives et sur les règles de confidentialité du traitement des informations médicales par l'assurance', 18 *Risques* (Apr.–June), 121.

obtaining and use of information on the health of insured persons or persons seeking insurance cover. In any event, even on the supposition that the tests are predictive for individuals, that does not help the insurer to price group insurance policies: in these, which are now widespread, the insurer is assessing the risk characteristics of the group as a whole, rather than that of the individual applicant.

Finally, it should be recalled that, until English law does away with the residual duty of disclosure, the applicant may be obliged to disclose information of this kind anyway, whether the insurer asks for it or not: 85 ff. above. In contrast, in Germany where non-disclosure does not avoid the contract unless the applicant was at fault (Versicherungsvertragsgesetz, Article 16.3), it is arguable that the importance and sensitivity of genetic information are such that, even if the applicant has such information, failure to disclose it is not fault. In current English law, of course, such an argument is not even worth running.

The Insurer as Licensor

Many a collector, whether of stamps, china, or plastic gnomes, has satisfactory cover for his collection under a household contents insurance. Then the time may come when the collection has reached a value that makes the insurer uneasy. He starts putting in the policy onerous conditions about the storage of the collection and insists on safes or starts to charge stiff rates. He may even require a schedule that catalogues every stamp. The message, of course, is that the insurer does not want to lose the business, but does not want to cover the collection. Probably the collector will find affordable cover with an insurer who specializes in that kind of business. Others may be less fortunate. In one instance, contents cover for (high risk) students and other persons in shared accommodation required that small valuables worth more than £50 be kept in a substantial cupboard with strong internal bolts and five-lever lock to British Standard 3621. This too is tantamount to saying 'don't buy these things or don't buy insurance from us'. In this case, however, specialist cover may not be available at all and general contents cover may have become unaffordable. Is that just 'life'?

The question has been the subject of serious debate in

connection with the EC Proposed Directive for Civil Liability for Damage Caused by Waste.[62] The possibility of compulsory insurance raised again the question whether, by providing, pricing, and withholding cover, insurers would effectively decide which businesses did business, and if they did do business, how they did it; in other words, whether that would or should make insurers 'licensors' of industry. Already marine insurers have driven old and unsafe ships to the breaker's yard and they could do something similar in other industries with potential for pollution. Should there be any constraint or control on the insurers? The question is not new. It arises every time there is a conflict of expectations—between insurers who consider that they have a right to choose their insured and the public which believes that, as regards some risks at least, it has a right to cover.

The 'Right' to Cover

The 17 year old in London who cannot obtain or cannot afford basic insurance cover to ride a motorcycle cannot (lawfully) ride a motorcycle. True, some will ride anyway, not least the streetwise cowboys who have found that the cost of paying fines for riding without insurance is less than the cost of insurance. However, for most young people the cost of cover is decisive, and they do not motorcycle. No doubt this pleases London taxi drivers, except perhaps those who realize that the cost of motorcycle cover is driving the young to buy cheap second-hand cars instead with which to make their own contribution to congestion in the capital.

A response of a different kind was heard in an American case.[63] It is that the effect of a clause excluding motor cover was an unacceptable deprivation of the basic necessities of life, a violation of the fundamental right to travel, and thus a violation of the Constitution. The argument failed, but on other grounds; the premises about the necessities of life and the right of travel were not disputed. In England, opinion does not appear to go that far but, in 1994, motor insurers faced attack not only from newspapers

---

[62] See e.g. J. I. J. Goldberg, 'An Uncertain Future: Retroactivity, Insurance, and the EC's Attempts at Environmental Legislation', 33 *Va. J Int. L* 684–715 (1993).

[63] *Mayo* v. *Nat. Farmers Union*, 833 P 2d 54 (Colo., 1992).

but also the Consumers' Association for 'cherry-picking' good risks. The assumption was that there is a 'right' to drive on the roads, hence a 'right' to insurance; that it was somehow 'wrong' that insurers should pick and choose. Similarly, the newspapers have sought to stimulate public debate over whether property insurers should be compelled to offer affordable cover for homes and business in the inner cities.

The Right to Select Risks

If anyone does drive without insurance, it is the industry (by means of the Motor Insurers' Bureau (MIB) and a 1 per cent levy on policies) that pays for any damage he does. To this degree at least insurers collectively take on drivers, many of whom no individual insurer would want on his books. This is not, however, in any sense a recognition of a driver's right to drive, but of the victim's 'right' to compensation. The MIB agreement was a special case of collective action, indeed of defensive action less for the driver's victim than for the industry itself—against the peril of 'government interference' that might ensue, if the motoring mayhem were uninsured.

The industry is wedded to the ethos of free enterprise. In 1994, for example, a journal leader spoke of 'the dangers of a Government presence causing distortions in the marketplace and creating a lame duck industry' like the car industry of the 1960s and 1970s, and concluded that, indeed, 'the industry does not want to wake up one morning and find itself effectively controlled by civil servants and Government ministers'.[64]

The individual insurer's perception of his role and responsibility in society does not see risk distribution as a primary goal, but rather a useful by-product of the natural operation of the free market. A natural market involves natural selection. Indeed, some insurers think that the cherries want to be picked out from the rotten apples: one has advertised motor insurance as 'taking careless drivers off your back'. Whether or not that is what the market wants, market forces push insurers in that direction. On the one hand, if an insurer does not refine his classification of risks

[64] *Post Magazine*, 30 *June* 1994, 13.

(or raise premiums and cater specifically for bad risks) his book of risks will contain too high a percentage of bad risks, who are being charged no more than the average premium, and he will lose money. On the other hand, one way to gain market share is to offer low risks lower prices. Moreover, except when classification is based on factors outside the control of the insured, such as age and sex, some believe that accurate risk classification encourages people to invest in loss prevention and thus further differentiate themselves from others who do not. Selection is a natural and normal part of the commercial process.

When the insurance industry was attacked for picking cherries, the ABI defended the practice as good underwriting, but, significantly perhaps, others who speak for the industry did not. There is a conflict of opinions and of interests—between those (usually in the industry) that highlight the risk-assessment or efficiency-promoting features of insurance classification and those (often outside the industry) that stress the risk-distributional function of insurance. Moreover, the latter point out that gains for one sector may mean losses for another, so that there is no net gain for society at large. To offer lower fire premiums to non-smokers may lead to smokers giving up smoking; but the consequence that is both more likely to occur and to be what the insurer is seeking is to attract new non-smoking applicants, who are believed to be better risks. This measure may reduce the losses paid by the particular insurer, but is not likely to lead to a significant overall reduction in loss in society as a whole. Similarly, some kinds of prevention, such as Neighbourhood Watch schemes, simply move the hazard to someone else's backyard without reducing the level of crime in the community at large.

The insurer's right to select implies a right to 'deselect'—to refuse renewal or to change the rules of engagement so radically that the former insured is effectively without cover (149 ff. above). In other words, the insured's licence to conduct relevant activity is withdrawn. Currently controversy arises out of liability insurers' step back by switching from occurrence cover to cover of 'claims made'.

Occurrences covered are acts (or omissions) of the insured occurring during the policy period, although the consequent claim by his victim may come later. Rating the cover requires prediction of the claims that will be made in the future. But the past is not necessarily a very reliable gauge of the future, especially as regards claims such as those arising out of toxic torts or professional negligence which may not surface until the distant future—called 'long tail' exposure. At the time of underwriting, it is difficult to anticipate not only the discoveries of science but also the legal and economic inflation over the years to come. In contrast, claims-made policies cover the insured against all claims that are made during the policy period, regardless of when the activity giving rise to the claim occurred. Rating this kind of cover is much less difficult, because only the claims that will be made during the imminent policy period have to be predicted.

As regards the risk beyond the imminent period, therefore, claims-made cover shifts much of the risk back to the insured. For instance, the successful claim of a single consumer against one tobacco company in respect of the consumer's lung cancer raises enormous implications for the future insurability of that company (and other tobacco companies). At the end of the current claims-made period, in the light of the now known potential for future claims of a similar nature, the company may find itself faced with either enormous rises in premium or a complete refusal to grant or renew cover at all. A claimant with cancer may find that he has fallen through a gap in the company's cover. Consequently, there has been something of a reaction against policies of this kind and, although enforceable in England, they have been outlawed, for example, in France and in Spain.

A Common Calling?

Insurers, it is argued, have the power to 'license' activity through the cost and availability of insurance and to 'legislate' through contracts, as well as the privilege of self-regulation and freedom from government interference. With this position of trust and influence, it is argued, goes a responsibility to provide cover. From the perspective of common law, underwriting has become a 'common calling', as once was the vocation of carriers and innkeepers. Like the carrier of goods, the motor insurer should always carry the risk, on appropriate terms. War risks apart, cover should always be provided—at a price. Indeed, some insurers have been advertising that every application will get a quotation. Like the common carrier of common law, the insurer holds himself out as being prepared to insure any person who applies for the kind of insurance he writes. Only if the insurer clearly and in advance reserves the right to refuse does the analogy fail altogether. All this is argument for reform; it is not yet law but it is an issue that will not go away in years to come.

8

Insurance and Law

The Insurer as God?

When drafts of international conventions 'reach the stage of a
diplomatic conference', the 'deus ex machina, the insurer, is not
mentioned in the cast'.[1] Thus spake Lord Diplock in 1970. His
words echo what had been said about the drama of domestic lawmaking too, both in Parliament and in the courts. However,
reticence about the role of insurance and insurers is less the rule
now than it was then.

The Role of Insurers in Litigation

The development of some parts of English law depends to a large
extent on litigation and litigants. The liability insurer can stifle the
development or refinement of liability law by smothering it with
settlement. Studies in Oxford showed that only a small proportion
of those people injured in accidents each year actually initiate
claims for damages; that 80 per cent of those claims are settled;
that generally the settlements, which are with claimants with little
idea of what their claim is 'worth', are for relatively small
amounts; and that in two thirds of cases the amount accepted is the
first offer made by the defendant's insurer.[2] The insurer is well
placed—and recent settlement of repetitive strain injury (RSI)
claims comes to mind—to make it unlikely that the question of
liability will be settled in law. When, however, insurers do fight it
is more likely to be on account of the size of the claim than the
importance of the point of law. If then the decision is in the
insurer's favour, he can snuff out the possibility of reversal on
appeal by a generous out-of-court settlement.

---

[1] Lord Diplock, 'Conventions and Morals', 1 *JMLC* 525 (1990).
[2] H. Genn, *Hard Bargaining* (Oxford, 1987), 13 ff.

In these circumstances, for the practitioner who must advise a client about his claim, what is the 'law'? Is it the statement of judges and the deductions of commentators from the tip of the iceberg that comes out in court, or is it rather the submarine movement of settlement practice? After all, the effect of legal rules in most cases is limited to whatever effect they have on the process of settlement. The insurer is the sophisticate of settlement. In the uncertainty surrounding the legal principles which form the basis of claims, the parties do not meet on equal terms.

The Effect of Insurance on Rules of Law

In the 1950s Viscount Simonds said that, when determining people's duties 'the fact that one of them is insured is to be disregarded' by the court.[3] Similar attitudes have been found in other countries as far apart as Australia and Germany. This remains broadly true of the particular defendant and the particular case in England today: one accountant should not have to bear a greater liability than another accountant because he has bought more insurance. But, as to whether accountants as a class should be liable, the insurance factor is ignored no longer.

In 1972, another senior judge said that liability and insurance 'are so intermixed that judicially to alter the basis of liability without adequate knowledge . . . as to the impact this might make upon the insurance system would be dangerous and, in my opinion, irresponsible'.[4] These are not the words of Lord Denning, although he did make statements of that kind, but the words of Lord Wilberforce who, unlike Lord Denning, was thought of as an articulate exponent of judicial restraint. Today, the substantive formalism of Viscount Simonds, who scrupulously left stones unturned, is a thing of the past. Courts are now slow to extend liability unless they believe that affordable insurance can be found to cover it: 283 ff. below.

Today the emphasis in tort is less on punishing the wrongdoer than on compensating the victim. Today, the importance of

---

[3] *Lister* v. *Romford Ice and Cold Storage Co. Ltd* [1957] AC 555, 576–7.
[4] *Morgans* v. *Launchbury* [1973] AC 127, 137.

insurance as a means of compensation is clear. It is right, surely, to say that

it is misleading to think of tort law as being the primary vehicle for ensuring payment of compensation to accident victims, with liability insurance as an ancillary device to protect the insured. It is more accurate to view insurance as the primary medium for the payment of compensation, and tort law as a subsidiary part of the process. [One] of the chief reasons why the great mass of personal injury claims arise out of road accidents and industrial injuries is that insurance is nearly always available in these cases.[5]

Indeed, the primacy of insurance in motor claims is reflected in the Road Traffic Act 1988, whereby matters such as late notice that normally defeat a claim by the insured against the insurer cannot be used in defence by the insurer against the victim.

Clearly insurance is important, and courts know that. Insurance responds to cover a new danger or a new liability. But is the reverse also true, that new rules of the general law are in some sense caused by insurers and insurance? One perception is that the shift of emphasis in tort from fault to compensation was partly caused by the introduction of compulsory liability insurance. In England the accuracy of this perception is far from clear. To test it we must first be clear about what we are looking for. What is the 'effect' of insurance?

One effect, the effect of the very existence of insurance cover, is that a case is decided in such a way that the insurance pays. This is the magnetic effect of money, the perennial attraction of any 'deep pocket' in a case; it is not special to insurance, but was found, for example, in the liability decisions against railway companies in the nineteenth century. The pull of money, of the insurance policy, is strongest in the United States where, more readily than in England, the plaintiff's lawyer is routinely able to find out how much insurance cover the defendant has. There is then a second pull up to the perceived limit in amount of the cover: the higher the plaintiff thinks it to be, the higher his expectation and the harder the bargaining for a settlement. In Australia also, recent

---

[5] P. Cane, *Atiyah's Accidents Compensation and the Law* (5th edn., London 1993).

cases allow the court to compel defendants to produce documents, including insurance policies.[6]

The second and more significant effect attributed to insurance is that the law itself is influenced by insurability. The influence may be seen in the very imposition or extent of civil liability or in liability that is framed so as to be targeted at a particular kind of insurer. Moreover, the influence, it is argued, may be particular or general. In the particular case of a particular contract, albeit a standard contract such as a building contractors' form, a term requiring one party to insure may determine and proscribe the liability of the other party. Clearly, this does occur. A more general influence is that insurability influences the lawmaker, Parliament, or judge, in the delimitation and development of liability law in general. This Chapter argues, however, that this kind of influence can be seen in the legislature, but, in England, much less in the courts than some of the proponents of the argument would have us believe.

Invisible Effects: Parallel Development

In the work of the courts, it is argued, legal rules 'have been "invisibly" affected by the existence of insurance'.[7] The invisible hand of insurance, it is argued, is seen less in particular cases than in general patterns of parallel development. Patterns of this kind were charted in the United States in the 1940s and 1950s. Like the 'invisible' hand of God in the world, however, where some such as Lord Denning[8] see the effect clearly others see only coincidence. In this Chapter, the contention is that the Denning perception is not at all apparent; and that, on the contrary, liability insurance is no more than a shadow that follows tort rather than vice versa. Indeed, it is a fearful and apprehensive shadow: a clear lesson of the debate about pollution, for example, is that any changes in the law create uncertainty, that uncertainty is bad for business, and

---

[6] *Gerah Imports Pty. Ltd* v. *The Duke Group Ltd* (1994) 68 ALJR 196, [1994] IJIL 201.

[7] B. A. Hepple and M. H. Matthews, *Tort: Cases and Materials* (4th edn., London, 1991), 883. See also A. Tunc, *International Encyclopedia of Comparative Law* (Tübingen, 1983), xi, pt. 1, para. 93.

[8] Rt. Hon. Lord Denning, *The Discipline of Law* (London, 1979), 280.

that insurers, far from leading the way and beating a new path for the law to follow, draw back, and decline business. Nonetheless, for those of the Denning school, the effects of insurance are said to be seen, in particular, in the law of tort.

Vicarious Liability

The Denning school points to vicarious liability which, it is true, is sometimes strict: there may be liability although the defendant has exercised reasonable care and skill. But the case proves too much, at least, unless it explains also why the liability occurs in some contexts (employment) but not others (contractors for sub-contractors).

Certainly, the institution of the National Health Service prompted courts led by Lord Denning to an extension of vicarious liability; but that is history. It is also a context in which science had made strides, such that it was possible, much more than before, to establish that someone had made a mistake. Since then, a feature of work patterns has been a move away from traditional employment to more flexible forms of relationship, part-time employment, and contract labour. This has been well documented by labour law[9] but appears to have escaped both the attention and the grip of the law of tort. As long as these relationships were outside the scope of vicarious liability, the purpose of vicarious liability, especially the distribution of loss through the employer's insurance and the pricing of his product, was undermined. Recently, vicarious liability has been expanded.[10] However, the driving factor seems to have been as much loss prevention as loss distribution. Again, the Denning argument from strictness is unconvincing.

Nuisance and Pollution

The Denning school also points to liability for dangerous escapes, toxic torts. There, however, the trend to strictness appeared to

---

[9] E. McKendrick, 'Vicarious Liability and Independent Contractors—A Re-examination' (1990) 53 *MLR* 770–84; R. Kidner, 'Vicarious Liability: For Whom should the Employer be Liable?' (1995) 15 LS 47–64.

[10] *Lane* v. *Shire Roofing Co. (Oxford) Ltd*, [1995] IRLR 493 (CA).

come to a halt in 1946. After that, it went into reverse, and writers began to assimilate nuisance generally with negligence. True, the reverse trend stopped in 1994 with the *Cambridge Water* case,[11] but that was not the work of the insurers. On the contrary, they have responded to greater strictness in the courts with restrictive drafting and to the greater strictness in proposed legislation with howls of protest.

Res Ipsa Loquitur

The rule *res ipsa loquitur*, whereby it can be inferred that the person in control of a damage situation has been negligent, is said to be a strict rule that has arisen in response to the draw of insurance. This is because the 'rule' is said to be strict, and puts the onus of proof (and cost of unexplained loss) on the better risk avoider, whose control of the situation makes his situation the one that is susceptible of the most precise risk assessment and rating. By increasing the procedural disadvantages of defendants, the 'rule' is said to be more a device for imposing strict liability.

An alternative view, however, is that the 'rule' is nothing more than recognition of a reasonable inference that there has been negligence, which the court is entitled to draw on the basis of probabilities. As long as the defendant is allowed to refute the inference by proof, there is no liability without fault. One may as well say that conviction of crime upon circumstantial evidence amounts to law of guilt without crime. Moreover, the rule goes back to the mid-nineteenth century, when insurance clearly did not influence liability in this way; and it is not clear that it is used more often today than before, if only because such cases may be more likely to settle. Nor is it clear that today the rule is applied much more strictly. The cases of the last thirty years appear to conflict, and, although the most powerful precedent can be construed as supporting a move in the direction of strictness, the most recent does not.[12] So, once again, the argument from strictness, this time with reference to *res ipsa loquitur*, is not convincing.

---

[11] *Cambridge Water Co.* v. *Eastern Counties Leather plc* [1994] 2 AC 264.
[12] e.g. *Ng* v. *Lee* [1988] RTR 298 (PC).

The Duty of Care

The central pillars of the Denning argument are the duty and standard of care. As regards the duty of care, one version of the argument is that the duty expanded, first by Lord Atkin and then Lord Wilberforce, under the influence of liability insurance; that, later, in the last quarter of the twentieth century, the duty contracted as liability insurance dried up. If this is true of the early years, then Winfield, in what has been described even by an exponent of the Denning school[13] as the seminal account of the development of duty of care, missed it.

In the second half of this century, expansion of the duty of care seemed to have gone furthest in *Junior Books*[14] in 1982. This seemed to bring on an attack of judicial agoraphobia, a feeling that the duty had gone too far, and the judges retreated in the direction of the trenches dug before 1932, trenches of 'incrementalism' and 'traditional categories'. But the argument, this time that the retreat on duty was a reflection of the withdrawal of unlimited liability cover in the insurance market, is once again unconvincing. First, limits were a feature of liability cover long before 1982. Secondly, the immediate response of insurers to *Junior Books* was not retrenchment and retreat, but, for one company at least, to offer expanded cover for what was perceived as the new and expanded liability for economic loss. Indeed, the strongest evidence against the argument is in the cases in which the courts declined to find a duty even though it was probable that liability insurance was or would have been available. Here again, there is no real evidence that the law followed insurance; rather, insurance followed the law.

The Standard of Care

Here the argument is that the courts have been more concerned with compensating claimants and rather less with whether defend-

---

[13] M. Davies, 'The End of the Affair: Duty of Care and Liability Insurance' (1989) 9 *LS* 67–83, 78, concerning P. H. Winfield, 'Duty in Tortious Negligence', 34 *Col. L Rev.* 41–66 (1934).
[14] *Junior Books Co. Ltd* v. *The Veitchi Co.* [1983] AC 520.

ants were at fault; that the trend in the standard of care expected of people has been for the standard to become stricter and more objective; and that this is because a liability insurer stands behind the defendant. In other words, insurance has had what was described as the magnetic effect of money.

The trend to strictness did not start with insurance: strict liability for torts was found long before compulsory liability insurance. The trend to strictness is certainly there, but it is not an unmistakable line in one direction. Nor is the trend even on all fronts. Away from the roads, the duty of care is often less strict.[15] The move to higher standards of care and to stricter liability on the roads might be explained apart from insurance. Perhaps it is entirely co-incidental that Lord Denning, who has had so much influence on this part of the law since 1945, learned to drive in 1941 but disliked it so much that he never drove again. Be that as it may, the driving cases may simply reflect a greater awareness that the jolly roadster of Bertie Wooster in 'the golden age' of motoring has become much faster; that there are a lot more of them; that they now damage not only the victim but society at large to the golden tune of nearly £1 million per fatality. That, moreover, is a sum which takes no account of the cost of damage to the environment, and which is often a lot higher when the vehicle does not do the job properly and the victim survives and needs long term care.

As regards greater objectivity, again the usual example is from motoring, the decision that the learner driver owes the same standard of care and skill as other drivers—not only to other road users but also to his own passengers.[16] The reason, however, was less compensation than the uncertainty that would be created by a variable standard of skill. Yet a variable standard is found in other contexts, and, once again one wonders whether the motoring cases are typical of the rest.

If indeed there is a trend to compensation, the causal role of insurance may be real but it is hard to prove. At best, the argument is like that of epidemiology, the study of the prevalence of specified diseases within a sector of the population: it measures

---

[15] e.g. the 'art' of valuation: *Luxmoore-May* v. *Messenger May Baverstock* [1990] 1 WLR 1009 (CA); R. Kidner, 'The Variable Standard of Care, Contributory Negligence and *Volenti*' (1991) 11 LS 1–23.

[16] *Nettleship* v. *Weston* [1971] 2 QB 691, 699–700 (CA); Cane, n. 5 above, 206.

results in that sector, but can only speculate about causes. It was epidemiology that first established the 'connection' between smoking and lung cancer which today is accepted. But, while there is currently more heart disease in Scotland than in Japan, it is still a matter of speculation whether or to what extent that is because the Scots drink more whisky and the Japanese eat more fish. The degree to which a statistical correlation establishes cause and effect depends in part on whether there are other possible causes and how many. Higher and harder standards of care may have causes other than insurance.

One possibility is that social attitudes have changed and are still changing. One change is that scientific determinism 'has replaced religion and magic as the way in which many ordinary people explain adversities. One consequence is that there is generally a search for causes and an attribution of responsibility or blame'.[17] For that and other reasons people are looking for scapegoats. So, in the realms of negligence, more liability for doctors, for example, may be the result not of more insurance but of changes in society. First, in the profession there is more understanding of medical cause and effect and there are more doctors willing to give evidence for claimants. Secondly, among patients there is more consumerism and litigation-mindedness, as well as more social conscience about and sympathy for the victims of our society and its products, and less awe of the men in white coats.

Damages

The belief is widespread that awareness of the existence of cover has an effect on the amount of damages awarded, especially damages awarded by juries; that juries award too much; and that the awareness has some effect too on the awards made by judges. To a degree this is probably true; however, it is hard to draw precise conclusions. Whereas English courts have sought to award full compensation for pecuniary loss, they have been relatively restrained in their awards for non-pecuniary loss, such as pain, suffering, and loss of amenity. This difference is not easily explained. It suggests that the pull of insurance is not as strong as

[17] B. Corby, 'On Risk and Uncertainty in Modern Society', *Geneva Papers on Risk and Insurance* 72 (1994), 235–43 at 238.

people might have thought, or, at least, that there are other more powerful considerations at work.

Another effect altogether is being attributed to the insurance factor in the United States. A popular theory there is that the amount of compensatory damages in a tort case should be assessed according to the 'insurance theory of compensation'. This theory sees a successful action in tort for damages as a 'port of entry' to insurance cover. From this perspective, the damages, it is argued, should be assessed according to an estimate of the insurance the claimant would have taken to cover the loss or injury, if he, the claimant, had planned for the contingency—the accident or mishap.

According to the theory, a utility-maximizing individual would incur the expense of an insurance premium if, by transferring dollars from the preloss state to the postloss state (via the insurance policy purchase), she would be transferring wealth from a state in which it yields less utility (the preloss state) to one in which it yields more (the postloss state). In fact, she would continue to make such transfers until the marginal utility of money in the preloss state was the same as in the expected postloss state. Once she reached that position of equality, she could no longer increase expected utility by transferring dollars to the postloss state. Hence, she would purchase no more insurance. Insurance theorists then apply these general guidelines to determine the insurance decisions that individuals would make as to specific sorts of potential losses.[18]

In other words, to the extent that the (wise and well organized) victim has insured against his actual loss, he or she recovers damages—but that is all the victim gets. For example, loss of income will be fully compensated. Loss of an unwanted wedding gift, however valuable, will not if, as is likely, the donee would not have chosen to insure it or insure it in full. Clearly, the theory is more easily applied to pecuniary losses than to non-pecuniary losses. Indeed, from the perspective of the wheelchair, it achieves heights of objectivity that might be regarded as chillingly remote. People's priorities and perspectives change when disability strikes. The theory is presently just a shadow on the western horizon of English law.

---

[18] E. S. Pryor, 'The Tort Law Debate. Efficiency, and the Kingdom of the Ill', 79 *Va. L Rev.* 91–151, 100–1 (1993).

Visible Effects: in Parliament

In the more distant past, the insurance industry did not speak with one voice and, consequently, was not well heard. Even with the formation of the British Insurance Association (BIA) in 1918, the industry was not greatly active in and around Parliament until shaken by the threat of nationalization in the period of Labour government commencing in 1945. Since then the BIA and the Association of British Insurers (ABI), its successor in 1985, have taken a lively interest in what is proposed in Parliament, ranging from proposed rules about dangerous dogs to the pension schemes for osteopaths. This the ABI is now well placed to do. Not only is it geared up to present the views of its member insurers, but in the Register of Members' Interests for the Parliament up to 1997, one member in ten declared financial links with the insurance industry. Yet it is not in Parliament, where insurance factors make for dull debate, that the industry is best able to influence opinion, but in the ministries charged with the legislation concerned; it is there that the ABI concentrates its fire. Two striking features of that fire are concern about limits on liability cover and limits on regulation of the insurance industry itself.

The extent of statutory liability is commonly tailored to the extent of cover that the industry can provide. In some instances what the industry is unable to provide is the enormously large sums required, but, more often, it is *unpredictably* large sums: in the famous flood warning of Cardozo J, it is 'liability in an indeterminate amount for an indeterminate time to an indeterminate class'.[19] So, when people say that a liability is uninsurable this usually means 'indeterminate to a degree that makes actuarial assessment by the insurer too imprecise for cover to be marketed at a price that will appeal to the relevant pool'. If insurers know the extent of their exposure, although the applicant may not like the rate, the insurers can nearly always quote.

In commerce, a clear example of the influence of insurance on legislation is provided by the evolution of the legislation, known

---

[19] *Ultramares Corp.* v. *Touche*, 255 NY 170, 179 (1931).

originally as the Hague Rules, that dictates the balance of risk and the burden of insurance between the parties to the carriage of goods by sea. The insurance factor has been central to the debate and, although it is not beyond doubt that the prevalent view of insurability was correct (287 ff. below), the view had a significant impact on the limit on the amount of liability. The availability of what was believed to be affordable insurance cover is also the premise behind certain other legislation, not least that which requires liability to be covered by insurance: the liability of motorists under the Road Traffic Acts and of employers under the Employers Liability (Compulsory Insurance) Act 1969. Finally, the most obvious case perhaps is 'catastrophe exposure', such as that of a serious nuclear 'incident', in which the cost of a possible claim is out of all proportion to the premium income derived from the class of insurance in question. Liability there is but only up to the limit that can be insured; see the Nuclear Installations (Licensing and Insurance) Act 1959. This is the position not only of the nuclear industry and of the power industry in England, but of aircraft operators in England and abroad.

The second feature is the industry's power of persuasion—that the industry should not be regulated or that rules, which are to apply to other sections of society, should not apply to insurers. The Law Commission[20] recommended changes in the law on non-disclosure and breach of warranty which an industry campaign managed to block. Equally, the power of the insurance industry as a lobby was seen in the insurance exemption from the Unfair Contract Terms Act 1977. When, however, the intervention came not from Westminster, but from Brussels, the industry's desire for exemption from the EC Directive of 1993 was frustrated. This might be seen as a defeat for an industry that has lost its influence, but it would be nearer the truth to see it as an orderly and tactical retreat in which, within the constraints imposed by the political climate, the industry remained influential. Crucially, the Directive does not apply to 'core provisions' of the insurance contract (230–6 above) and this exemption was developed from a proposal of the

---

[20] 'Non-disclosure and Breach of Warranty' (Cmnd. 8064, London, 1980). Cf. R. Lewis, 'Lobbying and the Damages Act, 1996' (1997) 60 M.L.R. 230–7.

ABI that reached the Commission via a European organization of insurers.

Finally, there has been a less direct kind of influence. A number of statutes obtained the necessary support in Parliament in part because of changes in the pattern of insurance or of changes in attitude brought about by insurance. The Law Reform (Contributory Negligence) Act 1945, whereby it became possible for a plaintiff to recover damages even though the plaintiff had been negligent, owed much to the spread of liability insurance. The abolition of the doctrine of common employment, whereby an employer was not liable to his employee for the negligence of another employee, was partly due to the complete change which the practice of employers' liability insurance had produced in the legal treatment of industrial accidents. The Law Reform (Husband and Wife) Act 1962, which enabled husbands and wives to sue each other in tort, was a response to a situation in which a spouse who had been injured in a road accident through the negligence of the other spouse was the only person in the world who could not claim damages from an insurance company. The influence of insurance has also been traced in the history of product liability.[21]

Visible Effects: in the Courts

The influence of insurance and insurers on the law developed by the courts is much less clear than the influence on legislation—both as regards patterns of development, the 'invisible' effects (274 ff. above), and as regards reasoning in particular cases. The courts may well allow themselves to be influenced by the primary effect of insurance, the magnetic effect of money, that draws the decision to available insurance: 284 below. The secondary effect, which tailors the law to the 'reality' of the insurance position, is another matter. This effect, the argument runs, is that the very imposition or extent of civil liability is influenced by insurability or is framed so as to be targeted at a particular kind of insurer rather than some other risk carrier. Influence in this secondary sense, it is submitted, is to be seen scarcely at all.

---

[21] J. Stapleton, *Disease and the Compensation Debate* (Oxford, 1986), 133. Generally, see Cane, n. 5 above, 201–2.

Available Insurance

As regards the primary effect, the magnetic effect of available insurance, at one level the influence of insurance may be general and almost subliminal. In the United States it has been contended[22] that 'insurers have repeatedly promoted the fear of liability in order to promote the demand for liability insurance. It is plausible that the fear of liability has been greatly exaggerated and that this exaggeration itself has greatly promoted liability by getting people to insure against it'. In other words, this is the role of insurance as a self-fulfilling prophecy but, as the author also observes, the magnitude of this effect is unknown and would be hard to measure.

The influence of insurance at a more particular level is both more obvious and better understood, This is the case of the judge who is consciously aware that one side is significantly more likely to have insurance to cover the loss and will incline a decision that way. Knowledge of general patterns of insurance cover must be distinguished from knowledge that a particular party to a case has cover. In 1994 a Crown Court judge found his way into the popular press when he awarded damages against an 82-year-old man, who had shot and injured the claimant—at a time when the claimant was attempting to break into the defendants's allotment shed. Hundreds of readers responded with anger and with donations to a fund to help the 'poor' old man pay. The judge's reply to the press was what he called the 'cream of the jest', that the 'poor' old man was insured. The appeal to the Court of Appeal was dismissed.[23]

The judge knew about the insurance because he had been told by counsel at the start of the trial. What he did not know, it seems, is that judges are not supposed to know that sort of thing. That is theory; in practice, they often do. They always know, of course, when insurance is compulsory. The judge who goes to lengths to find the motorist negligent does so not because he dislikes motoring but because he believes that, if Parliament has ordained compulsory insurance, public policy favours compensation, and that the motorist has cover and, probably, the claimant does not.

---

[22] K. D. Syverud, 'On the Demand for Liability Insurance' 72 *Tex. L. Rev.* 1629–1653, 1639 (1994).　　　　　[23] *The Times*, 3 Nov. 1995.

The reverse may also be true. A case in New Zealand concerned whether a motorist whose illegally parked car caught fire and damaged a building should be liable to the building owner in tort. The likelihood that the owner of the building would have fire insurance being greater than that the motorist would have motor insurance that covered that kind of liability was a factor against liability.[24] Few objections are raised, except that it is factor that may distort the law of tort. In these cases the likely insurance cover was obvious. Less obvious but no less important is the court's perception of whether insurance is available to cover economic loss.

Controversy continues over whether and when there should be liability in tort for economic loss caused by negligence. Whether liability is indeed desirable or not is not our concern. The immediate interest of the controversy is the role of insurance or, rather, perceptions of insurance in the debate—not least because sometimes the court's perception has been mistaken.

In Canada a ship with important cargo and a careless captain hit a railway bridge. On a typical day before the accident the bridge was crossed by thirty-two freight trains hauling in total 1,530 freight wagons. The foreseeable consequence of the accident was that traffic could not cross the bridge until it was made safe some weeks later, and that a wide range of manufacturers, carriers, other businesses, and, especially, the plaintiff railway company would lose money. The case was *Norsk* in which, in an admirable but controversial attempt to get to grips with the economics and insurability of the situation, the Supreme Court decided (by four to three) that the loss was recoverable by the railway.[25]

If the claim had been brought in England, it would have failed. English law says that that is economic loss, for which the 'ship' is not liable because it owes no duty of care. The main reason is the 'floodgates' argument,[26] that otherwise there would be too much

---

[24] *Mayfair Ltd* v. *Pears* [1987] 1 NZLR 459, 462 (CA).

[25] *Canadian National Ry. Co.* v. *Norsk Pacific SS Co.* [1992] 1 SCR 1021. See D. Cohen, 'The Economics of *Canadian National Railway* v. *Norsk Pacific Steamship*', 45 *U Toronto LJ* 143–62 (1995). Cf. B. S. Markesinis and S. Deakin, 'The Random Element of their Lordships' Infallible Judgment' (1992) 55 *MLR* 619–46. Cf. also B. Feldthusen and J. Palmer, 'Economic Loss and the Supreme Court of Canada' 74 *Can. B Rev.* 427–45 (1995).   [26] n. 19 above.

liability and that the world of enterprise and of commerce would
come to a halt. The assumption, of course, is that the liability is
one for which there is no affordable insurance. Insurers can
usually quote. 'Yes, sir, we will cover your 18-year-old son and his
new Golf GTI, and the premium will be £6,000!' Available cover is
one thing, affordable cover is another. Indeed, in *Norsk*, one
argument against liability for economic loss limited by foreseeability alone was that liability would hit hard at non-business
people, such as the holidaymaker who starts a fire. The premise
was that such people would be unlikely to have cover, which is
surely correct. In *Norsk*, however, one argument accepted by the
majority in favour of liability for economic loss was that that was
the only way the claimant could recover loss of profit, as such loss
was not insurable—which is clearly not correct. Loss of profit is an
established line of insurance business.[27]

In England, when the House of Lords decided against the
recovery of economic loss in cases such as *Murphy*,[28] it is not
apparent that the House was better informed. Did the House
know, for example, that, circumscribed by the rules of causation,
such loss is recoverable in countries like Holland? The Supreme
Court there, as in Italy, has held that when someone negligently
cuts a power supply, that person is liable for all foreseeable
consequences, physical and pecuniary. Did the House know that,
in France, the vehicle liable for a crash is liable for the foreseeable
economic consequences of the congestion? These liabilities are
insurable and insured. Last, but surely not least, did the House
know that insurance cover for liability for economic loss was
available in England?

Atiyah's assertion that 'it is really high time (in both England
and America) that lawyers informed themselves about . . .
fundamental matters of insurability in new tort cases and saw to it
that the courts were also informed',[29] is surely true; but can
anything really be done about it? The difficulty seems to be that of

---

[27] See Riley, *Business Interruption Insurance* (7th edn., London, 1991), chs. 7
and 8.

[28] *Murphy* v. *Brentwood DC* [1991] 1 AC 378.

[29] P. S. Atiyah in a lecture (1992) quoted by Derrington J: 'The Effect of
Insurance on the Law of Damages', in P. Finn (ed.), *Essays on Damages* (Sydney,
1992), 153–191, 187.

getting the relevant information (242 ff. above), and, moreover, information that is up to date. The court can indicate to counsel that it wants the information before the court. However, this kind of information, notably that about claims experience and cost, may have to come from insurers who regard it as commercially sensitive, and may thus be hard to obtain.

Efficient Insurance

If insurance is available to one side only, that may be all that the court needs to know, and then, if it wishes, the court can shift loss in that direction: insurance has its primary effect (273 above). In a leading case, however, having found that *both* sides were insured, Lord Denning concluded that the insurance factor cancelled out[30] and turned to other factors in the case. However, if indeed both sides are insured, there remains the further question, which insurance is the more efficient and thus perhaps the insurance that should carry the loss? But, again, there is the associated question, is this an issue which the courts are in a position to resolve?

Occasionally, the answer is clear. *Coggin*,[31] for example, concerned vicarious liability for the negligence of a crane driver. The House held that the driver was the employee of his general employer and not of the client, for whom he was moving goods at the time, because the identity of the client might change from one day to the next. That mattered, because it meant that the general employer was the better insurer—not least in the sense of the one more able and more likely to see to the insurance needs of the driver against illness, unemployment, and accidents.

In other cases, the answer is less obvious. In some of them the judges have reached confident but conflicting conclusions. They cannot all be right, and one must wonder about their sources. In most cases, however, judges do not mention insurance. The main reason seems to be that they know that the insurance implications of the case are important, but they also know that they do not know enough about them to let the decision turn on the point. This is an honest diffidence that is found in the highest courts of the

---

[30] *Photo Production Ltd* v. *Securicor Transport Ltd* [1978] 3 All ER 146, 154.
[31] *Mersey Docks and Harbour Board* v. *Coggin and Griffiths Ltd* [1947] AC 1.

Commonwealth, as well as in England.[32] The present contention is that, with the utmost respect, they are right: mostly, judges do not because they cannot and probably, in most cases, they should not. The issue is often very difficult.

One reason for the difficulty is that it is not usually an isolated question but is made more complex by being part of a broader question. In *Norsk*, for example, the question, as one of the judges saw it, was whether the claimant railway 'was better placed to protect itself from the consequences' of the business losses because, like the other claimants, it had 'access to the full range of protective options', which included not only first party commercial insurance and self-insurance, but also contracts with both the bridge owner and the railway's customers.[33] Another reason, the main reason, is that the courts have insufficient information. Even as an isolated issue, the merits of one kind of insurance over another may be very difficult to assess. In *Norsk*, the court asked whether the total cost (premiums and transaction costs of all affected businesses) was significantly greater for (their) loss insurance than the cost of liability insurance to potential wrong-doers such as the shipowner. Again, in the case of an action against a public body such as a health authority, which may well be self-insured, the question is whether it is 'efficient' to make the public body pay? By 1995 the NHS was paying £125 million in compensation for negligent treatment, a rise of over 50 per cent on 1993. Assuming that it is economically efficient to make the NHS pay, there is a further question: is it socially and politically desirable that the payment should come from funds allocated to public purposes, such as health care, rather than from other sources? It has been well argued that special considerations apply to public bodies as defendants.[34] And, in any of these cases, when the court decides, can it be sure that the loss will be allocated to a sufficient degree and with sufficient certainty to avoid the wasteful

---

[32] High Ct. of Australia: *Caltex Oil (Aust.) Pty. Ltd* v. *Dredger 'Wilhemstad'* (1976) 11 ALR 227, 265. Sup. Ct. of Can: *Canadian National Ry. Co.* v. *Norsk Pacific SS Co.* (1992) 91 DLR (4th) 289, 350. HL: *Morgans* v. *Launchbury* [1973] AC 127, 142–3; and *Marc Rich & Co. AG* v. *Bishop Rock Marine Co. Ltd (The Nicholas H)* [1996] 1 AC 211, 228–9, *per* Lord Lloyd.

[33] n. 25 above, 349, *per* La Forest J.

[34] See Markesinis and Deakin, n. 25 above, 631.

cost of overlapping cover?[35] As before (242 ff. above), we seem to be encountering the problem of briefing the court. It is scarcely surprising that, more often than not, courts are silent. With this in mind, let us now look at some situations in which the efficiency of insurance has been significant.

Tort: Loss or Liability Insurance—in General

An exceptional judge, who 'proves the rule' of judicial silence on the issue of efficient insurance, was Lord Diplock. 'As a judge in the lower courts, Diplock was regarded as analytically outstanding, iconoclastic, and outspoken' and, although he shared some of intellectual ability and the values of Lord Wilberforce, he had 'less of the modesty and caution'.[36] As President of the Restrictive Practices Court he strode with confidence into the realms of economics. As a leading member of the British Maritime Law Association, he was well able to fathom issues of insurance as they affected the carriage of goods by sea and was deeply involved in the debate when the international liability regime (the Hague Rules) was revised. So, he brought to his role as a judge an unusually high degree of experience of the impact of insurance on certain branches of commercial law. Even so, he may have got it wrong.

Lord Diplock was not, of course, the first judge to be aware that a liability system based on fault is an expensive way to administer accident losses; and that the benefits received by victims from the defendant's liability insurance are less in relation to cost than those received under private loss insurance. The Pearson Commission calculated that the system cost 45 pence of every £ of insurance premium.[37] The corollary is the supposition, which is much influenced by motor insurance and which the authority of Lord Diplock established in English judicial thought, that, generally, loss insurance is cheaper and more efficient than liability insur-

---

[35] On this problem see K. S. Abraham and L. Liebman, 'Private Insurance, Social Insurance and Tort Reform', 93 *Col. L Rev.* 75–118, 94 ff. (1993).
[36] R. Stevens, *Law and Politics* (London, 1979), 562.
[37] *Royal Commission on Civil Liability and Compensation for Personal Injury*, 1978, Cmnd. 7054, para. 83.

ance.[38] It was Lord Diplock who described the insurer as the 'deus ex machina' of the liability scene. But, even if one can start from agreement about the appropriate definition and model of economic efficiency, scrutiny shows that both the script and the plot are much less simple than Lord Diplock would have had us believe. Here are some of the arguments.

First, loss insurance is argued to be more efficient because it is more focussed. The victim's estimate of how much loss insurance he needs is likely to be more accurate than the wrongdoer's estimate of how much loss he can cause: the wrongdoer does not usually know who his victim will be. For example, the railway has a better idea of how much it will lose from closure of a railway bridge than the shipowner who hits it and closes it. The owner of a factory has a better idea of the effect of a fire on his factory and his business than the adjacent road repairer responsible for the fire.

Against this argument, first, it is said that the 'vice' is less vice than virtue; that it is a 'fail-safe' feature that liability cover is usually drafted in more general terms than loss insurance and, consequently, any unexpected dimension of the subject-matter insured is more likely to be covered. Secondly, it is said that, sometimes, liability insurance is preferable because the wrongdoer has a better idea of whether there will be any damage at all—damage caused by him, the person best placed to avoid it. This is true sometimes of professional liability, but less true, perhaps, of the motorist convinced that he is at least as good a driver as anyone else.

Secondly, it is argued for loss insurance that, in some cases at least, victims, whose interests are paramount, prefer it. This is mainly because it is settled more favourably to the victim. On the one hand, the victim may be required by his loss policy to bear the first layer (£x) of loss: an excess or deductible. On the other hand, the victim may get less from the liability insurer because the liability, and thus the indemnity, is reduced by any contributory

---

[38] Diplock, n. 1 above, 529; see further G. Calabresi, 'First Party, Third Party, and Product Liability Systems', 69 *Iowa L Rev.* 833–51 (1984); S. A. Rea, Jr., 'Economic Analysis of Fault and No-Fault Liability Systems', 12 *Can. Bus. LJ* 444–71 (1987); P. S. Atiyah, 'Personal Injuries in the Twenty-first Century', Paper to the Society of Public Teachers of Law, 16 Mar. 1996. Cf. M. Nell and A. Richter, *Optimal Liability: The Effects of Risk Aversion, Loaded Insurance Premiums, and the Number of Victims*, Geneva Papers No 79 (Apr. 1996), 240–53.

negligence. Moreover, he may find the money due harder to get: the loss insurer usually hopes to have a continuing relationship with the victim, whereas the liability insurer neither expects nor hopes to see the victim ever again, and has no such incentive to pay promptly or in full, or to give the benefit of any doubt.

Again, however, this second argument for loss insurance is coloured by motor insurance, and has less relevance, for example, to carriers' liability insurance: the carrier may well want to see the victim (and his cargo) again, and will be unhappy if his insurer does not pay quickly and in full. Moreover, the victim may not be solely concerned with getting the most compensation. There is certainly a feeling in society, but one that is hard to quantify, that it is 'only fair and right' that the wrongdoer should be the one to pay, whether damages or liability insurance premiums. Psychologists tell us that, sometimes, receiving the compensation *from the wrongdoer* is necessary to produce the victim's sense of satisfaction.[39] Journalists tell us that today this is coupled with a sense in victims that someone else should be seen to be to 'blame' and to pay rather than the 'victim' himself; and, less often perhaps, that, if the responsibility is left to be carried by his own loss insurance, the finger is left pointing too much at him rather than someone else. Indeed, Cane may well be correct in his conclusion that the efficiency argument, that puts the loss on the one who can more efficiently insure against it, is based on notions of paternalism and distributive justice which are alien to the common law tradition[40]—and to the preferences of many victims.

The third argument for loss insurance is, depending on the context, also one for liability insurance; it is the spreading argument. Manufacturers, for example, are better able to insure against damage or injury done by their products than those who use them, and the cost of liability insurance can be spread with less pain among the buying public as a whole than would be the case if a particular user were saddled with all of his own loss. Again, carriers by sea are bigger buyers of insurance (and hence a better known risk) than cargo owners and, as such, can buy cover more cheaply. To this, however, the carrier might reply that, on the

---

[39] G. T. Schwartz, 'The Ethics and Economics of Liability Insurance', 75 *Cornell L Rev.* 313–65, 334 (1990).

[40] P. Cane, *Tort Law and Economic Interests* (2 edn., Oxford, 1996), 427.

contrary, a major loss is more cheaply spread over a number of cargo (loss) insurers than a single liability insurer. Indeed, in the case of carriage by sea, the argument between loss insurance and liability insurance has been going on for much of this century, and is far from having been resolved. One reason for that is the inherent difficulty of the issue, but that may not be the only reason. Another, it appears, is that, although apportionment of risk does have some effect on the levels of damage and cost, it is less significant than has been believed in the past; and that consequently the carrier has insufficient incentive to research the matter and provide the information needed to fuel the debate to some kind of conclusion: the result is that the data that are available are unhelpful, and the court which seeks to be helpful may be nothing of the kind. In particular, reasons given in the past for putting a ceiling on the liability of carriers (risk prediction, avoidance of ruinous loss) do not bear serious scrutiny.[41]

Fourth, an argument for loss insurance is that the wrongdoer's liability to the victim and the insurer's liability to the wrongdoer are issues more likely to raise difficulties of fact and law than any such questions under loss insurance. This argument reinforces the second, as any difficulties give the insurer a stick with which to beat down the claim. It is also an argument that the transfer of loss to the liability insurer is likely to be less certain and that uncertainty creates cost. However, although bright clear lines do reduce uncertainty, the cost factor cuts both ways. It points to the development of legal rules which spread loss over as few insurers as possible. A no-liability rule may, for example in the case of carriage, lead to multiple first party loss insurance, with greater associated transaction costs.

Further, perhaps this is (again) a point in the debate to suggest that the criterion of efficiency is not low cost alone. In the central case of motor insurance, for example, the smaller and cheaper is the vehicle, the more vulnerable the occupants, the greater the likely loss, and the more expensive the insurance. But if that led to lower premiums for larger vehicles, that would not be acceptable to those concerned about the environment. Moreover, in some

---

[41] As regards carriage, see the seminal study: J. Basedow, *Der Transportvertrag* (Tübingen, 1987), 505 ff. More generally, see J. N. Adams, 'The Economics of Good Faith' (1995) 8 JCL 126–37.

contexts, loss insurance, if associated with strict duties,
the deterrent effect of tort liability. Not on the roads, it is tr
deterrence derives less from liability than from fear of injury o
disqualification; but in other cases, such as professional liability,
the damage to reputation caused by liability may be significant.

After all this time and after much debate, the winner of the
argument is not clear. This alone suggests that further debate may
be fruitless, and is reinforced by the argument that, from the
beginning, the debate was false, because it is fruitless to compare
things unless, in essential respects, the comparison is of like with
like. As Stapleton points out, the risk covered by loss insurance

is the risk of damage being suffered, howsoever caused, be it by someone
else's tort or not (let us call this risk T+NT), and this is different from that
in relation to which liability insurance is taken out, namely of the insured's
tort causing the damage (let us call this risk T).[42]

This may explain why loss insurance has not been universally
preferred. Strikingly, liability insurance remains the route to
recovery for many victims of personal injury. This is reflected in
regimes for the liability of employers and of producers, as well as
motorists. This Chapter argues that the issue is difficult, that the
debate has no winner, that any general conclusions for loss
insurance or for liability insurance are suspect, and that perhaps
the Australian judge, who said that the merits of loss insurance
should not be assumed but should be tested in each situation,[43]
was right.

Tort: Loss or Liability Insurance—Commercial Practice

Situations are found in which loss insurance is indeed preferable to
liability insurance—and thus the court may be inclined to negative
a duty of care actionable in tort. An example is a major airport,
with associated engineering and passenger facilities (shops, park-
ing, conference centre) and, of course, aircraft: larger aircraft hold
400 people, with great potential for loss of revenue if the aircraft
are immobilized. The situation poses a formidable liability for any
contractor who might cut wires or drop a lighted cigarette. For

---

[42] J. Stapleton, 'Tort, Insurance and Ideology' (1995) 58 MLR 820–45, 831.
[43] Stephen J in *Caltex* n. 32 above, 265.

adequate liability cover the overall cost
portion to the value of the global activity,
en more stark in particular cases. The van
ordon bleu beefburgers requires almost as
rer of the radar. Another situation, posing
he large construction site, such as that
lding of a new airport terminal. In such
urt minded to negative duty justify its
decision and draw a line that lawyers can explain to their clients?

Here at least, if the information can be accessed by the lawyers, insurance sometimes provides a broad answer. The practice or pattern of insurance indicates the burden of insurance that is preferred by people in the situation and, probably, the one that is most efficient: the practice is not only an explanation for the line but a marker for the line itself. First, the exorbitant cost of a multiplicity of individual liability insurances may, as we have just seen, be the reason for drawing the tort line against liability. But, secondly, if, as is likely, the airport owner or the head contractor has taken out insurance to cover both the loss and the liability of all those legitimately on site, that insurance is both a confirmation of the commercial reality against multiple individual cover, and also a conceptual marker: tort law tells us that the duty of care, which might otherwise have been owed by one person to others, may be affected by the contractual framework created between them. The courts will respect this. Commercial practice is a factor important to courts deciding what the law ought to be; this is because certainty and predictability are furthered if the law reflects the practice.

Another such situation is that of the bailee who, for goods in his charge, takes not (only) liability insurance but loss insurance. The law has responded to clear commercial practice with the 'commercial trust': the bailee is allowed to recover from the insurer the full value of goods lost or damaged, even though the loss is not his, and he then holds the money for the bailor, the actual loser. Insurance practice overrides the general rule of law that only the loser can enforce a right to indemnity. Again, in the case of the bailee who happens to be a carrier of goods under the Hague Rules, the Rules are both cause and effect of an established pattern of liability based on a certain distribution of risk and of the burden of insurance. This was a significant element in the recent decision of the House of Lords against a duty of care for classification societies to owners of damaged cargo.[44]

Finally, but less surely, the very practice of *not* taking out insurance may also tell the court something about the appropriate allocation of risk. In *Norsk*, one of the judges agreed that:

if the business community accepts a rule of non-liability for indirect economic losses without securing insurance protection against them by a relatively inexpensive method, then this fact at least suggests that these losses do not present a social problem serious enough to justify the cost to society in providing for their compensation by the most expensive method in its arsenal—liability based on fault. In other words, if the business community is insured, then there is no point in shifting the loss from one insurance company to another at high cost. If the business community is not insured, then that reveals that other ways of defraying such losses are perceived as superior to insurance and the problem is not that serious.[45]

Contract: Terms

The cost of insurance affects the parties' choice of contract terms, for example, terms for the carriage of goods. Under the international carriage conventions (such as the Hague Rules for carriage by sea) shippers can increase the liability of the carrier above the standard conventional limit in amount by making a declaration of the value of the goods shipped; the effect is to transfer risk from the consignor (and his cargo insurer) to the carrier (and his liability insurer). Declarations are rarely made. This is because, in the event of a declaration, although the cargo insurer would lower his premium, the carrier would raise the freight charge by an amount greater than the decrease in premium; so, clearly, the shipper would lose more than he saved and thus has little incentive to make the declaration. All this is because there are so many risks covered by the cargo insurance that the prospect of recovery in respect of one of them has little influence on the amount of the premium, whereas the risk of liability to the cargo owner is one of the main risks insured under the carrier's liability insurance, and is a significant factor in the amount of premiums.

Again, when one party introduces contract terms to exclude or

---

[44] *The Nicholas H*, n. 32 above.
[45] n. 32 above, 350 (citation omitted), *per* La Forest J.

limit his liability, the reasonableness (and thus the interpretation) of the terms depends in part on the availability of insurance. The issue arises mainly under section 11(4) of the Unfair Contract Terms Act 1977, but courts had taken this line before the Act. For example, the insurance factor led the court to favour exemption for the supplier of a service for a relatively small fee who was responsible for a large amount of damage to the property serviced;[46] indeed, some clauses purport to 'limit the risk to an amount conveniently insurable'. Another such case is that of the bailee of property. If his charges are low and the property is something like a car for which the owner is likely to have loss insurance, courts favour bailee exemption. If, however, the owner is less likely to have cover, e.g. household furniture insured at home but not while in temporary storage, and given that the law allows bailees to insure the property of others as if it were their own (the 'commercial trust', 294 above), courts are less likely to favour exemption. Even the providers of large-scale services may be treated in this way by standard form contracts such as forms, applicable to building contractors whether the work be large or small, and the allocation of risk and of the burden of insurance in this way has been respected and applied by the courts.[47]

Contract: Damages

In *Bredero*, County Council P sold land to defendant D, who developed it and made a large profit. To do so, D broke a covenant with P concerning the density of the development. P's action for damages, the difference between the sale price and the higher price P could have demanded to agree the actual development, failed. P had suffered no loss as a result of D's breach. To award P the sum claimed would, said Steyn LJ, be 'a dramatic extension of restitutionary remedies . . . to confer a windfall in each case on the aggrieved party'. This was not justified mainly because of its 'wide-ranging impact on commercial law: uncertainty about the amount of damages and 'a tendency to discourage

---

[46] *Photo Production*, n. 30 above, 851.
[47] See *Scottish Special Housing Assn* v. *Wimpey Construction UK Ltd* [1986] 2 All ER 957 (HL).

economic activity'.[48] The latter seems to be reference to the idea of 'efficient breach', which tolerates breach of contract if the effect is to generate more wealth. A further reason, said the judge, was that liability insurance premiums would rise, and that would be against the public interest.

The judge assumed that relevant insurance is available, but, generally, it is not. Liability insurers usually exclude contractual liability (deliberate or not). Deliberate breach is excluded because it poses a moral hazard: the insurance itself is an inducement to bring about the peril (deliberate breach). If the insured can get the profit and also get an indemnity for the cost, damages to the aggrieved party, this increases the risk and thus the unpredictability of the insurer's exposure—which is also heightened in such a case by the 'legal hazard', i.e. the relatively high chance that cases of this kind will go to court. So, if breach of contract is covered at all, cover is likely to be costly and limited. Steyn LJ's weighting of the insurance factor is correct only if deliberate breach is covered often enough to have a significant effect on premiums in general—which, it seems, it is not.

Conclusion

The conclusion is that Bishop was right, concerning the efficient distribution of economic loss, when he said that courts do not have enough information to make the requisite technical judgment in each individual case.[49] In many instances this appears to be true also of the insurance factor; and judges are aware of this. Consequently, there is scant reason to believe that judicial perception of insurance has influenced significantly the rules of liability. The influence of insurance and insurers is seen most clearly in Parliament, in the form of persuasion, and in the courts in the conduct of litigation. In each case, the influence has been mostly to moderate or restrict liability.

[48] *Surrey CC* v. *Bredero Homes Ltd* [1993] 3 All ER 705, 715 (CA).
[49] W. Bishop, 'Economic Loss in Tort' (1982) 1 *OJLS* 1–29, 13.

9

The Sequel: Perceptions of the Past and of the Future

Certainty and Security

This book has shown that rather different perceptions of insurance exist among those concerned, as well perhaps as too little talking and too much mutual suspicion. One cause of this is ignorance riding on the back of the maxim that time is money and must be saved at all costs. Another is the state of the law, the nature of its rules, and the degree of uncertainty. People believe that, if any dispute arises with insurers, insurers have an unfair advantage under the law.

Insurance is a drama in which the actors need to know their lines: what to say and when to say it—which means knowing what the others will say too.

The insured wants peace of mind and security: the certainty of cover against the slings and arrows of outrageous life. A study in Holland suggested that in common law countries there is more emphasis on personal independence and responsibility, and, consequently, less felt need for predictability than in other countries in the study, among them Austria, Belgium, France, Germany, Italy, Spain, and Switzerland.[1] Be that as it may, for order and stability in society, law and what is built upon it must be certain; and there is scant reason to believe that in England people find either insurance or insurance law predictable enough.

The insurer too wants certainty—certainty about the risk insured so that he can rate it and insure it, effectively and profitably. Uncertainty, whether it concerns changes in the law or changes in the weather, is the bane of insurers. To rate risk the insurer studies both: 38 ff. above. As regards law, the insurance

---

[1] G. Hofstede, 'Insurance and the Product of National Values', *Geneva Papers* 77 (1995), 423–9.

industry has an effective presence in Parliament. As regards the physical features of risk, it studies ways in which risk can be predicted, managed, and controlled. With this information the individual insurer circumscribes his exposure by carefully drawn contract terms, including terms designed to encourage and educate the insured to reduce the risk and the extent of loss. In doing that the insurer has moved from the role of actuary to that of advisor and risk manager, with an associated change in the nature of his legal liability to the insured: 143 ff. above. Enormous energy and skill are behind the very professional drive of the insurance industry to achieve all this. Research about risk and the writing of cover is collective and co-ordinated to a degree not found in the past and not found today in many other countries of the world.

In matters of cover large companies have managers to manage risk, managers who may well be a match for the insurers with whom they deal. Others, small companies or consumers, are not. People have neither the training nor, it seems, the instinct to counter risk, for they are mostly mistaken in both their fears and their certainties: 6 ff. above. Their fears are not in proportion to the risk; they do not fear what threatens them most, and their responses are misplaced. So are their certainties. They look for anchor points but grab at straws—the comforting anecdote of Uncle Ed who smoked fifty cigarettes a day and lived to the age of 80.

If people's response to risk is to buy insurance, frequently they do not understand what they have bought: 119 ff. above. The persistence of some complainants to the Insurance Ombudsman in the teeth of the wording of their policies shows a stubborn devotion to perceptions of what cover ought to be, rather than what it is. Evening classes in the interpretation of insurance policies, side by side with scale modelling and Spanish for beginners, are not a serious option. Still, for an educated modern society an understanding of risk is fundamental, and that, in an ideal world, it should be part of the curriculum of continuing education is an attractive suggestion. People would make better decisions about risk and about insurance, and a better deployment of their assets. Moreover, people might learn not to expect too much of insurers or of the 'plain' English of policies insurers write.

People would learn that, in language as in law, certainty is relative, and that absolute certainty is unattainable. Until then the most we can hope for is policies which are as plain as is reasonably possible to the people who buy them, policies which fulfil, as far as sensible rating permits, the reasonable expectations of people with an aversion not only to risk but also to small print; and rules of law which, to their legal advisers at least, are as clear as can be reasonably contrived. It was the celebrated American judge, Cardozo J, who said[2] that he was:

much troubled in spirit, in my first years on the bench, to find how trackless was the ocean on which I had embarked. I sought for certainty. I was oppressed and disheartened when I found that the quest for it was futile. I was trying to reach land, the solid land of fixed and settled rules, the paradise of a justice that would declare itself by tokens plainer and more commanding than its pale and glimmering reflections in my own vacillating mind and conscience. . . . As the years have gone by, and as I have reflected more and more upon the judicial process, I have become reconciled to the uncertainty, because I have grown to see it as inevitable.

Certainty of Law

If absolute certainty cannot be reached, it is nonetheless the end of a road that the law should take as far as it reasonably can. 'It is the province of the law of contract to draw the future into the present.'[3] To ring fence the future requires firm points of reference and clear lines. The 'great object in every branch of law, but especially in mercantile law, is certainty'.[4] These words of Lord Mansfield in 1809 have been echoed down the years. Whether in business or in the affairs of consumers, uncertainty of law means cost—in drafting to provide against what the law might mean and, ultimately, in lost opportunities because of what it might not mean or in litigation to settle what it does mean.

In 1993 a leading commercial judge, Sir Christopher Staughton, concluded that he did not know 'how otherwise one can demonstrate that business people prefer certainty, unless it be by the choice of English law for their contracts, and standard forms of

---

[2] B. Cardozo, *The Nature of the Judicial Process* (New Haven, Conn., 1921), 166.
[3] J. Kohler, *Philosophy of Law* (transl. A. Albrecht, New York, 1914), 136.
[4] J. A. Park, *A System of the Law of Marine Insurances* (6th edn., London 1809), 202.

contract compiled by reference to English law'.[5] Chosen it is. Perfect it is not—neither commercial law in general nor insurance law in particular.

Certainty of Insurance Law

In insurance law, the certainty sought by Lord Mansfield has been largely achieved on some points. On the one hand, the insurer benefits, for example, from a hard-and-fast interpretation of time limits for notice and, moreover, for payment of premiums: the courts in life insurance cases have not followed land law down the track of relief against forfeiture to soften the effects on life assurance when premiums are tendered late: if the insured does not pay on time the cover comes to an end. On the other hand, the insured benefits, for example, when the insurer is hoist by the petard of what is prominent in the insurer's documentation rather than allowed to escape through the interstices of small print. To a very limited degree English law recognizes something like a rule whereby the reasonable expectations of the insured about the cover are fulfilled, as long as those expectations are based on a reasonable view of what the insurer has said.

When the law is hard and fast, however, mostly its effects seem to be hard for the insured. The courts have responded with exceptions, but sometimes, for example concerning insurable interest and commercial trust, the exceptions look strained and even puzzling—not only to the insured but also to the solicitor seeking to explain them: 28 ff. above. Sometimes the insurers, to their credit, do not insist on their strict legal rights; but when the insurer has waived a point in people's favour, they may well wonder whether they can be at all sure that the insurer will do the same next time.

Indeed, the trail of uncertainties starts right at the beginning when someone comes for insurance. The first problem is that the product may not be easy to understand. The main benefits may be clear; the exclusions and conditions may not. When insurance is sold, the law shows more concern about the accuracy or completeness of what the applicant says to the insurer than with

[5] 'Good Faith and Fairness in Commercial Contract Law' (1994) 7 *JCL* 193–6, 194.

what the insurer says to the insured. True, the Association of British Insurers (ABI) has published a code that requires sellers to point up the exclusions. How carefully they do this is disputed. Anyway, buyers are driven by the prospective benefits of what they are buying; most of them, naturally enough, want to believe that the product is as good as it is presented to be.

If they are wise, buyers are aware of their ignorance and turn for advice. Today, as in the past, the person to turn to is the broker; but today they may not find the knowledge they seek. Brokers today are under pressure. They are under pressure of competition from alternative outlets that purport to provide the public with cheaper insurance products. They are under pressure of time, not only to save money, but also to meet the expectations of the client; but they lack both the time to learn about new products and the time fully to explain them to the client: 64 ff. above. Anyway many buyers are not wise; they simply do not ask for advice. Surveys suggest that many people do not understand what brokers are for or why they might need them. Indeed, it sometimes seems that some brokers do not either.

Today brokers are seeking a new role in a changing scene; consequently they are sending out confusing signals to a confused public. The law, too, as it affects brokers and other agents, is sending some confusing signals by allowing dual agency and conflicts of interests: 48 ff. above. In a scathing judgment back in 1989, Purchas LJ said that:

To the person unacquainted with the insurance industry it may seem a remarkable state of the law that someone who describes himself as a Lloyd's broker who is remunerated by the insurance industry and who presents proposal forms and suggested policies on their behalf should not be the safe recipient of full disclosure.[6]

Whether the broker is a Lloyd's broker or not, if a client ever asks 'whose side this broker on?', the answer is sometimes surprising.

When people have bought their cover—when they have signed the form and perhaps received a policy, they think that is that and get on with living; but as buyers of insurance they may be in something of a fool's paradise. Although they should have been

---

[6] *Roberts* v. *Plaisted* [1989] 2 Lloyd's Rep. 341, 345 (CA) concerning disclosure of material information: 83 ff. above.

alerted by the proposal form or by the broker that they have to disclose material information, without painstaking advice from someone such as a broker, buyers will not know what is material and what has to be disclosed: 85 above. If they have not disclosed the very last detail, the cover can be set aside at the discretion of the insurer. Moreover, if they have paid premium, it is commonly paid to the broker and, occasionally, a buyer finds that, for one reason or another, the broker has not passed it on to the insurer; and that until it is passed on there is no cover at all.

Mostly, of course, people manage to buy perfectly sound and sensible insurance. Then they forget about it until, as is quite usual in practice, they get a reminder to renew (and would be outraged to be told that they are not entitled to reminders and that it is up to them to check dates) or they make a claim. So, for example, having 'sorted out' his accident cover, holidaymaker Peter then discovers the thrills of bungee jumping. When he hits the water and is hurt, however, he discovers that it is a dangerous pastime, that his insurer agrees—and that his insurer has excluded it from his cover. Or he jumps safely but, when he comes home and falls on the stairs and claims, he is told by his insurer that his bungee jumping may not have broken his neck but it has broken something called a warranty in the policy; and that when he jumped, weeks before he slipped on the stairs, his cover ended automatically. If he is lucky, Peter may be told about the Insurance Ombudsman, who takes a rather different view of these 'warranties' and, eventually, perhaps after many months of 'reconsideration' by the insurer, his claim is paid.

At the same time, accountant Jane who has bought professional liability cover has a bad day at the office and gives a client some careless advice. When the writ arrives, she finds that her insurer is not obliged to defend her at all or, if the insurer decides to do so, that the insurer does not want to settle quietly but wants to make a stand, make her a test case on a difficult marginal point of what her lawyer calls economic loss and the rule in *Hedley Byrne*. All this is going to cost Jane a great deal, both in damage to her business reputation and what she will have to pay for liability cover in future. Meanwhile, her garage, which bought cover against environmental impairment liability (EIL), finds that the policy definition of pollution is complex and not at all what the garage expected; after all, why should there be cover for damage done by the great flood of oil from the burst pipe but not for that from the seepage from the defective pipe with a small crack that nobody noticed?

Jane may, however, feel a bit less foolish and a bit less annoyed than her immediate neighbours, who thought that 'all-risks' cover meant what it seemed to say, but then found that it does not. Indeed, Jane found that even the very definition of 'insurance' is unclear. That was of little immediate concern to her but of grave concern to her other neighbour, who is 'something in the City'; for years that neighbour had been selling the public life insurance on the basis that that kind of life insurance qualified as a tax-efficient investment, only to be told one day by a court of law that it was not life insurance at all.

Surprises like this are not usually sprung until the insured brings a claim. At that point the insured may find other surprises too. The exporter whose briefcase was stolen during deep and difficult negotiations in Gangtok, when the telephone lines were down, is told by the insurer, on getting back to London, that any claim will be rejected because notice of loss is too late or because the precise contents of the briefcase cannot be proved or because documentary evidence from the Gangtok police was not obtained. Or the exporter may be told that business trips to Sikkim are 'material to the risk' and that what happens there is not covered at all because the insurer was not told about the planned trip in advance.

In practice, of course, insurance is not such a lottery as these tales may suggest. Whatever the strict black letter of the law may say, insurers, sometimes prompted by the Insurance Ombudsman or by the press, often take a softer line. They waive their strict rights under the contract or under the law, they turn blind eyes to late dates, they make 'ex gratia' payments. But if the insured are to have any certainty, any real sense of security, they need to know what the insurer will do *before* the insurer does it; they need to be sure that the insurer who was kind last time will be kind next time. They want to know why so much depends on the discretion, however benign, of the insurer. Is there not still something in Williston's belief[7] that most people prefer an inanimate rule to

[7] S. Williston, *Some Modern Tendencies in the Law* (New Haven, Conn., 1929), 95.

dependence on the 'unbridled will' of their fellow men and women? People who buy locks for their doors wants to be able to sleep peacefully in the knowledge that they are secure. People who buy insurance too want to know that their cover is secure. However, insurance law 'remains, in certain respects, unfairly favourable to insurers'. This view is to be found not in any publication of the Consumers Association, although it might well have been, but in the report (paragraph 64) to the Personal Investment Authority by a leading judge of his time, Lord Ackner.

At no time is the truth of this observation more evident that in the amount of discretion that the law allows insurers, especially when a claim is brought and the insurer smells fraud. Quite apart from the tried and tested use of 'technical' defences, such as late notice or non-disclosure (181–5 above), the law gives the insurer almost infinite discretion to delay payment until the claimant cracks or simply gives up. There is evidence that a considerable proportion of the stress suffered by plaintiffs in personal injury cases is a product of deliberate strategy by insurers defending the action and the inability of solicitors, for reasons of resources, organization, and experience, to move the claim forward.

Insurers are mostly fair and honourable people, but it was a senior member of the insurance industry who warned against people in the claims department who pick up a file and look for a spine to shiver down: 181 ff. above. The evidence of history is that few people can be trusted with power; that discretion is power; and that it does not follow at all that because the power is small on the scale of history that the chances of abuse are small too. 'There never was a man who thought he had not law but his own will, who did not soon find that he had no end but his own profit.' That was the view of an historian[8] many years ago. It is still the view of English law that no man or woman should be judge in his or her own cause. The perception of this book is that too often insurance law is such that the insurer is just that. Fair and just perhaps, but judge nonetheless. So, what can be done about the law of insurance? Before trying to answer that question we must first answer another. What what can be expected of the people who buy insurance, the insured?

---

[8] Edmund Burke, *Impeachment of Warren Hastings*, 17 Feb. 1788.

The Nature of People

Expectations of Speed and Convenience

People tend to assume that, if something can be done more quickly than before, it is being done better than before. People who want fast food, convenience food, also want other purchases to be fast and convenient, especially tedious ones like insurance: this is ignorance riding on the back of the view that time is money and money must be saved at all costs, and that buying things should be fun. Lingering over the purchase of a new coat may be a pleasure, lingering over insurance cover is not—that is the perception of the insurer or broker afraid of losing market share, and it is probably correct. However, although speedy selling of standard insurance products that have been around for years may well be viable, there is real doubt about that when the products are new and complex.

The insurance industry rightly prides itself on product innovation. Scarcely a week passes by without the announcement of some ingenious new policy, with a new range of terms. For common kinds of product, such as house contents insurance, *Which* draws up tables to help the persistent consumer make meaningful comparisons. However, like the technical specifications of hi-fi, insurance terms are studied only by the enthusiast or the obsessive. Too often, buyers do not really know what they are buying from sellers, who do not know much more than the buyers about what they are selling.

That is why, when a well-known seller of socks and sandwiches started to sell financial products in 1995, the range was limited to simple standard cover. For anything less simple, people need guidance to see that the cover will meet their needs and suit their purposes. They need an adviser like the insurance broker; the broker is the retailer who has something of the role and the responsibility of the High Street retailer under the Sale of Goods Act. Moreover, when people buy directly from insurers, the person representing the insurer, employee or agent, has a similar role and responsibility himself or for the insurer—a selling situation not unlike that of the manufacturer with its own shops. If buyers do seek the advice of these people, they have every reason to expect competent advice; but, as we have seen, too often they do not get it.

Moreover, none of this avails the growing number of people who buy by telephone. Estimates are that 'telesales' will account for 80 per cent of motor cover and 20 per cent of house contents cover by the year 2000. For these transactions, the most that can be hoped is that terms will be monitored or censored by the Insurance Ombudsman (201 ff. above) or by the consumers' organizations (235 above). Like buyers of canned food, to ensure that they do not get a can of worms buyers of insurance must depend on the quality control and scrutiny of someone else.

Distrust

Whatever the Ministry of Agriculture may say about the safety of certain food products, some people will not believe it and will not eat them. Sureness and certainty depends not only on the public perception of the products but also on their perception of those who provide them. One source of uncertainty and expense in the insurance market today is the mutual distrust of insurer and insured. Certain economists argue that, generally, business is done better in a spirit of trust and mutual confidence than one of outright competition. A prominent opponent[9] of competition wrote of trust as a 'rational economic tool' to secure long-term relationships and compensate for market weaknesses such as information imbalance. Even a prominent advocate[10] of competition has contended that the largest costs in a modern economy are transaction costs, and that these are minimized in an atmosphere of trust—in contrast to an atmosphere in which everyone tries to take advantage of everyone else, and no-one moves without a lawyer. He goes on to warn against economic ideas imported from the United States which come laden with cultural presuppositions— among them the view that, because people cannot be trusted, formal methods of enforcing competition between them are essential. He concludes that the American emphasis on the law as an enforcement mechanism is a part of American culture which does not travel well.

[9] Will Hutton, *Guardian*, 21 Oct. 1995, concerning F. Fukuyama, *Trust: The Social Virtues and the Creation of Prosperity*, (London, 1995).

[10] Samuel Brittan, *Financial Times*, 18 Nov. 1993, with reference to Mark Casson, *The Economics of Business Culture* (Oxford 1993).

An assessment of the argument for trust is beyond the scope of this book, but there is little in the insurance market-place to suggest that the argument is misconceived. Indeed, in Europe a leading member of the insurance industry wrote that, whatever strategy is adopted by insurance companies to retain market share in future, there is one immutable constraint: the insurance industry must have the trust of its customers. It must be seen to honour its commitments, and industry strategy must ultimately be geared to increasing the security underlying each and every policy.[11] This being so, what can be done about it in England?

Trust: Image

For the public to trust insurers requires, it seems, a change in the image of insurers. When the well-known seller of socks and sandwiches launched financial products in 1995, it sold only on an 'execution basis': it offered simple and clear information 'on the label' and made it clear that it was not offering advice about the terms. With emphasis on the company's general reputation built up over many years in the retail trade, the centre of the company's marketing strategy was the quality and reliability of what it had sold in the past: 'Trust us again!'.

Reliability implies not only consistency of performance but transparency. People need to 'know where they are' not only with the product but also with the producer. A relationship in which the stronger party first holds out the hand of friendship but then, come the claim, pulls back in suspicion or even hostility is a recipe for nothing but disappointment, disillusionment, and even a sense of betrayal. Nor does this help the balance sheet because, usually, it costs the insurer less to keep existing customers than to find others to replace them. Insurers who were tough on claims in the past now find it hard to shed the image of 'cheats in bowler hats' projected, unfairly no doubt, by the popular press. A better image means a softer response to claims, the point of contact which, all agree, makes the greatest mark on the memory of the customer. In the medium term, self-interest alone suggests that insurers should strive for a better relationship with the insured, one less of

---

[11] H. Schulte-Noelle, 'Challenges for Insurers in the Nineties', Geneva Papers on Risk and Insurance, No 72 (1994), 287–303, 301.

confrontation than of co-operation. Clearly some insurers, especially in the life sector, are moving in this direction. However, they should be aware that both to retain the predictability associated with the paradigmatic contract of the past, and to obtain the trust and co-operation which maximizes the mutual benefits of the long-term contract in future is not possible. The one can only be achieved by some sacrifice of the other.

Trust: Information

For insurers to trust the public will, it seems, also require a change in the insurers' image of the public; but here the iniative lies not with the public but with the insurers, and lies in education, education about insurance to remove false expectations and education about fraud. Already there are signs that people are beginning to understand that insurance fraud is not a sport but a form of cheating, and that it is they who, ultimately, bear the cost of fraud. As with other kinds of crime, the best way of reducing the level of fraud is to raise the level (and thus the fear) of detection. Of great significance, therefore, to the relationship between insurer and insured is that the chance of detection has been much increased by the computer, CUE: 180 above.

Although CUE may increase the confidence of the insurer it does not, of course, necessarily lead to trust—on either side. On the contrary, one consequence of CUE may be that there is not more but less trust on each side—on the insurers' side because they feel that with CUE behind them they do not need to trust the insured, and on the side of the insured because of what they feel about computers. The perception persists that, like speed cameras on roads, computer checks are 'not cricket'; that like some other miracles of science, computers put too much power in the hands of the wrong people or, at least, people who cannot always be trusted. Recently newspapers told of the policeman who was sacked for keying a car registration number into a police computer—to trace the lady owner and to ask her out. The impact of the story, however, was less in the end than the means: abuse of central computers. Many people are deeply suspicious about the use of information by networks of computers available to public authorities, to branches of government, and to the police. Some will see CUE as one more strand in the web of the Orwellian state.

The ABI has published a Data Protection Code of Practice. The Code (2.2) suggests a bland statement in the proposal form to inform the proposer that his 'details will be passed to and used or held by other members of the XYZ Group'; and that, if the information is to be available to third parties, the proposer must be told. On the one hand, clearly some people will not like the idea at all. On the other hand how many people seeking motor insurance, for example, will realize that a small English company called Churchill belongs to a large Swiss company called Winterthur? And is the parent company a third party? Once people know what others might know about them, the prospect is likely to make them uneasy and, once again, distrustful and uncertain.

The Code (2.2) also states that the purpose of any enquiry must be explained to proposers unless it is reasonable to expect them to know. But how many proposers know that what is said in a motor proposal may be checked against what they said in a fire proposal five years earlier to another insurer in the group? Again, how many people know that data submitted for the purpose of quotation, but which does not lead to a contract, may also be held? And (7.1) that, although insurers are encouraged to depersonalize such data, where this is practical, to prevent the identification of a particular individual', 'data held only for historical, statistical or research purposes may be held indefinitely'? This kind of information, the Code (2.10) asserts, people should expect to be held; so the person does not have to be notified at all. Indeed, this is a category of data exempt from access by data subjects, who have no means of ensuring therefore that they have been depersonalized (8.2). No more have insurers effective means of ensuring, as required by the Code (2.11), that when information comes via an intermediary, the intermediary has 'fairly represented' the position to the client. It is difficult to believe that anyone concerned enough to read the Code will be reassured by its contents. The Code is now being reviewed by the ABI.

The Law of Co-operation

Modern writers on the law of contract have stressed the importance of long-term contractual relationships, and some have argued for changes in the law of contract to accommodate and encourage these 'relational' contracts. This book suggests (146 ff. above), however, that the insurance relationship, long term as it may well be, differs in significant respects from other paradigms of the long-term contractual relationship; that insurance is still served by rules of law that are black in letter and clear in outline; and indeed that some existing rules are not nearly clear enough. While advocating more trust between insurer and insured, it is argued here nonetheless that the insured should not have to trust the insurer's discretion about resort to rules of law, such as technical defences, which favour the insurer rather than the insured; but that, as far as can reasonably and possibly be, the insured should have the firm support of predictable insurance contract law.

Still, some aspects of the relationship cannot be based entirely on law like that. Indeed, one suggestion is that long term contractual relationships are a sociological rather than a legal category in which, as some writers have put it, 'short-term maximizing behaviour is rejected as opportunistic'. On the contrary, it is said, as in any kind of partnership, the parties should aim at 'utility-maximization indirectly through long-term co-operative behaviour manifested in trust and not in reliance on obligations specified in advance'.[12] One way of facilitating co-operation is by resort to external norms deriving from trade or industry practice. Relational contracts, they argue, require the rejection of immediate *individual* self-interest as the measure of economic rationality, and its replacement by common interest as this measure. Self-interest in these contracts is sufficiently served by co-operation.

The interest of that argument for relational contracts lies not only in its intrinsic merits but in its resonance with current legal developments on a wider front, in particular, with the doctrine of contractual good faith, which has now crossed the Channel from Brussels to underpin contracts at large. For contracts of insurance this may well offer a new legal foundation for the insurance relationship. This kind of good faith requires of the parties a spirit of co-operation (233 above); and it requires of the court, within the limits of the information available (242 ff. above), a more purposive interpretation of the contract terms and an associated

---

[12] D. Campbell and D. Harris, 'Flexibility in Long-term Contractual Relationships: The Role of Co-operation' (1993) 20 *J. Law & Society* 166-91, 167, 180.

assessment of the reasonable expectations of the insured (125 ff. above).

The Nature of Law and of Language

Like many goals in life certainty of law is one that should be sought, but sought in the awareness that it is a goal that will never be perfectly attained; and that it is 'not a valid objection to legal doctrine that it will not always be easy to know whether the doctrine is to be applied in a particular case. The law has to face such embarrassments.'[13] Many a legal question is one of degree; one answer often shades into another.

An associated problem lies in conflicting traditions of the common law. On the one hand, as we have seen, the law seeks to respect people's need to know where they stand. On the other hand, the common law distrusts rules that are general, and prefers the 'incremental' development of rules case by case, inch by inch. Of liability for economic loss, for example, it was said in the Canadian Supreme Court that uncertainty 'is inherent in the common law generally. It is the price the common law pays for flexibility, for the ability to adapt to a changing world. If past experience serves, it is a price we should willingly pay, provided the limits of uncertainty are kept within reasonable bounds'.[14] Likewise, in a report for the Governor of the Bank of England concerning the law affecting financial markets, Lord Alexander accepted that the promotion of legal certainty is of fundamental importance, but conceded that some uncertainty 'is inevitable as market practice almost always moves more quickly than the law supporting it. There is thus always a risk that a gap between the law and the markets may exist'. If the law is too rigid, it may inhibit developments in law and practice which become desirable as conditions change. Nonetheless, he went on, it is 'essential that, where the law is not or cannot be known with complete certainty, this gap should be as narrow as possible. At the very least, predictability of response should be present'.[15]

---

[13] *Dashwood* v. *Magniac* [1891] 3 Ch. 306, 364, *per* Bowen LJ (CA).

[14] *Canadian National Ry. Co.* v. *Norsk Pacific SS Co.* (1992) 91 DLR (4th) 289, 368, *per* McLachlin J.

[15] *Final Report of the Legal Risk Review Committee*, paras. 1.2 and para. 2.1.

To this end, the terms of insurance contracts are drawn with care and consideration; but neither the quest for precision nor the scarcely consistent campaign for 'plain' English will ever avoid all ambiguity: 121 ff. above. Because the law has to be expressed in words, and words have a penumbra of uncertainty, marginal ambiguity is bound to occur. This being so, the function of the judge is not simply to administer the law and apply the contract. The judge must look not only to the letter of the law and the wording of the contract, but also to the purpose of both. The application of the EC Directive, for example, to unfair insurance terms (234 above), while good for the insured in the longer run, will do little for certainty in the shorter term. It will, however, be consistent with a process of demystification, whereby insurance law is brought more clearly into the frame of the general law of contract. This, it is submitted, is something that can and should be done in the cause of certainty. If, as is also submitted here, it is too much to expect the insureds to understand every clause of their contracts and the law that sustains it, at least something can be done to ensure that their advisers, solicitors, or barristers, can do it for them. The law, said Williston, 'must be applied by men engaged in practical affairs and by so many of them that to be useful legal doctrine must be capable of being understood and stated by men who are neither profound scholars nor interested in abstract thought'.[16]

This would be a real response to a real need. Insurers are specialists in insurance and, as needs must, in insurance litigation. Mostly, solicitors are neither; and in the field of litigation in particular solicitors are often no match for insurers. Of course, barristers and some solicitors too do specialize in litigation at large, but insurance law is likely, at best, to be a dim recollection of a chapter tucked away at the end of a course on commercial law. The law schools offering a course on insurance law as such are few and far between, and that is unlikely to change. With diminishing resources to meet the increasing demands of other, often more novel and more fashionable, options, more space in the syllabus for insurance law is unlikely. Anyway, it may not even be desirable. In practice, lawyers with less and less time to meet the demands of courts and clients for more and more speed do not

---

[16] n. 7 above, 127.

have the resources either of time or of training to learn enough. Lawyers in practice have to make do with what training they have got; and that means, mainly, the law of contract.

The Nature of Insurance Contract Law

Neither insurance nor insurance law functions or develops in isolation. Fleming speaks of 'a symbiotic relationship' between the law of tort and liability insurance.[17] Indeed an interrelationship can be seen between the conditions of insurance contracts, not only for liability but for other risks, and a whole range of behaviour on the part of the insured. Behaviour has been the traditional concern of criminal law, tort, and, in specific ways, contract law. But now the insurance contract too has become a regulator. Insurers, concerned with risk-management and loss prevention and thus with the moral hazard, promise cover only if the insured observe a 'code' of conduct: they cover house contents only if certain locks are fitted, they cover road hauliers' liability only if certain anti-theft devices are installed. One set of rules (contract) supports another set of rules (conduct).

The main questions of symbiosis here, however, concern the role of insurance *law*. Is there such a degree of conceptual affinity between insurance law and the general law that the one influences the other? And, if so, can insurance law be understood in terms of the general law? In their role as advisers, both the intermediary and the insurer operate squarely within the general law of contract and, to a marginal degree, the law of tort. So the question of affinity becomes whether and to what extent insurance contract law is different in content from the general law of contract.

Common Law

The work of insurance intermediaries, whether they act for the insured or for the insurer, is governed by the general law of agency, although the law is sometimes ignored in practice. Insurance contracts, whether contracted through intermediaries or not, are concluded like other contracts. Acceptance meets offer or

[17] J. G. Fleming, *The American Tort Process* (Oxford, 1988), 21. See also C. von Bar, *Das Trennungprinzip*, AcP 181 (1981) 289–327; and above 274 ff.

counter-offer in the usual way. Even at Lloyd's the customary market rituals have been squeezed into the template of offer and acceptance. Insurance contracts do not require any special form and, apart from marine contracts, do not even have to be in writing—although in practice a document such as a policy is commonly used. In short no difference: insurance contracts are concluded like other contracts.

Performance of the contract by the insured is mainly the payment of premium. With the exception of some special rules about the recovery of premium, the rules of law that apply to the payment of premium are the general rules of law for the payment of money. When the courts have sought to soften the consequences of non-payment (forfeiture), they have done so with general rules of law such as waiver. Performance of the contract by the insurer is mainly the provision of cover—the promise of payment in the event of a stated contingency. Cover, the insurance 'product', is, of course, quite different from what is sold in a supermarket, but one important similarity in law lies in (the rules of) interpretation, i.e. the specification of the kind of product being sold, its quality, and contents. Again, in general no difference: insurance contracts are interpreted like other contracts. In particular, there is a presumption that any word that has an established meaning in some other part of the law is used in the same sense in the insurance contract; but, of course, a presumption can be rebutted to give way to exceptions, and here we do find some differences between the law in general and the law of insurance.

One exception lies in the rule of causation: the insurance rule of proximate cause is narrow; it is said to accommodate the desire of insurers for predictable levels of exposure. A strict rule of this kind is sometimes applied to general contractual exclusions, but it is prominent in insurance law. A second exception is that some words and phrases (e.g. loss, fire, all-risks: 159 ff. above) have acquired a crust of case law which gives them their own colour, and this, of course, is the colour of the insurance context. Moreover, certain categories of insurance term are not only different from general contract categories but utterly confusing in their apparent similarity. Although insurance 'exclusions' are like other 'exclusions', 'conditions' and 'warranties' are understood quite differently in insurance contracts. Even so, to some extent the same can be said of other standard contracts, such as charterparties or building contracts; and on the important issue of the effect of a breach of warranty, the House of Lords has now brought insurance law back into the broad line of general contract law: 133 above. Finally, interpreters of insurance contracts have begun to talk about the 'reasonable expectations' of the insured; this kind of heresy, if that is what it is, is not limited to insurance contracts.[18] Whether this approach (to all contracts) is truly contractual or whether it is so 'objective' and removed from the likely intentions of the parties as to be really 'tortious', as it is described in the United States, is another matter; the point here is that on this issue insurance contracts are treated in the same way as other contracts.

Elements, notably mistake and misrepresentation, that vitiate other contracts also vitiate insurance contracts, and in the same way. Strikingly, however, insurance contracts are also vitiated by non-disclosure; this is indeed a very special rule of insurance law: 80 ff. above. In 1915 a treatise on non-disclosure set out a general principle of disclosure which, it was maintained, applied to most kinds of contract. In the second edition of that work, not published until 1990, the authors had retreated from such a general view of non-disclosure.[19] Explanations of the rule based on general ideas of implied term or fiduciary duty have also been rejected. The rule is an aspect of the insurance duty of good faith. This is not the rule of good faith which is beginning to emerge in the general law of contract, as that goes beyond disclosure; but the convergence of the two or, more likely, the absorption of the narrow insurance rule in a wider contract rule for all contracts is a real prospect. Even now, as regards the degree of inducement that triggers a remedy, the House has recently aligned non-disclosure with misrepresentation, and thus with general contract law.[20] More-over, except that the Misrepresentation Act 1967 does not apply to non-disclosure, the insurer's remedy for non-disclosure, rescission, is *mutatis mutandis* the same as that for misrepresentation, and thus a remedy of the general law.

---

[18] See Clarke, *Law of Insurance Contracts*, 15–5B.

[19] G. S. Bower, *The Law Relating to Actionable Non-Disclosure* (2nd edn., London, 1990) 85 ff.

[20] *Pan Atlantic Ins. Co. Ltd* v. *Pine Top Ins. Co. Ltd* [1995] 1 AC 501.

In the case of contingency insurance, such as life insurance, the action to enforce the insurer's promise is an action for debt like any other. In the case of indemnity insurance, however, the action has been described as an action for damages but damages 'in a somewhat unusual sense'.[21] This is no more than the politeness demanded of a first instance judge inhibited by precedent: if the payment of indemnity is indeed a payment of damages, insurance law is eccentrically out of line. This apart, in other respects such as the assessment of loss the basic rule of indemnity, according to which the insured recovers no more than his actual loss, is very similar to the principle of indemnity in tort; and cases from tort are often cited: 186 ff. above.

Finally, when the insurer raises defences, legal argument is often based on waiver or estoppel—very much the same refrain heard again and again in relation to other kinds of contract. Indeed, waiver has a prominent part in insurance law and practice. Insurers sometimes choose to respond to insurance claims in a way that is more generous to the insured than is strictly required, either by the letter of the contract or the letter of the law. Nothing special about that alone, of course, except perhaps in the degree. Not only do insurers pay against the 'better' judgement of their lawyers or the 'uncharitable' views of their own claims departments, but the industry has codes of conduct which urge insurers not to insist on certain of their legal rights, for example, not to rescind unless the insured's misrepresentation was careless or fraudulent. Moreover, these and other extra-legal considerations of 'good insurance practice' and of what is 'fair and reasonable in all the circumstances' are the 'rules' that guide the Insurance Ombudsman.

Statute

Apart from the requirement of disclosure, the main differentiation of insurance contracts has come not from the courts, not from those with any conceptual feel for the jurisprudence, but from elsewhere, mainly from Parliament. When new rules of law were brought in by statute for exclusion clauses in contracts, they did

---

[21] *Jabbour* v. *Custodian of Israeli Absentee Property* [1954] 1 WLR 139, 144, *per* Pearson J; cf. Clarke, n. 18 above, 28–2.

not apply to insurance contracts: the Unfair Contract Terms Act 1977. However, on the one hand, exclusion of insurance in that Act is evidence of the persuasive power of the industry rather than of any inherent difference between insurance contracts and other contracts; and, of course, some other kinds of contract were also excluded. On the other hand, similar legislation of European origin did not exclude insurance contracts: 234 above. Not surprisingly, there are some special statutory rules for insurance contracts. But, with one reservation, they are of marginal importance.

The reservation concerns the Contracts (Applicable Law) Act 1990. This establishes rules for all contracts, with certain exceptions. The exceptions include insurance contracts (but not re-insurance contracts) on risks situated in the EC which are not left to be governed by national rules (previously governing all kinds of contract) but for which a special regime is established. This is a marked differentiation of insurance contracts, but its significance to the present discussion is tempered in two respects. First, the special regime allows a result that does not differ as markedly as first impressions might suggest from the general contract rules in the Act. Secondly, the view is widely held that a special regime for insurance contracts is not justified.[22]

Contract or Contracts?

In the past decisions in certain contexts, such as shipping, construction, and insurance, have had considerable influence on the development of English contract law. The influence has been mutual. Again and again, courts faced with particular issues in insurance cases have recognized a familiar issue of general contract law and treated it as such. The general law, mostly the law of contract, provides a frame of reference from which, by education, inclination, and tradition, the English lawyer proceeds. The general law provides a substratum from which the judge can draw if a rule of 'insurance law' is not apparent. This is not a weakness of insurance law but a source of strength. It is not a palliative; it is a standard procedure because, in the words of a

---

[22] See F. Reichert-Facilides (ed.), *International Insurance Contract Law in the EC* (Deventer, 1993).

eading judge, it is desirable 'that the same legal principles should apply to the law of contract as a whole and that different legal principles should not apply to different branches of that law'.[23]

In the last 100 years many established branches of law have developed new branches. This is partly the complexity that comes with growth; but it is partly the result of the associated concentration of human time and energy—and the associated ignorance of wider perspectives of law—the high priest syndrome, that revels in modern legal mystique, that elevates a narrow view and the associated vice of ignorance into the virtue of specialization. The law is better applied if it is better understood. Insurance contract law should be something which the legal profession recognizes and to which it can relate. The presumption should always be against those who assert that it is or should be different. This book shares the view of a leading American writer in the field, that insurance law is 'not an exotic species that belongs in a legal zoo, but a system that is subject to and part of the same regime of principles and policies that constitutes the rest of the law'.[24] Insurance contracts are still largely seen by lawyers as commercial contracts, and it is in the area of commercial contracts that classical contract law survives in its purest form.

Effective insurance depends on effective insurance contract law, and that depends on effective contract law—depends, however, only to a degree. The court, the draftsman, the commentator, each might do worse than to recall the words of Sam Johnson: 'How small the part of all the hearts of men endure, that laws or kings can cause or cure.' Insurers are neither gods nor kings, but they can and do do much to ease the financial and psychological burdens of what men and women must endure. So too the laws with which insurers must work. They could do more.

---

[23] *The Hansa Nord* [1976] 1 QB 44, 71, *per* Roskill LJ (CA).
[24] K. S. Abraham, *Distributing Risk* (New Haven, Conn., 1986), 9.

Bibliography

ABRAHAM, K. S., *Distributing Risk* (New Haven, Conn., 1986).

ACKNER, LORD, *Report on a Unified Complaints Procedure* (Personal Investment Authority, July 1993) (the Ackner Report).

BAYERISCHE RUCK (ed.), *Risk is a Construct* (Munich, 1993).

BEATSON, J. (ed.), *Good Faith and Fault in Contract Law* (London, 1995).

BIRDS, J., *Modern Insurance Law* (3rd edn., London, 1993).

CANE, P., *Atiyah's Accidents Compensation and the Law* (5th edn., London, 1993).

CLARKE, M. A., *The Law of Insurance Contracts* (3rd edn., London, 1997).

CLARKE, MICHAEL, 'Insurance Fraud' (1989) 29 *Brit. J of Criminology*.

COCKERELL, H. A. L. and GREEN, EDWIN *The British Insurance Business* (2nd edn., Sheffield, 1994).

COHEN, D., 'The Economics of *Canadian National Railway* v. *Norsk Pacific Steamship*', 45 *U Toronto LJ* 143.

CORBY, B. 'On Risk and Uncertainty in Modern Society', *Geneva Papers on Risk and Insurance* 72 (1994), 235–43.

DICKSON, G. C. A. and STEELE, J. T., *Introduction to Insurance* (2nd edn., London, 1984).

FAURE, M. G., 'The Limits to Insurability from a Law and Economics Perspective', *Geneva Papers on Risk and Insurance* 77 (1995), 454.

GENN, HAZEL, *Hard Bargaining* (Oxford, 1987).

ITOH, J., 'Challenge to the Future', *Geneva Papers on Risk and Insurance* 72 (1994), 334.

KLINGMULLER, E., 'Liability Insurance in the Federal Republic of Germany', *Geneva Papers on Risk and Insurance* 56 (1990), 330.

LEWIS, RICHARD, 'The Regulation of Insurers and the Long Term Security of Structured Settlements' [1994] IJIL, 75.

LOEWENSTEIN, G. and MATHER, J. 'Dynamic Processes in Risk Perception', 3 *J Risk & Uncertainty* 155 (1990).

MILLER, DAVID S., 'Insurance as Contract: the Argument for Abandoning the Ambiguity Doctrine', 88 *Col. LR* 1849 (1988).

SCHULTE-NOELLE, H., 'Challenges for Insurers in the Nineties', *Geneva Papers on Risk and Insurance* 72 (1994), 287.

SLAWSON, DAVID S., 'Standard Form Contracts and Democratic Control of Lawmaking Power', 84 *Harv. LR* 529 (1971).

TREITEL, G. H., *The Law of Contract* (9th edn., London, 1995).

VERMAAT, A. J., 'Uninsurability: a Growing Problem', *Geneva Papers on Risk and Insurance* 77 (1995), 446.

WAGENAAR, W. A., VAN KOPPEN, P. J. and CROMBAG, H. F. M., *Anchored Narratives: The Psychology of Criminal Evidence* (Hemel Hempstead, 1993).

WILS, W. P. J., 'Insurance Risk Classifications in the EC', (1994) 140. J.L.S. 449.

Index